THE EXORCISM OF SATAN

"In *The Exorcism of Satan*, Josh Howard thoroughly and expertly handles the subject of the devil's defeat by the King of Kings. In addition to discussing Satan's final fate as revealed in the book of Revelation, he also shows readers why Christ's resurrection signifies that the church already is victorious in the present age. I commend to you this important and uplifting volume."

Matthew R. Akers, PhD
Associate Dean of Doctoral Programs &
Director of the Hispanic Institute
Mid-America Baptist Theological Seminary, Memphis, TN

"Of making many books on eschatology there is no end, but this work adds a unique contribution to the field that does not weary the body. *The Exorcism of Satan: The Binding of the Strong Man by Christ the King* examines the overlooked theme of satanic defeat within the realm of eschatology and the 'already/not-yet' view championed by George Ladd. Joshua Howard carefully develops a robust canonical eschatology that is grounded in the biblical text and shows what assurance Christians may have today knowing that Satan has been bound by Christ the King. I warmly commend this work."

Jason P. Kees, PhD
Adjunct Instructor
Midwestern Baptist Theological Seminary and Spurgeon College
Kansas City, MO

"For too long, evangelical thinking and writing about Satan has either been well-nigh non-existent or limited to those apt to find a demon behind every bush. I'm thankful, therefore, for Josh's work, which uses careful exegesis to demonstrate a marvelously joyful truth: the Seed of the woman has indeed crushed the serpent's head, even as we wait with a sure hope for the Serpent's full and final destruction at the last day."

Mitchell W. Kimbrell, PhD
Senior Pastor
Christ Memorial Church, Williston, Vermont

"Some books on spiritual warfare so focus on Satan that the enemy receives more attention than the Bible gives him. Others so emphasize the ongoing battle that the reader is almost defeated before he or she finishes reading the book. Still other books spend more time speculating on Satan than on teaching Scripture. This book avoids every one of these errors. It rightly situates the story of Satan in the context of God's overall victory, both in this age and in the age to come. It properly emphasizes satanic defeat, recognizing that Satan has been defeated, is being defeated, and will be defeated. This work is thoroughly biblical, convincingly walking through the Scriptures to show the defeat of a foe who still wars against us. It will inform you, challenge you, caution you, encourage you, and strengthen you—all at the same time."

Charles Edward Lawless, Jr., PhD
Professor of Evangelism and Missions & Dean of Doctoral Studies
Southeastern Baptist Theological Seminary, Wake Forest, NC

"The work of Satan in the present era and his influence in the lives of believers and unbelievers is a topic of perennial concern as well as apathy and neglect. Thankfully, Josh Howard offers the discerning reader a fascinating and challenging addition to this subject. His interpretation of inaugurated eschatology as an 'exorcism' of Satan offers a new lens through which to view the present age and the place of the evil one in it. I am delighted to see the publication of this helpful study and pray for its wide dissemination within the body of Christ."

John Mahony, ThD
Professor of Theology (retired)
Nesbitt, MS

"Josh Howard addresses an important but often overlooked area of the study of the end times. Jesus has defeated Satan, and Scripture speaks of Satan as presently bound. But what exactly does this mean? Dr. Howard carefully analyzes the biblical teaching about the exorcism of our defeated foe—what Satan can and cannot do until the Lord's return. This is a thorough and compelling book that addresses and answers many of the questions students of eschatology have about this fascinating topic."

Kim Riddlebarger, PhD
Author of *A Case for Amillennialism* and *The Man of Sin*
Visiting Professor of Systematic Theology, Westminster Seminary, CA

THE EXORCISM OF SATAN

THE BINDING OF
THE STRONG MAN BY
CHRIST THE KING

JOSHUA P. HOWARD

SERIES EDITOR:
OWEN STRACHAN

The Exorcism of Satan:
The Binding of the Strong Man by Christ the King

Copyright © 2022 Joshua P. Howard

All rights reserved. No part of this book may be used or reproduced in any manner whatsoever without written permission except in the case of brief quotations embodied in critical articles and reviews. Direct your requests to the publisher at the following address:

Published by

Free Grace Press
815 Exchange Road, Ste. 101
Conway, AR 72032
(501) 214-9663

email: support@freegracepress.com
website: www.freegracepress.com

Printed in the United States of America

Scripture quotations are from the ESV® Bible (The Holy Bible, English Standard Version®), copyright © 2001 by Crossway, a publishing ministry of Good News Publishers. Used by permission. All rights reserved.

ISBN: 978-1-952599-54-5

For additional Reformed Baptist titles, please email us for a free list or see our website at the above address.

"So comes snow after fire,
and even dragons have their endings."

— J. R. R. Tolkien,
The Hobbit, or, There and Back Again

Contents

Preface to the Series - Dr. Owen Strachan	xi
Preface	xiii
Acknowledgements	xv
Abbreviations	xvii
Chapter 1: Consequences of Satanic Exorcism in This Age	1
The Eschatological Consequences of Satanic Exorcism	3
Satanic Exorcism as an Intermediate Defeat	5
Satanic Exorcism as the Hope of Inaugurated Victory in This Age	6
Defining Terms	8
Chapter 2: Systematic Evidence of Satanic Exorcism in This Age	17
An Approach to Satanic Exorcism in Christ's First Coming	18
Satanic Exorcism in the Overlap of This Age and the Age to Come	31
The Theological Deficit Concerning the Effects of Satanic Exorcism	36
Toward Building a Doctrine of Satanic Exorcism	45
Remaining Questions	46
Chapter 3: Satanic Exorcism in the First Coming	49
Satanic Authority Prior to the First Coming	50
Demonic Exorcisms as Proleptic Victory	66
Five Common Features in Gospel Exorcisms	76
Satanic Exorcism in the Gospels	78
Chapter 4: Satanic Exorcism in this Age	99
The Conquering Christ: Christus Victor	99

Divine Warrior	101
Deliverance from This Present Evil Age	103
Authority over Rulers and Powers	106
Satan's Cosmic Destruction	115
The "god of this world"	125
Chapter 5: Satan's Power and Authority Curtailed	**131**
Inability to Accuse	131
Loss of Satanic Authority over the Nations	146
Satanic Deception as Revolt	157
Chapter 6: Satanic Assault Persists in this Age	**173**
Matthew 6:13	173
Matthew 12:43–45 // Luke 11:24–26	175
Satan's Persistent Influence	177
Satan's Ongoing Attacks	183
Satan's Cosmic War	192
Satan's Future and Final Defeat	198
Chapter 7: Conclusion	**205**
Summary of Findings	206
Contribution to the Field	210
Appendix 1: Lexical Parallels	**213**
Appendix 2: Satanic Passages Analysis	**215**
Bibliography	**223**

Preface to the Series

Dr. Owen Strachan

The New Studies in Theology (NST) series exists to enflesh sola Scriptura. In the monographs represented by this line, readers will explore various doctrines of Scripture from a hermeneutic that is both intellectually rigorous and intentionally doxological. This is not academic theology for its own sake. The NST aims at helping pastors, theologians, and other students of the sacred Word know the deep things of God. The scholarship unveiled here is unapologetically extensive, but the overall goal of NST texts is to communicate a grand vision of God, his gospel, his kingdom, and his providential work in all creation.

Under the leadership of Dr. Jeffrey Johnson, the founder of Free Grace Press, we have launched the NST in conscious thankfulness for a similar series edited for decades by D. A. Carson. The New Studies in Biblical Theology (NSBT) volumes helped bring biblical theology, developed so fruitfully by Geerhardus Vos and others, back to the fore. We pray that the NST will do the same with sound doctrine, albeit with a broader disciplinary purview than the NSBT. The method of the authors in this series is to work first at the level of the text (exegetical theology), to understand the thematic progression of the subject matter through the canon (biblical theology), and to arraign the canonical material into overarching principles and convictions that are biblically faithful (systematic theology). It is this final category that occupies the lion's share of our attention in the NST.

This is no exercise in atomized interpretation. Our authors seek conversation, wisdom, help, and serious insight from the historic church (historical theology). Further, they work hard to answer questions raised in the gaps of the text, thinking logically (philosophical theology). But it is the biblical text itself that has center stage in NST volumes; it is the Word that consumes our attention, drives our thinking, and measures our doctrinal conclusions. Sola Scriptura is not a mere slogan or a message on a coffee mug. For NST authors, sola Scriptura is our method as much as it is our message. We believe the ongoing promotion of biblical authority honors the Lord and promises to strengthen Christ's blood-bought church (see Isaiah 66:2).

In this volume, Joshua Howard serves up a rich exegetical-theological meal. He shows us that the exorcistic works of Christ are not merely signs of deity (though they surely and gloriously are). More than any previous theological volume has done, Howard casts the entire ministry of the King as an exorcism of Satan from the earth. Howard fits this principle, derived from close exegesis of numerous texts, into the framework of inaugurated eschatology. The reader will come away informed by Howard's study and in awe of the God who has triumphed over the devil through the life, ministry, death, and resurrection of his obedient Son.

This is theology for the sake of the church. It is richly biblical, consonant with confessional conviction, conversant with leading scholars, but above all, bent on helping us understand the Word. To paraphrase Luther, reflecting on the marvel of the Reformation, the Word is everything in this volume. Christ is robed in power in this volume. The defeat of our terrible enemy is achieved in this volume. Our hope is hard won but certain in this volume. In these pages, as in the created order that God rules, the devil has been robbed of his power over the church, the clock is counting down the days until the Son's return, and the church militant will very soon be the church triumphant. Indeed, the first rays of that eschatological triumph already peek through the clouds. The celestial city is distant but visible.

In this book, you will find much to enjoy. Here is theology for God's people. Here is real biblical and canonical insight. Here is sola Scriptura in action.

Dr. Owen Strachan
Provost & Research Professor of Theology
Grace Bible Theological Seminary
Series Editor, NST

August 2022

Preface

The Exorcism of Satan: The Binding of the Strong Man by Christ the King is an approach of canonical eschatology that builds toward a systematic-theological doctrine of satanic exorcism in this age. In a seminary class early in my theological studies, I was introduced to the tension of the already/not-yet nature of the kingdom in the New Testament, and I quickly became fascinated by the field of eschatology. As I continued to read and research, it became clear that satanic defeat was an area of scholarly deficit in eschatology, and one that provides imminent hope for the believer. After reading a passing remark in a commentary on John's gospel that referred to satanic defeat as an "exorcism" event, I became confident that the New Testament uses the language of exorcism to describe Satan's defeat in the work of Christ, situated within the greater eschatological flow of the canon. From this initial fascination, the current study has taken shape.

SDG,

Joshua P. Howard

Battle Creek, MI

Acknowledgements

This work represents the culmination of a spark that sprang from a word in an obscure commentary footnote and subsequently grew into a flame as I explored the theme of satanic exorcism throughout Scripture. Eventually, this flame blazed into a fire that led to this current project. I am particularly grateful to my parents, Dr. Paul and Melissa Howard, who faithfully provided a great measure of support, encouragement, and prayer for me during my theological studies. I am indebted to Dr. John Mahony for initially stirring my interest in eschatology, and for later shaping my theological thoughts and encouraging me to reflect deeply on the things of Scripture. I am grateful to Dr. Mitch Kimbrell, who taught me to love and work in the Greek of the New Testament. Dr. Rustin Umstattd and his family selflessly opened their home and table to me during my seminar visits at MBTS, and I am so thankful for their friendship and encouragement. I am thankful for the help, guidance, and wisdom of Dr. Owen Strachan and Dr. Jason Kees, men of strong scholarship and godly leadership who helped shape this project. I am also thankful for the publishing staff at Free Grace Press for believing in this project and seeing it through to completion. Finally, my strongest advocate and closest confidant has always been my wife, Marci, and I truly cannot envision this book without her love and support—what follows is dedicated to her.

Abbreviations

AB	Anchor Bible
BBR	*Bulletin for Biblical Research*
BDAG	Bauer, Walter, Frederick William Danker, William F. Arndt, and F. Wilbur Gingrich, eds., *A Greek-English Lexicon of the New Testament and Other Early Christian Literature* (3rd ed.)
BEB	*Baker Encyclopedia of the Bible*
BECNT	Baker Exegetical Commentary on the New Testament
BibSac	*Bibliotheca Sacra*
BST	Bible Speaks Today
CBR	*Currents in Biblical Research*
CTJ	*Calvin Theological Journal*
CTM	*Concordia Theological Monthly*
CTR	*Criswell Theological Review*
CurTM	*Currents in Theology and Mission*
DBL	*Dictionary of Biblical Languages with Semantic Domains: Greek*
DCB	*Dictionary of Christian Biography, Literature, Sects and Doctrines*
DDD	*Dictionary of Deities and Demons in the Bible*
DJG	*Dictionary of Jesus and the Gospels*
DNTB	*Dictionary of New Testament Background*
EBC	Expositor's Bible Commentary
EuroJTh	*European Journal of Theology*
EvQ	*Evangelical Quarterly*
Hor	*Horizons*

HTR	*Harvard Theological Review*
Int	*Interpretation*
IJST	*International Journal of Systematic Theology*
ISBE	*International Standard Bible Encyclopedia*
JSHJ	*Journal for the Study of the Historical Jesus*
JAET	*Journal of Asian Evangelical Theology*
JBL	*Journal of Biblical Literature*
JETS	*Journal of the Evangelical Theological Society*
JSNT	*Journal for the Study of the New Testament*
LALGNT	*Lexham Analytical Lexicon to the Greek New Testament*
LBD	*Lexham Bible Dictionary*
LNTS	Library of New Testament Studies
NAC	New American Commentary
NCC	New Covenant Commentary
NDT	*New Dictionary of Theology*
NICNT	New International Commentary on the New Testament
NICOT	New International Commentary on the Old Testament
NIDNTT	*New International Dictionary of New Testament Theology*
NIGTC	New International Greek Testament Commentary
NIVAC	NIV Application Commentary
NSBT	New Studies in Biblical Theology
NTL	New Testament Library
ODCC	*Oxford Dictionary of the Christian Church*
OTL	Old Testament Library
PNTC	Pillar New Testament Commentary
Presb	*Presbyterion*
RCS	Reformation Commentary on Scripture
REC	Reformed Expository Commentary
RevExp	*Review and Expositor*

RTR	*Reformed Theological Review*
SEÅ	*Svensk exegetisk årsbok*
SJT	*Scottish Journal of Theology*
SSBT	Short Studies in Biblical Theology
SwJT	*Southwestern Journal of Theology*
TDNT	*Theological Dictionary of the New Testament*, eds. G. Kittel and G. Friedrich
ThTo	*Theology Today*
TJ	*Trinity Journal*
TLNT	*Theological Lexicon of the New Testament*
TMSJ	*The Master's Seminary Journal*
TNTC	Tyndale New Testament Commentaries
TOTC	Tyndale Old Testament Commentaries
TR	*Theological Review*
WBC	Word Biblical Commentary
WDCT	*Westminster Dictionary of Christian Theology*
WTJ	*Westminster Theological Journal*
WW	*Word and World*
ZECNT	Zondervan Exegetical Commentary on the New Testament
ZAW	*Zeitschrift für die alttestamentliche Wissenschaft*
ZNW	*Zeitschrift für die neutestamentliche Wissenschaft und die Kunde der älteren Kirche*

Chapter 1

Consequences of Satanic Exorcism in This Age

A knowledge of history can prove quite helpful in life. Even a somewhat frail or anemic view of history is surely better than having no sense of history at all. Stories of civilizations now gone, sagas of heroes now forgotten, and a grasp of the sheer breadth and depth of history can give an individual a special sense of one's place in a grand story. Knowing what has come before can ground and root us in our own part of the story, even giving us perspective on what is yet to come. Further, not all history is of the same type; some parts are uplifting, some parts are quite confusing, and some parts are downright horrifying. Beyond its ups and downs, one of the great benefits of history is that it gives us a more balanced perspective—a sense of our place in this world, and how we got here.

What then does history have to do with theology? We may cautiously observe that Scripture is not *just* history, but Scripture is certainly a most unique *type* of history—one given to us by God Himself. The grand story of Scripture shows us that we are part of a saga—one that stretches from God's words of creation echoing over the deep (Gen 1:2–3) all the way through to the Lord God radiating his magnificent light throughout all redeemed creation (Rev 22:5). God reveals this magnificent saga to us in Scripture, and the better we understand Scripture, the better we understand the God of Scripture—as well as our place and purpose in that unfolding story.

As I began devoting myself more fully to the study of Scripture, the clearer it became that there was a theme of spiritual conflict that was quite prominent in this story. God was in the process of defeating evil (and our accuser Satan), and that picture of his victory seemed particularly evident in the New Testament accounts that spoke of Christ's earthly ministry. A battle seemed to have taken place—a tremendous defeat of the forces of darkness, one that forever changed the landscape of human history. It also seemed that the New Testament writers assumed that knowing about this victory would impact the way Christians lived in a rather dramatic way.

If an army fights in a worthy conflict against a despicable foe, receiving word of the opposing army's defeat should be monumental news with immediate and lasting effects. There may still be fighting ahead as the good army advances and the remnant of the enemy's troops may still roam the battlefield, but if the war has been won, then the entire dynamic of the conflict should change. Indeed, it *must* change. The victorious soldiers have cause to celebrate, a reason to march forward in confidence, and motivation to push forward with all exertion toward the victory that has been achieved.

In a similar vein, Christians are given something in Scripture very similar to the declaration of a battlefield victory. Christians are assured in Scripture that Christ has conquered Satan, bound him as a captive enemy, and subsequently liberated all enemy territory in this world. This picture is one of triumph—a truly victorious description of Christ's conquest. It is a depiction that should dramatically change the way Christians live, concerning both how we view the end and how we live in the present.

In the pages that follow, I would like to suggest a rather simple proposition. The proposition itself is quite modest, but its impact should be transformational to the way we live and the hope that we hold. I would like to suggest that Satan is a defeated foe—in a very real and tangible sense. This defeat of Satan is not just a symbolic defeat that holds no power, but it is a real, ongoing, and dramatic defeat that has changed the very battlefield of Scripture. I would further suggest that Satan's defeat is in keeping with Christ's manifest defeat of the earthly forces of darkness that He encountered during his earthly ministry—a ministry which accomplished the defeat of Satan as Jesus's culminating work. In that regard, we may accurately and biblically say that Satan has been "exorcised" from his place in this world. Satan's defeat is therefore not a theological outlier, but it lies at the very core of Christ's incarnational work.

I would like to suggest that if these things are true—that is, if Satan is a currently defeated foe who is restrained by the conquering hand of Christ—that we, as Christians, should frame our lives and beliefs in keeping with this truth. My estimate is that most believers do not consider themselves truly victorious in this world, and the outworking of that errant belief can be damaging to both our theology and our practice. The defeat of Satan is a key foundational element in how we perceive the overarching storyline of Scripture, particularly concerning the way end-time events are being accomplished. In the pages that follow, I would like to invite you to consider what Scripture tells us about the defeat of our enemy—and to live accordingly. If this victory of Christ is true, it should change the very tenor of our lives as believers.

The Eschatological Consequences of Satanic Exorcism

This treatise focuses on the present eschatological manifestation of satanic exorcism in this age, situated within the biblical narrative following Satan's initial fall from heaven and prior to his future (final and ultimate) defeat. There are eschatological effects of satanic exorcism—his defeat incurred substantial, identifiable consequences. These eschatological consequences are essential in qualifying the nature and extent of Satan's defeat. A theological appraisal of satanic exorcism clarifies the current limitation of satanic power as well as the parameters regarding satanic limitation.

The doctrine of satanic exorcism thus illuminates a midpoint in the cosmic state of spiritual warfare and emphasizes the eschatological overlap of *this age* and *the age to come* that is present in Christ's victory. Satanic exorcism and defeat occur within the context of spiritual warfare since it acutely concerns the satanic powers and authorities operating in this world and among the nations. Christ inaugurated his eschatological victory during his first coming through the activity of publicly exorcising demonic spirits, while the peak of his exorcistic ministry came in the exorcism of Satan himself from this world. A working understanding of the spiritual realm helps to properly situate satanic exorcism, though these related themes are infrequently addressed in many contemporary theological works.

Twentieth and twenty-first century work in eschatology has benefited dramatically from the insights of biblical theology and has brought greater sensitivity to the inherently eschatological nature of the New Testament.[1] There is a frequent New Testament refrain that Christ has achieved victory over Satan in his first coming. Christ has cast out and judged the satanic ruler of this world (John 12:31; 14:30; 16:11) and bound the satanic inhabitant of this world so that his territory might be liberated (Matt 12:22–32; Gal 1:4). Christ has observed Satan being cast down in defeat (Luke 10:18), even as Christ has triumphed over every satanic power and authority (Col 2:15; Heb 2:14; Eph 1:20–23, 3:10). Satan, the deceiver, is now thrown down from his place of power, and his current judgment is that he may no longer successfully accuse the elect due to the completed redemptive work of Christ (Rev 12:7–12; Rom 8:33, 38–39). Therefore, because of Christ's expulsion of Satan, Christ now commissions his disciples in his power and authority and instructs them to proclaim his victorious name among the nations (Luke 10:1–20; Matt 28:18–20 // Mark 16:14–18* // Luke 24:44–49 // John 20:19–23).[2] The power and personification of satanic lawlessness is currently bridled (2 Thess 2:1–12), and Satan himself is explicitly restrained from deceiving the nations and thereby forming an apocalyptic rebellion (Rev 20:1–3).

The New Testament theme of satanic defeat in contemporary scholarship is frequently buried beneath a thick accumulation of ongoing disagreements over eschatology—eschatological arguments that are often replete with complicated charts, fiercely held presuppositions, and a plethora of hermeneutical approaches.[3] Perhaps wary of the quarrelsome excesses of the past, many churches effectively eliminated eschatology from their doctrinal teaching. Some regard eschatology's reliance on supernatural divine intervention to be unpalatable (or intellectually embarrassing) to the modern mind, and still others are wary of the wildly errant apocalyptic

---

1 Vern S. Poythress, "Currents within Amillennialism," *Presb* 26.1 (2000): 21. Poythress notes that recent scholarship in eschatology has correctly stressed a focus on inaugurated fulfillment and the eschatological hope of the new earth from a biblical-theological perspective.

2 Throughout this work, double slashes indicate parallel passages under consideration. Disputed passages are denoted using an asterisk.

3 Robert H. Smith, "Eschatology of Acts and Contemporary Exegesis," *CTM* 29.9 (1958): 641. Smith holds that the division in eschatology can be summarized with the question: "In what ways are history and eschatology related?" This question will either be answered through God's revelation, which links the two concepts together, or by bifurcating history and eschatology entirely.

predictions that have understandably produced a guarded skepticism in many listeners.

Nevertheless, despite the distaste that eschatology holds for some, eschatology communicates a timeless message of hope for the people of God—one that guards against an unhealthy, destructive attachment to the world and, conversely, an outlook of despairing escapism from it.[4] Suffering precedes glory—victory through suffering is the Savior's path, and likewise, it is the eschatological path of all of Christ's followers to varying degrees. Eschatology is vitally necessary in a world whose final judgment is fast approaching, and it is urgently needed in the church, which must focus its eyes and fix its gaze on the Savior.

Satanic Exorcism as an Intermediate Defeat

Satan's defeat may be aptly described as a cosmic exorcism—Satan has been cast-out from this world by the work of Christ (John 12:31), defeated and curtailed in his activity and power. Few scholars have addressed the concept of satanic defeat using the paradigm of exorcism, and satanic exorcism is discussed even less frequently with theological ends in view. Satanic defeat, understood as cosmic exorcism, draws on the similar theological themes of Christus Victor and Jesus as the divine warrior. Christ has victoriously defeated Satan in his first coming, and He has decisively conquered the forces of evil.

The doctrine of satanic exorcism also illustrates the inbreaking of God's kingdom in the present age—Christ's first coming conclusively established his kingdom over and against the kingdom of darkness (Matt 4:17 // Mark 1:15). Christ has authoritatively defeated Satan, and Satan has been exorcised positionally due to the triumphant advance of God's kingdom. Satan is now cast down, restrained, and defeated—yet his assaults and persecutions against the church continue, nonetheless. In the age before Christ's

---

4 S. H. Travis, "Eschatology," in *NDT*, 228–31. Craig Blomberg observes that "it is ultimately only eschatology which completes an adequate Christian theodicy," and further that "a healthy understanding of the inaugurated eschatology of the New Testament will save us from the twin errors of a despair or defeatism that attempts to do nothing for this world but save souls from it and the currently more prominent mistake of replacing a hope for a supernaturally recreated universe with utopian socio-political programs for this world." Craig L. Blomberg, "Eschatology and the Church: Some New Testament Perspectives," *Themelios* 23.3 (1998): 19.

first coming, Satan (after his initial fall from heaven) still enjoyed a measure of authority and power in *this age*, while in the consummation of *the age to come*, he will be finally defeated and wholly removed (i.e., consigned to the lake of fire; Rev 20:10). Satan's inaugurated defeat is an eschatological theme that runs throughout the paradigm of satanic exorcism—a significant and perceptible defeat has taken place, yet he is still an active enemy of the church. The restraint of Satan is both specific and real, yet the consequences of satanic exorcism in the present age should not be conflated with an indiscriminate and complete cessation of evil.

In the wake of Christ's work accomplished in his first coming, there is a biblical paradox that emerges in the New Testament: Christ now reigns, and Satan is now defeated (inauguration), while correspondingly Christ will reign and Satan will be defeated (consummation). This paradox involves the overarching concept of a two-age eschatology. The time between Christ's first and second comings entails an experience of the old age passing away, giving way to the new age that is present due to Christ's work. In biblical terms, we recognize that *this age* is both present and passing away, while *the age to come* has begun in Christ while it yet awaits a future consummation. Satanic exorcism emerges as an intermediate victory in our current time between the ages (i.e., in the overlap of the ages) since the age to come has begun in the first coming of Christ. The two-age paradigm's eschatological framework is the background of this systematic approach to the particular focus area of satanic defeat.

SATANIC EXORCISM AS THE HOPE OF INAUGURATED VICTORY IN THIS AGE

A brief assessment of current world events may cause one to ask the question: How can the Bible speak of Satan being exorcised, restrained, or castout from this world in any real sense?[5] In the current experience of the New Testament overlap of *this age* and *the age to come*, Satan has been defeated, restrained, and cast out in the work of Christ's first coming—yet his attacks and influence are still palpable as this age remains but is passing away. The

---

5 R. Fowler White, "Agony, Irony, and Victory in Inaugurated Eschatology: Reflections on the Current Amillennial-Postmillennial Debate," *WTJ* 62.2 (2000): 161–76. White begins his article with the provocative question: "How dare we speak of the victorious reign of Christ and his church in our culture or any culture?"

consummation of Christ's second coming is still yet to come. A robust examination of satanic defeat in this age requires a "fully biblical inaugurated eschatology," one that surveys the victorious theme of perseverance amid persecution that stretches across the biblical narrative.[6] The New Testament exposition of satanic exorcism reveals certain aspects of satanic defeat, notably: Satan's inability to deceive the church; his inability to prevent the gospel from spreading; and his inability to stir up the world into a premature cataclysmic rebellion. Satan's inaugurated exorcism is expressed within eschatological confines and parameters—thus, the church will experience present victory amid fierce opposition and persecution from the forces of evil in this world.

The following study will examine satanic exorcism in this age as an intermediate eschatological victory with particular attention directed toward the effects of that exorcism in the current overlap of the ages. The present work will trace a basic outline of satanic defeat through the biblical canon, with its primary focus concentrating on the New Testament depiction of the current state of satanic exorcism.[7] An analysis will ensue of the ongoing effects of Christ's first coming regarding the accomplishment of satanic exorcism from this world. The eschatological doctrine of satanic exorcism clarifies that in Christ's first coming, he achieved victory over Satan by exorcising him from the place of power and authority that Satan previously occupied. Thus, satanic exorcism describes a divine limiting of satanic power in this age, even as satanic attack and persecution persists while this age is in its final days (Heb 1:2). In conclusion, this study will observe key elements of Christ's cosmic exorcism of Satan in this age, while making observations about the effects of this exorcism.

---

6 White, "Agony, Irony, and Victory," 162. White primarily refers to the church's experience, but this observation holds true for God's people in both the Old Testament and New Testament.

7 The present study will give only limited attention to the state of satanic power and authority described in the Old Testament and to satanic judgment in the (future) second coming.

Defining Terms

Eschatology

In its most basic sense, the term "eschatology" is associated with the theological study of the last things.[8] As a combination of the Greek words ἔσχατος (*last*) and λόγος (*word*), the study of eschatology typically occupies the final pages of systematic theology books as a means of discussing the concluding future events that are to take place in redemptive history. Though it is not improper to discuss and categorize such ultimate, final matters in systematic theology, it is more helpful to recognize eschatology in a broader biblical sense—as a historical movement toward a final goal and an eternal new order.[9] A robust view of eschatology is especially valuable for the church since eschatology is both a future hope and a present and necessary component of thoroughgoing biblical study. Presently experienced eschatology is a significant New Testament theme, as G. K. Beale observes. Beale rightly notes, "It should not be astonishing to discover that eschatology is a dominant idea in the New Testament. In fact, it is not an overstatement to say that to understand New Testament eschatology, one must have some acquaintance with how the New Testament authors viewed eschatology or the 'end times.'"[10] Eschatology entails the final things in redemptive history, yet it also describes the movement through which those events are presently

---

8 Wayne A. Grudem observes, "The study of future events is often called 'eschatology,' from the Greek word *eschatos* (ἔσχατος), which means 'last.' The study of eschatology, then, is the study of 'the last things.'" *Systematic Theology: An Introduction to Biblical Doctrine* (Downers Grove, IL: Inter-Varsity Press ; Grand Rapids: Zondervan, 1994), 1091. See also BDAG, s.v. "ἔσχατος"; S. H. Travis, "Eschatology," 228–31.

9 Geerhardus Vos, *The Pauline Eschatology* (Phillipsburg, NJ: P&R, 1995), 1. Michael Horton accurately contends that eschatology is not merely a bookend to systematics, observing that eschatology precedes soteriology. T*he Christian Faith: A Systematic Theology for Pilgrims on the Way* (Grand Rapids: Zondervan, 2011), 906. Beale echoes Vos, observing, "Such an understanding of the latter days that views them as arriving only at the very end of history needs rethinking. The phrase 'latter days' occurs numerous times in the New Testament and often does not refer exclusively to the very end of history, as we typically think of it. This wording is used frequently to describe the end times as beginning already in the first century." *A New Testament Biblical Theology: The Unfolding of the Old Testament in the New* (Grand Rapids: Baker Academic, 2011), 130.

10 Beale, *New Testament Biblical Theology*, 129. Beale advocates that eschatology is the dominant theme of New Testament theology, the lens through which responsible readers must view the storyline of Scripture.

realized. Eschatology does not solely occur in the closing chapters of the New Testament but runs throughout the entire canon of Scripture. [11]

A robust and thorough understanding of eschatology should recognize the full forward thrusting movement of various themes in Scripture that are in motion toward a final goal, a movement that flows from the very outset of the redemptive saga to its final consummation. Keith Mathison observes,

> Eschatology in a broader sense, however, concerns what Scripture teaches about God's purposes in Christ for history. As such, eschatology does include a study of the consummation of God's purposes at the end of history, but it also includes a study of the stages in the unfolding of those purposes.... [A] study of biblical eschatology must include a study of Christ's first advent as well as his second. [12]

A robust understanding of eschatology gives believers a theological context for our place in the flow of the redemptive saga, containing elements both personal and global, present and future. The *telos* (goal or aim) of eschatology that emerges from this understanding recognizes that the new creation is neither a wholesale destruction of the old nor merely a return to it.[13] God has redemptive plans for the created order, and those redemptive plans involve an eschatological escalation toward a new created order in which all the promises of God find their ultimate consummation. The *telos* of eschatology recognizes the reclamation and restoration that are found

---

11 Anthony A. Hoekema, *The Bible and the Future* (Grand Rapids: Eerdmans, 2000), 6.
12 Keith A. Mathison, *From Age to Age* (Phillipsburg, NJ: P&R, 2014), 2.
13 Anna Case-Winters observes that eschatology must be distinguished between end and beginning, *terminus* (i.e., endpoint) and *telos* (i.e., goal or purpose)—*Endzeit ist Urzeit*. Case Winters's view is similar to Moltmann's discussion of the goal (*telos*) of history compared to its end (*finis*), though not extending to Moltmann's conclusion of a "theology of hope." See Anna Case-Winters, "The End? Christian Eschatology and the End of the World," *Int* 70.1 (2016): 63; Jürgen Moltmann, "The End as Beginning," *WW* 22.3 (2002): 222; contra Robert H. Mounce, *A Living Hope: A Commentary on 1 and 2 Peter* (Eugene, OR: Wipf & Stock, 2005). There is also a theme of cataclysmic purification in Christ's return (cf. 2 Pet 3:10; Isa 34:4), on which, see the discussion in Hoekema, *Bible and the Future*, 280–81. Hoekema favors viewing the cosmic fire of 2 Peter 3:10 as referencing a purifying restoration; cf. Thomas R. Schreiner, *1, 2 Peter, Jude*, NAC 37 (Nashville: Broadman & Holman, 2003), 384ff; contra Robert H. Mounce, *A Living Hope: A Commentary on 1 and 2 Peter* (Eugene, OR: Wipf & Stock, 2005), 143; David Alan Black, Katharine G. L. Barnwell, and Stephen H. Levinsohn, *Linguistics and New Testament Interpretation: Essays on Discourse Analysis* (Nashville: Broadman & Holman, 1992), 265.

in the redemptive flow of what is accomplished in the work of Christ, concluding with Christ's reclamation and restoration of his people even amid the fiery judgment that accompanies his return (see 1 John 4:17; 2 Pet 3:7).

Satan

Satan is a crucial character in this biblical study, yet finding explicit biblical references to Satan entails far more than a detailed word study might suggest.[14] The doctrine of Satan is often relegated to the periphery of theological studies, either to satanology or to the larger subcategory of angelology. Analysis of Satan is frequently regarded as a tangential topic of doctrinal speculation that is probably best avoided due to the anti-supernatural tendency of modern scholarship. The same tendencies seem to be true for the eschatological category of satanic defeat.[15] Modern studies in satanology and demonology have made effective use of recent discoveries of extant extra-biblical materials, including first-century Jewish and Pseudepigraphal writings. However, these extra-biblical sources are of varying degrees of effectiveness and certainly cannot suffice as a theological foundation.[16]

In the biblical narrative, Satan emerges as a shadowy spiritual figure who only irregularly surfaces in the narrative plot and typically occupies a secondary focus in the passages in which he does make an appearance.[17]

---

14 Breytenbach and Day observe: "Σατάν and Σατανάς are transliterations of the Heb śāṭān (cf. [LXX] 3 Kgdms 11:14.23; Sir 21:27) or Aram śāṭānā' and mean 'adversary.' In such instances 8HevXIIgr and the LXX translate the Hebrew expression with *Diabolos* →Devil, meaning 'the Slanderer.' *Ho Satanās* (rarely used without article) thus designates the opponent of God. In the New Testament *Satanās* and *Diabolos* can refer to the same supernatural being (cf. Rev 20:2) and can thus be interchanged (cf. Mark 1:13 and Luke 4:2). This highest evil being can also be referred to as *ho ponēros* ('the evil one,' cf. Matt 13:19) and *ho peirazōn* ('the tempter'—cf. Matt 4:3: 1 Thess 3:5)." Cilliers Breytenbach and Peggy L. Day, "Satan," in DDD, 726–27.

15 Derek R. Brown, "The Devil in the Details: A Survey of Research on Satan in Biblical Studies," CBR 9.2 (2011): 200.

16 See an explanation of the development of "Satan" in Second Temple literature and modern writings (including Dante's *Divine Comedy* and Milton's *Paradise Lost*) in Robert W. Canoy, "Time and Space, Satan (Devil, Ancient Serpent, Deceiver, and Accuser), and Michael in Revelation," RevExp 114.2 (2017): 259. For additional ANE material on Satan, see the discussion of "διάβολος" in Hans Bietenhard, "Satan, Beelzebul, Devil, Exorcism," in NIDNTT, 3:468ff. Also see Roy D. Kotansky, "Demonology" in DNTB, 269–73; Alan Richardson, "Satan," in WDCT, 521–22.

17 For further reading on the development of sociological constructions about Satan alongside ANE cultures, see Richard H. Hiers, "Satan, Demons, and the Kingdom of

His recorded legacy begins in the Fall narrative of Genesis 3 (leading to the *protoevangelium* promise in Genesis 3:15), yet he receives relatively sparse theological mention in the Old Testament.[18] There is development in the biblical disclosure of Satan in the Old Testament (Job 1–2 and Zechariah 3 contain recognizable references), and there is increasing recognition of a personified power of evil at work in this fallen world—with a growing use of the title "the Satan" or "the adversary."[19] Nevertheless, even though various details about Satan's activities become apparent, his origin and descent into evil remain obscure, as Scobie observes:

> In Job 1 and Zech 3 "the Satan" is an angelic being, and therefore presumably created by God. According to Col 1:16, the various "powers" were all created through Christ. Since Satan and the powers are portrayed as opposed to God, it is a fair assumption that they are thought of as having rebelled against God. Jude 6 (cf. 2 Pet 2:4) merely hints at a belief in fallen angels .... John 8:44 says the devil "was a murderer from the beginning," and 1 John 3:8 says "the devil has been sinning from the beginning"; "from the beginning" *(ap' arches)* could suggest a rebellion before creation.[20]

Satan's origins may be disappointingly hazy, yet the opening chapters of Genesis introduce his work in the context of deception and accusation.

God," *SJT* 27.1 (1974): 35–47; Merrill F. Unger, *Biblical Demonology: A Study of Spiritual Forces at Work Today* (Grand Rapids: Kregel, 2012), 244. Some scholars have also observed a tendency to present satanic passages in harmonic unison in Old Testament studies, while New Testament studies focus more on individual passage references. See Brown, "The Devil in the Details," 214.

18 Satan's presence, or even his "legacy" through the serpent's influence, in the Genesis 3 narrative is not a universally recognized interpretation and has many detractors in scholarship. On the *protoevangelium* as a prophetic forecast of ultimate satanic defeat, see Mathison, *From Age to Age*, 26n40; Hoekema, *Bible and the Future*, 4–5. On the frequency of occurrence of the name "Lucifer" for Satan, see discussion on Isaiah 14:12 in Charles H. H. Scobie, *The Ways of Our God: An Approach to Biblical Theology* (Grand Rapids: Eerdmans, 2003).

19 Scobie, *Ways of Our God*, 243.

20 Scobie, 268. Scobie discusses the translation of "Day Star" (הֵילֵל, *hêlēl*) in Isa 14:12 as "*lucifer qui mane oriebaris*" in the Latin Vulgate, a translation that enabled many to identify Isaiah's "Day Star" with Satan (or "Lucifer" as a personal name for Satan). Scobie maintains that a consistent biblical-theological perspective will recognize Christ as the true Day Star. Scobie, 264. Scobie argues that possible references to Satan in Isaiah 14:4–21 and Revelation 8:10–11 (cf. 9:1–11) are more tenuous and speculative.

Satan's work of deception induces humanity's rebellion against God and ultimately brings destruction and death upon the divine image-bearers.[21] Though Satan occupies a role of accusation and destruction, Christ defeated him and cast him down from his prosecutorial role when Satan "fell from heaven" through Jesus's death, burial, resurrection, and ascension (Luke 10:17-18; John 12:31; Rev 12:9).[22] Satan's capacities as an angelic being are now limited in this age following the work of Christ.

The current study will adopt two approaches for surveying the biblical material concerning Satan, comparably found in Charles Scobie's work.[23] First, "Satan" will be retained as a personal title that recognizes the evil spiritual being who functions as the biblical archetype of evil. Though many biblical titles likely refer to this figure, the moniker "Satan" has the benefit of functioning as both a title and a descriptive designation.[24] Second, this study will solely focus on the nature of Satan's defeat and will not attempt to speculate as to his origins. Scobie correctly observes: "The New Testament has much to say about Satan and the various forms in which the powers of evil manifest themselves. But no more than the Old Testament does it speculate on the origin of God's adversaries."[25] Satan appears in the New Testament as an evil power over the rulers, powers, and authorities of this age—yet the work of Christ effectively exorcises him.[26] Further discussion

---

21 Canoy, "Time and Space, Satan," 262. Canoy cites G. K. Beale, *The Book of Revelation: A Commentary on the Greek Text*, NIGTC (Grand Rapids: Eerdmans, 1999), 656. Cf. Hans Bietenhard, "Satan, Beelzebul, Devil, Exorcism," 468.

22 Bietenhard, "Satan, Beelzebul, Devil, Exorcism," 468; Canoy, "Time and Space, Satan," 264.

23 See appendix 2 for a list of biblical passages that have been proposed to refer to Satan.

24 Satan is called by his proper name (Gr. Σατανᾶς [Satanas]; ; Heb. "שָׂטָן") or, often, by the moniker of "Accuser" (κατήγωρ) or "Devil" (διάβολος; diabolos). Scobie, *Ways of Our God*, 243; Millard J. Erickson, *Christian Theology, 3rd ed.* (Grand Rapids: Baker Academic, 2013), 448; Louis Matthews Sweet, "Satan," in ISBE, 2693. A study of the New Testament uses of *satanas* (σατανάς) and *diabolos* (διάβολος) along with 30 other terms for Satan reveals 137 likely occurrences (149 possible) in a total of 74 percent of New Testament books. See Thomas J. Farrar and Guy Williams, "Talk of the Devil: Unpacking the Language of New Testament Satanology," JSNT 39.1 (2016): 72–96; Thomas J. Farrar and Guy Williams, "Diabolical Data: A Critical Inventory of New Testament Satanology," JSNT 39.1 (2016): 40–71.

25 Scobie, *Ways of Our God*, 267.

26 Scobie, 265. Scobie notes, "For the New Testament these [supernatural/spiritual] powers are real. They have been defeated by Christ in the decisive battle of the war between good and evil, though they will be eliminated only at the final consummation."

of Satan's name, work, and biblical appearances in both the Old Testament and the New Testament will be developed in later chapters.

Exorcism

Exorcisms commonly occur in the Gospel narratives, and a defining characteristic of Jesus's exorcisms is his spiritual authority over the demonic realm.[27] Jesus is the one who exorcises demons, the "exorcist" par excellence. The closest Greek equivalent for the English gloss "exorcist" is ἐξορκιστής, though this word is infrequent in its New Testament usage (cf. ἐξορκιστῶν, Acts 19:13). In the New Testament, exorcism is typically described using the more common verb ἐκβάλλω ("to drive out, expel").[28] Though the word usage concerning exorcism varies in the New Testament, it is evident that "the phenomenon of exorcism is much more widespread than the infrequent use of the cognate noun and verb suggest."[29]

Exorcism in the present study will reflect the five criteria laid out by Cook and Lawless (given in the context of demonic possession): 1) God's kingdom brings conflict with the kingdom of darkness; 2) demons can physically control an inhabitant; 3) many demons can simultaneously inhabit a host; 4) demons resist leaving a host; and 5) demons fear Jesus and his authorized spokesmen.[30] Exorcism includes a transference (or reclamation) of the element of authority—authority that is typically expressed as ἐξουσία in the New Testament. Authority involves a power dynamic in the spiritual realm—it is something that is claimed by Satan (Matt 4), yet Jesus powerfully wields it (Matt 12; cf. Eph 6) and subsequently delegates it to his disciples (Matt 28:18–20).[31]

---

27 William F. Cook and Charles E. Lawless, *Spiritual Warfare in the Storyline of Scripture: A Biblical, Theological, and Practical Approach* (Nashville: Broadman & Holman, 2019).
28 Bietenhard, "Satan, Beelzebul, Devil, Exorcism," 473. Other lexical variations of *exorkistēs* reveal varying definitions that do not match biblical realities, such as "one who expels demons by the use of magical formulae." Sweet, "Exorcism, Exorcist," 1067. *Ekballō* has a softer semantic range such as "send out" or "remove." See BDAG, s.v. "ἐκβάλλω."
29 Bietenhard, "Satan, Beelzebul, Devil, Exorcism," 473.
30 William F. Cook and Charles E. Lawless, *Spiritual Warfare in the Storyline of Scripture: A Biblical, Theological, and Practical Approach* (Nashville: Broadman & Holman, 2019), 61–62.
31 The concept of authority will be addressed in greater detail in chapter 3 of the present work.

Deception

Deception is a significant component of satanic strategy. Deception is often rendered by the Greek term πλανάω (and its cognates; see Rev 20:3,8; Matt 24:4–5), and it is closely related to the concept of human rebellion against God (cf. πλανῆσαί, Deut 13:5 LXX).[32] The common Hebrew equivalent for πλανάω is העה, a term that, in the LXX, often refers to "being led astray" or "deceived" (Deut 27:18) or wandering without direction or purpose (Job 12:25; Isa 35:8).[33] Deception distracts an individual away from a pursued goal, often leading to the destruction of the one who is deceived. Believers are warned against deception that leads to destruction (ἐξαπατήσῃ, 2 Thess 2:3), just as the serpent deceived Eve in the Garden to their mutual destruction (ἐξηπάτησεν 2 Cor 11:3; see also ἠπατήθη and ἐξαπατηθεῖσα in 1 Tim 2:14 with the fall in Genesis 3 in the background). Satan is described in Scripture as the "great deceiver." Indeed, Satan "deceives because it is part of his personality to do so."[34] Deception is a quality of Satan whereby he seduces people into believing a destructive lie (Gen 3), a quality that is also exercised in the New Testament by demonic spirits (1 Tim 4:1–2, 1 John 4:1). [35]

Elements within Judaism anticipated the advent of deception in the last days occurring alongside suffering in the covenant community—deception that would be subtle, drawing those away from the faith, and ultimately leading to their destruction (Dan 11:30–45, cf. 2 Thess 2:3).[36] Satan uses deception as "one of the primary means" against humanity.[37] Beale observes:

---

32 The idea of "revolt" connected with deception is found in George Eldon Ladd, *A Commentary on the Revelation of John* (Grand Rapids: Eerdmans, 1972), 262. Others view deception in a soteriological sense, as in Gregory H. Harris, "Satan's Work as a Deceiver," *BibSac* 156.622 (1999): 190–202.

33 *LALGNT*, s.v. "πλανάω"; Michael R. Jones, "Apostasy," in *Lexham Theological Wordbook*, eds. Douglas Magnum et al., Lexham Bible Reference Series (Bellingham, WA: Lexham, 2014).

34 Harris, "Satan's Work as a Deceiver," 190.

35 Harris, 190–202; "Falsch, Falschheit," in *Calwer Biblical Lexicon: Biblisches Handwörterbuch* illustriert, ed. Paul Zeller (Stuttgart: Verlag der Vereinsbuchhandlung, 1912), 175.

36 Beale, *New Testament Biblical Theology*, 156, 190, 202. See also Vos, *Pauline Eschatology*, 111.

37 Erickson, *Christian Theology*, 448. Erickson does, however, categorize 2 Cor 4:4 and 1 Thess 2:18 as "deception" passages (alongside 2 Cor 11:14–15), with Rev 12:9 and 20:8,10 also referenced.

It is clear that persecution and deception in the ecclesiological community started in the first century and has continued ever since.... At that time [the climax of the tribulation], persecution and deception, which formerly have affected only part of the church throughout history, will be present throughout the worldwide church, at which point Christ will return a final time (see Rev 11:1-13; 20:1-10).[38]

Paul warns believers to beware those who "deceive [ἐξαπατῶσι] the hearts of the naive" (Rom 16:18), while also recognizing that "the God of peace will soon crush Satan under your feet" (Rom 16:20; see Gen 3:15). [39]

Subsequent chapters will develop further the aforementioned terms ("eschatology," "Satan," "exorcism," and "deception"). Definitions have been provided in this opening chapter to provide clarity, as the subsequent discussion will regularly employ these concepts. The ensuing chapters will interact with these terms in far greater detail, discussing the biblical warrant for each, while also building upon the theological theme of satanic exorcism in this age.

---

38 Beale, *New Testament Biblical Theology*, 203.
39 Beale, 219, 221–22.

Chapter 2

Systematic Evidence of Satanic Exorcism in This Age

The New Testament consistently affirms that Christ authoritatively defeated Satan in his first coming—cosmically exorcising Satan from this world. Satan's exorcism means that he is defeated and restrained in this present time; therefore, the doctrine of satanic exorcism is one that provides immeasurable hope and encouragement for Christians who will continue to experience victory through suffering until the consummation of Christ's second coming. The church has always struggled with the tension of the eschatology of this age—a tension that involves recognizing Christ's decisive defeat of Satan while simultaneously understanding that suffering and evil persist in this world (and even appear to worsen in particular times and places). This inaugurated perspective produces an apparent paradox: Satan is exorcised from this world and his authority is curtailed, yet the evils of satanic attack and persecution persist. This eschatological paradox may be clarified by developing a robust theology of satanic exorcism, one that clarifies the Christian call to perseverance and victory through the persecution and evil that lingers in this age.[1]

The church's victory in this age is realized in a similar manner as Christ's victory in his first coming. Just as Christ suffered, his church will also suffer—yet it is precisely through this Christological (or "Christ-patterned") suffering that true victory is realized for the Christian (John 16:33).[2] This

---
1 White, "Agony, Irony, and Victory in Inaugurated Eschatology," 162. White terms this approach a "fully biblical inaugurated eschatology."
2 Horton observes that this inaugurated victory is a "theology of the cross"—an eschatology concomitant with experienced suffering in this age. See Horton, "Eschatology After Nietzsche: Apollonian, Dionysian or Pauline?," *IJST* 2.1 (2000): 29. A study by Köstenberger, Stewart, and Makara likewise picks up on the theme of eschatological

chapter will survey some of the representative perspectives that illuminate the area of satanic exorcism, particularly in its function as an eschatological paradigm. This chapter will focus primarily on modern works that have had substantial influence on the subject of satanic exorcism.[3] After surveying these scholarly works, the theological themes that begin to emerge will help to frame the remaining discussion of the dynamic of satanic exorcism within the two-age eschatological paradigm.

An Approach to Satanic Exorcism in Christ's First Coming

G. K. Beale

How can the New Testament account of satanic exorcism be described in a way that is both biblically accurate and theologically meaningful? A helpful approach to this question is to frame the concept of satanic exorcism within the greater interpretive lens of a balanced whole-Bible eschatology. This interpretive approach is the assertion of G. K. Beale, who suggests that eschatology should function as a sort of interpretive lens through which we view the biblical storyline—an interpretive approach that calls for a comprehensive and robust understanding of biblical eschatology. To serve as an appropriate interpretive lens for biblical interpretation, Beale defines eschatology as "the [biblical] movement toward the new-creational reign, with other associated eschatological concepts being understood as subcategories."[4] Eschatology encompasses the progressive movement through the redemptive saga of Scripture, culminating in the last days and entailing all the dynamics that lead to that redemptive conclusion. Beale recognizes that some may object to such a definition, but he maintains: "We may say that eschatology originally preceded soteriology, but with

---

victory-through-suffering, specifically keying in on Jesus's teaching that his disciples would suffer in this present age (the church age), even as the generation he was addressing would suffer judgment in the impending destruction of the temple in the first century. See Andreas J. Köstenberger, Alexander Stewart, and Apollo Makara, *Jesus and the Future: Understanding What He Taught about the End Times* (Bellingham, WA: Lexham, 2018).

3 Compare the binding of Satan and the millennium in Augustine of Hippo, *City of God*, trans. Henry Bettenson (New York: Penguin, 2004), Book 20.7. Certain relevant works not discussed in this chapter will appear in later chapters.

4 Beale, *New Testament Biblical Theology*, 23. By this definition, satanic exorcism would be one such subcategory.

the fall, eschatology is now restoration from sin followed by a consummation of an eternal new creation."⁵

Eschatology incorporates all of God's purposes for his creation, including the redemptive purposes accomplished in the person of Christ. Christ's first coming is the high point of this unfolding redemptive saga—an eschatological inauguration in which Jesus's demonic exorcisms and satanic defeat (binding of the "strong man" of Matt 12:19 // Mark 3:27 // Luke 11:21–23) attest to his victory over both sin and Satan (achieving victory where the first Adam had failed).⁶ Whereas Adam's failure brought sin and death to all humanity, Christ's conquering work through the cross and resurrection now brings redemption and life (Rom 5:12–21; 1 Cor 15:21–22). There is also an eschatological progression of spiritual warfare that is consistently present in the background of the biblical saga, a cosmic spiritual battle that is occurring just beyond men's ability to see—yet one into which Scripture gives occasional glimpses. Beale contends that this cosmic spiritual battle is one that involves Satan's initial fall from heaven through sin (exemplified through the serpent in the Garden), followed by Satan's defeat in Christ's first coming (explored in the following chapters), and finally comes to full realization in the conclusive defeat that will occur when Christ returns.

The chronological timing of Christ's eschatological defeat of Satan is not explicitly clarified in Scripture—Christ's death, burial, resurrection, and ascension are clearly of primary importance (1 Cor 15:3–5); however, specific passages that describe Christ's defeat of Satan are chronologically imprecise regarding where they occur within the events of the first coming (Luke 10:18).⁷ While this present study will maintain that satanic defeat is accomplished throughout the entirety of Christ's first coming, Beale places the main emphasis of spiritual victory (and concomitant satanic defeat) on Christ's resurrection.⁸

---

5 Beale, 89; cf. also 24, 178.
6 G. K. Beale and Mitchell Kim, *God Dwells among Us: Expanding Eden to the Ends of the Earth* (Downers Grove, IL: InterVarsity Press, 2014), 90–91, 142–43. Beale and Kim's study includes an analysis of the binding of the "strong man" in parallel with demonic exorcism, but satanic exorcism is not explored any further in the work (see 90–91).
7 Beale places primary weight on the resurrection and ascension. See G. K. Beale with David H. Campbell, *Revelation: A Shorter Commentary* (Grand Rapids: Eerdmans, 2015), 177.
8 G. K. Beale, "The Millennium in Revelation 20:1–10: An Amillennial Perspective," CTR 11.1 (2013): 29–62.

In his works, Beale regularly incorporates the conception of God's presence in this world as it is expressed through the temple—explicitly noting that the temple is a cross-canonical theme encapsulating God's presence, the task of his people, and the spread of his glory throughout all creation.[9] What God commenced in Eden is being fulfilled and restored to fruition in a new-creational design—one that provides canonical unity through the overarching theme of eschatological consummation.[10] Though some readers of the biblical narrative have regarded man as a practically neutral character in the biblical story, Beale contends that a robust eschatology reveals humanity's creational purpose for reflecting God in his creation, alongside of man's sinful choice to reflect the Serpent instead of the Creator.[11] The resultant condition is that rather than humanity (following Adam) ruling in creation by glorifying the Creator, man's rebellion instead leads to Satan's perverse exercise of authority in this world and a perversion among the created order.[12]

Beale's work emphasizes the conquering role that Christ exercises in his first coming, a role of conquest over the satanic kingdom that occurs alongside the establishment and advance of God's eternal kingdom.[13] Christ appears in the first coming as the conquering Son of Man (Matt 24; see Dan 7:13–14), the one who overcomes Satan's kingdom in fulfillment of Old Testament prophecy.[14] The prophetic expectation that builds from Daniel 7 is of the impending overthrow of God's enemies; yet, this Danielic expectation is realized by the Son of Man who paradoxically (or, as Beale asserts, ironically) fulfills his triumphant enthronement through what appears to

---

9 G. K. Beale, "Eden, the Temple, and the Church's Mission in the New Creation," JETS 48.1 (2005): 5–31.

10 Beale, *New Testament Biblical Theology*, 93. Beale further develops the theme of "temple," advancing that the New Creation is a fulfillment of the former temple (272–273), and further, that Christ is the ultimate fulfillment of the temple theme of the Old Testament (632). For further discussion of the new-creational paradigm, see Beale with Campbell, *Revelation*, 33–34.

11 G. K. Beale, *Redemptive Reversals and the Ironic Overturning of Human Wisdom* (Wheaton, IL: Crossway, 2019), 54–55.

12 Beale describes Satan's derailment of Adam's vice-regency as a divinely-instituted ironic judgment. Beale, *Redemptive Reversals*, 84–85. Similar is the observation of Robert R. Recker, who maintains that Satan occupies the eschatological role of a false ruler, a "usurper" and "imposter." Robert R. Recker, "Satan: In Power or Dethroned?," CTJ 6.2 (1971): 135.

13 Beale, *New Testament Biblical Theology*, 428–29. Beale's focus on Christ's conquering role is an example of the Christus Victor theme of the atonement.

14 Beale, 191–92, 400, 200–203, 147–50.

be a shameful and humiliating death. Christ conquers, but the work of his victory is accomplished in a way that many did not expect.

Nevertheless, it is precisely through Christ's sacrificial, atoning death that his first coming is both fulfilled and consummated (Matt 16:21; Luke 9:22; Ps 8; cf. Dan 7:21–22, 7:18, 24–27), and the Christian is therefore called to follow in discipleship in this same manner of Christological suffering (Rev 2).[15] In a time when many modern religious individuals cannot even entertain the actual possibility of the spiritual realm (much less its theological consequences for this age), Scripture demonstrates that Christ's first coming brought defeat to our spiritual enemy through the establishment of his eternal kingdom and rule (Ps 2:8–9).[16] Beale concludes that the defeat and exorcism of Satan is Christ's initial fulfillment of our future hope (Rev 1:17–18; Dan 2:44–45).[17]

The paradox of victory-through-suffering initially makes it difficult to speak in precise terms about the conditions of Satan's currently defeated (exorcised) state. Beale recognizes that Satan has suffered an eschatological defeat that extends throughout the church age, yet this defeat and binding are temporary and partial in their effects. The partial effects of satanic defeat are readily observable in the evil that is persistently occurring in this world, though Scripture provides greater clarity than merely subjective experience.[18] Satan's defeat transpires at the intersection of *this age* and *the age to come*, forming a key eschatological component to understanding Christ's victory (see Figure 1).[19]

The age to come has essentially invaded the realm of *this age*, bringing the inauguration of assured victory even while *this age* is, nevertheless, passing away.

Beale explains that Satan's restraint results from Christ's victory over Satan, leading to God's corresponding protection of his elect against satanic deception (see Rev 9:4).[20] Satan and the forces of evil seek to deceive

---

15 Beale, *Redemptive Reversals*, 99–103.
16 Beale, 167–68.
17 Beale, 177
18 Beale, "Millennium in Revelation 20," 153, 202, 216–18.
19 Vos, *The Pauline Eschatology*, 36–38.
20 Beale with Campbell, *Revelation*, 38. Beale identifies the binding of Satanic activities by means of the "keys" (chapters 3 and 20) as an area that can benefit from further elucidation.

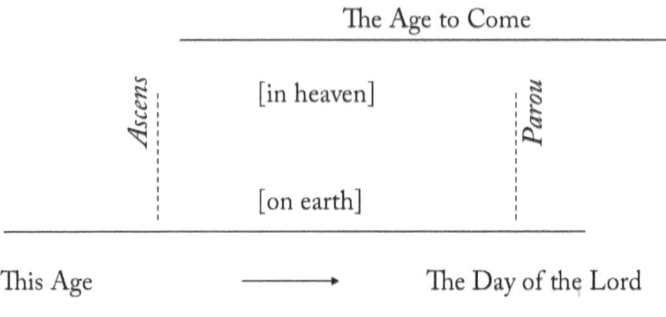

FIGURE 1

the lost to their destruction. As Beale notes: "Those who abide in spiritual darkness must be plagued by the forces of darkness, whose work it is to draw the dark curtain of unbelief permanently over the spiritual eyes of the ungodly, who are intractable in their unbelief."[21] Satan previously exercised a degree of power and authority in this world that has now been curtailed through Christ's work on the cross (Rev 12), a power that he offered to Jesus in the wilderness temptations (Luke 4:5–8 // Matt 4:8–10).[22] The New Testament describes Satan as the one who deceives (Rev 20:3, 12:9), yet he is also described as the one who has been evicted from the heavenly realm and cast into the abyss—a realm that Beale describes as a realm of limited satanic operation (Rev 9 and 20), the "opposite of heaven."[23]

Beale's evaluation is that Satan is defeated due to Christ's work (accomplished in his death and resurrection), and that victory subsequently extends throughout the entire period of the church age, even amid suffering and persecution.[24] The defeat and restraint of Satan are described in different ways in Scripture: an expulsion and fall from heaven (Rev 12 and 20); a binding of the "strong man" (Matt 12:29 // Mark 3:27 // Luke 11:21); a fall from heaven as the disciples are given power (Luke 10:19–19; John 12:31); and a disarmament in which this foe is rendered powerless (Col 2:15; Heb

---

21 Beale with Campbell, *Revelation*, 179.
22 Beale, *New Testament Biblical Theology*, 253; George Eldon Ladd, *The Presence of the Future: The Eschatology of Biblical Realism* (Grand Rapids: Eerdmans, 1974), 118–19.
   Beale emphasizes the role of the cross in satanic defeat.
23 Beale, "Millennium in Revelation 20," 37–38, 41.
24 Beale with Campbell, *Revelation*, 253.

2:14). All these events describe a significant (and yet not comprehensive) restraint of Satanic power.[25]

Satan's restraint does not result in an unqualified, complete, and total cessation of all satanic activity but instead refers to a specific limitation of power and authority for a specific purpose.[26] Beale shows that Satan's restraint primarily impacts his ability to deceive and destroy (two concepts that will prove to be inseparably related). Due to Christ's victory, Satan is no longer able to deceive the nations, nor is he allowed to bring defeat to the church of Christ through a premature revolt of the nations against God.[27]

Beale elsewhere clarifies the nature of Satan's restraint by observing that he no longer possesses the previously exercised authority over death (1:18; cf. Matt 12:29 // Mark 3:27 // Luke 11:21), he cannot prevent Christ from drawing the nations to Himself (John 12:31), and he cannot deceive the nations concerning salvation.[28] Kim Riddlebarger echoes Beale's perspective on the effects of satanic restraint:

> The imagery that Satan is presently bound means that he cannot deceive God's people *en masse* nor can he attack the covenant community with relative impunity as he did before the coming of the Messiah. This is evident by reviewing the broad course of redemptive history. Satan deceived Adam in Eden, resulting in sin and the curse of death coming upon the entire human race. Through the agency of Israel's pagan neighbors, Satan prevented the nation from fulfilling its assigned role in the promised land as a light to the nations. Adam desired to be like God. Israel desired to be like her pagan neighbors.[29]

---

25 Beale, "Millennium in Revelation 20," 38–39. See a related discussion on satanic restraint in Ladd, *Presence of the Future*, 149; Recker, "Satan," 141–42.
26 Beale, "Millennium in Revelation 20," 38, 40–41. See Revelation 3:7–9, 9:2–3, and 20:2–3.
27 Beale, *New Testament Biblical Theology*, 420.
28 Beale, "The Millennium in Revelation 20," 39–40; so also Sam Storms, who posits that Satan is unable to deceive the nations, accuse Christians, or impede gospel advance— though not prevented from persecuting the church. See Sam Storms, *Kingdom Come: The Amillennial Alternative* (Fearn, Scotland: Mentor, 2013), 429n7, 439, 444, cf. 433ff.
29 Kim Riddlebarger, *A Case for Amillennialism: Understanding the End Times*, exp. ed. (Grand Rapids: Baker Books, 2013), 211.

Like Riddlebarger, Beale ties satanic deception to the biblical-theological commission that commenced in Eden, showing that Satan deceived "God's first covenant community" of Adam and Eve—thus temporarily hindering humanity from fulfilling its mandated commission.[30]

Although the first Adam failed, the last Adam has now come and restrained the serpent so that this defeat might not be repeated. Beale observes the paradox of victory and triumph achieved through ostensible loss and doom: "Christ ironically defeated satanic forces spiritually by allowing himself to be nailed to the cross, and it is in this ironic manner that the end times begin."[31] Christ began the last days in the redemptive work of his first coming, defeating Satan through the apparent defeat of death on a cross. Beale draws together the themes of inaugurated satanic defeat and Christian suffering in an appeal to Christian perseverance, viewed through a decidedly Christ-centered eschatological lens.

Benjamin L. Gladd

Closely related to Beale's approach to eschatology is the approach taken by Benjamin Gladd. Gladd explains the eschatology of the New Testament from the stated perspective of inaugurated eschatology,[32] ensuring that Christ's victory (and the concomitant defeat of Satan) is a presently enjoyed reality, even while evil and persecution continue alongside this victory. Gladd's work significantly clarifies the inaugurated overlap of *this age* and *the age to come*—an eschatological overlap that produces a situation in which the kingdom of God is operating contemporaneously with the satanic tribulation of this age (see Figure 2).[33]

---

30 Beale, "Millennium in Revelation 20," 41.
31 Beale, *Redemptive Reversals*, 160. Recker likewise observes, "Christ is now the Lord of the nations, and conversely, Satan no longer has the freedom and the authority to deceive nations as a whole—no longer can he keep them shrouded in demonic darkness (Rev 20:3)." Recker, "Satan," 137–38.
32 Gladd refers to this phenomenon as a "redemptive-historical idealist" view. See G. K. Beale and Benjamin L. Gladd, *The Story Retold: A Biblical-Theological Introduction to the New Testament* (Downers Grove, IL: InterVarsity Press, 2020), 466.
33 This construct is similar to the two-age schema of Geerhardus Vos. The present illustration is adapted from Beale and Gladd, *Story Retold*, 43.

Israel's history "Old Age"	Kingdom	New Eternal Cosmos
	Tribulation	

FIGURE 2

The advance of God's kingdom is significant in the New Testament narrative, regularly producing spiritual conflicts (i.e., demonic exorcisms) as the advance of the kingdom brings the precursory blessings of the age to come. The kingdom is being established in an inaugurated state, though in a manner that George Eldon Ladd describes as "fulfillment without consummation."[34] Ladd asserts that such is the mystery of the kingdom (μυστήριον; Matt 13:11 // Mark 4:11 // Luke 8:10)—that Christ is at work prior to its consummation, an *already* victory ahead of the *not-yet* consummation.[35] Thus, the church simultaneously experiences a defeated satanic foe and the final, dying attacks of that evil opponent.

Christ victoriously commences the establishment of the kingdom in his victory, and Gladd shows that the demonic exorcisms performed by Christ and his followers in the Gospel narratives function as public evidence of the spiritual advance of the kingdom. Gladd demonstrates that Christ fulfills Old Testament prophecy through his defeat of Satan throughout his earthly ministry (Matt 21:44; cf. Dan 2:34), beginning with his successful overcoming of the wilderness temptations (Matt 4:1–2 // Mark 1:12–13 // Luke 4:1–2) and concluding in his commissioning of the disciples (Matt 28:18–20).[36] Christ fulfilled what humanity had failed to accomplish. In contradistinction to Israel succumbing to sinful temptation and failing to evict the pagan nations from the promised land, Christ perfectly resisted

---

34 Ladd, *Presence of the Future*, 222. Ladd's "eclectic" approach to the book of Revelation is permeated with the tension of inaugurated eschatology, focusing on the advent of the kingdom of God (Gottesherrschaft).
35 Ladd, *Presence of the Future*, 144–45, 225. Ladd establishes that "before the eschatological appearing of God's Kingdom at the end of the age, God's Kingdom has become dynamically active among men in Jesus' person and mission." Ladd, Presence of the Future, 139.
36 Beale and Gladd, *Story Retold*, 53–57. The timing of both Satan's defeat (concerning the wilderness temptations) and the purpose of demonic exorcisms in kingdom advance are debated topics within inaugurated eschatology. Beale and Gladd observe that the disciples are appointed in the aftermath of Jesus successfully resisting satanic temptation. See Beale and Gladd, *Story Retold*, 54.

temptation and drove Satan from this very world.[37] Gladd observes that Scripture describes Christ victoriously crushing the head of the serpent (Gen 3:15; Isa 11:13, 29:5) and decisively liberating his people from the grip of satanic defeat.[38]

Anthony A. Hoekema

Similar to Beale's approach, Anthony Hoekema presents eschatology as a dominating biblical theme, a theme that permeates the entire Christian experience and frames one's approach to biblical interpretation.[39] Hoekema shows eschatology to be a broad theme that is both present and future, both personal and global, both inaugurated and not-yet-consummated.[40] Hoekema further demonstrates the two-age eschatological paradigm by illustrating that the eschaton prophesied by the Old Testament is now fulfilled in the New, though it is fulfilled in an inaugurated manner that has begun but has not yet concluded.[41]

Hoekema stresses the biblical continuity that results from robust biblical eschatology, while he also recognizes the drastic transformative effects of the current inbreaking of the age to come. There is a constant eschatological tension within the New Testament, a tension that Hoekema aptly describes as an *already/not-yet* tension that exists between two coalescing ages and two colliding spiritual kingdoms.[42] Kim Riddlebarger likewise describes this New Testament tension using the illustration of a stretched

---

37 Beale and Gladd, 53.
38 Beale and Gladd, 57, 72.
39 Hoekema, *Bible and the Future*, 1, 3.
40 Hoekema, 1. Hoekema's work is correspondingly divided into "inaugurated eschatology" and "future eschatology."
41 Hoekema, 14, 18. Hoekema's work bears much in common with scholarly work in the area of inaugurated eschatology by G. K. Beale and Oscar Cullman (see Hoekema's reference to the former authors' V-Day/D-Day illustration, 21), as well as the two-age eschatology exemplified by Geerhardus Vos (Hoekema, *Bible and the Future*, 20–22, 39; see a sketch of Vos's framework on 298ff.). Hoekema's inaugurated two-age approach is shared by Sam Storms, who likewise observes Satan's restraint lasting throughout the church age. Storms contends that Satan's restraint primarily impacts his ability to deceive the nations (i.e., his ability to incite them to war against God and prematurely bringing Armageddon), their ability to accuse Christians, and their ability to impede gospel advance—though in no way does Satan's restraint impede his ability to persecute the church. Storms, *Kingdom Come*, 429n7, 433, 439, 444.
42 Hoekema, *Bible and the Future*, 15, 34–37, 52, 68, 180.

rubber band. When the necessary (eschatological) tension is not adequately recognized and maintained, the rubber band can snap into divergent perspectives that inevitably over-emphasize either the futuristic or the fulfilled components of eschatology.[43] Exercising the "prophetic perspective" so often employed in eschatology by the biblical writers, Hoekema employs a Christological hermeneutic that frames Christ's first coming as the decisive event in human history—an event that gives meaning both to all that preceded it and all that follows it.[44] Hoekema observes: "Because of the victory of Christ, the ultimate issues of history have already been decided."[45]

Hoekema examines the function of demonic exorcisms in the ministry of Christ, and he concludes that demonic exorcisms and satanic restraint function as hallmarks of the establishment of Christ's kingdom reign. [46]George Eldon Ladd similarly explains that the advent of the kingdom is inseparably tied to Christ's defeat of evil, and the New Testament recognizes the inaugurated defeat of Satan in the accomplished work of Christ (see Luke 10; Rev 12; John 12).[47] Hoekema shows that demonic exorcisms indicate the present advance of the kingdom and satanic restraint extends for the entirety of the church age (though ongoing persecution reminds Christians that they live in the latter days).[48] Ladd similarly observes: "Jesus's exorcism of demons means the binding of Satan; and the mighty works of his disciples mean that Satan has been cast down from his place of power."[49]

---

43 Kim Riddlebarger, *The Man of Sin: Uncovering the Truth About the Antichrist* (Grand Rapids: Baker Books, 2006), 35–36. Riddlebarger, in this example, is explicitly warning against the positions of dispensationalism and preterism.

44 Hoekema, *Bible and the Future*, 9, 29, 156. Hoekema also shares the hermeneutic of "progressive parallelism" for the book of Revelation with that of William Hendricksen. See Hendricksen, *More Than Conquerors: An Interpretation of the Book of Revelation, 75th anniv. ed.* (Grand Rapids: Baker Books, 2015), 233.

45 Hoekema, *Bible and the Future*, 69, 177.

46 Hoekema, 46–47. Similar is George Eldon Ladd, who interprets Christ's demonic exorcisms as examples of precursory victories over Satan. See Ladd, *Presence of the Future*, 151–52. Ladd correctly observes that the nature of Satan's binding lies in the prevention of worldwide deception leading to revolt, yet he incorrectly observes this binding occurring in a yet-future scenario. Ladd, Commentary on the Revelation of John.

47 Ladd, *Presence of the Future*, 153, 156–57, 183.

48 Anthony A. Hoekema, "Amillennialism," in *The Meaning of the Millennium: Four Views*, ed. Robert G. Clouse (Downers Grove: InterVarsity Press, 1977), 163, 177–78; Hoekema, Bible and the Future, 134–35, 227–28.

49 Ladd, *Presence of the Future*, 257.

Hoekema observes that the biblical narrative indicates that Satan exercised a degree of power and authority over the nations in the Old Testament. At the same time, his current restrained state (Rev 20:1–6) provides the divine reclamation of eschatological authority necessary for Christ to triumphantly commission his disciples to the nations (Matt 28:18–20).[50] Satan is bound from deceiving the nations (ἔδησεν/δέω in Rev 20:2, cf. δήσῃ/δέω in Matt 12:29), enabling the unimpeded accomplishment of the Great Commission.[51] Hoekema observes that Satan's restraint prevents him from deceiving the nations in two regards: (a) in preventing the gospel (and its spread); and (b) in leading the nations into premature rebellion.[52]

William J. Dumbrell

William Dumbrell examines eschatology as a canonical theme that stretches across the biblical account (what he calls a "consistent" eschatology), using an interpretive approach that bears the defining marks of the two-age schema.[53] Similar to Beale, Dumbrell contends that eschatology is a "lens" through which the whole biblical story may be viewed, and therefore eschatology is an especially illuminating perspective for the biblical narrative that stretches from Eden to the new creation.[54] Dumbrell marks several features of satanic defeat that are realized in Christ's victory, observing that Satan is cast out of heaven (John 12:31, cf. Luke 10:18) in an eschatological description that makes use of exorcistic language.[55]

Christ's victory on the cross led to an inaugurated cosmic defeat of all satanic rulers and authorities, while Dumbrell recognizes that all ongoing opposition to Jesus's plan (whether by the Jews or his disciples) is satanic in origin, as it is opposed to the eschatological mission of Christ.[56] Dumbrell observes that Christ's victory expelled Satan from the place of power he

---

50 Hoekema, "Amillennialism," 161–62.
51 Hoekema, *Bible and the Future*, 228–29, 238.
52 Hoekema, "Amillennialism," 162, 181.
53 William J. Dumbrell, *The Search for Order: Biblical Eschatology in Focus* (Eugene, OR: Wipf & Stock, 2001), 260. Dumbrell refers to the two-age schema as "consistent" inaugurated eschatology.
54 This lens is what Dumbrell calls "whole-Bible" eschatology. Dumbrell, *Search for Order*, 9, 11.
55 Dumbrell, *Search for Order*, 253. Dumbrell's assertion is a possibility, though it is more probable that these passages refer to an exorcism of Satan from this world.
56 Dumbrell, *Search for Order*, 190–91, 253, 298–300.

previously held, and Satan's restraint runs throughout the church age in an expectation of the coming New Jerusalem.[57]

T. Desmond Alexander

The divinely instituted role of man's vice-regency over creation is a critical component in William Dumbrell and T. Desmond Alexander's work. Alexander expounds biblical-theological themes from Eden to the New Jerusalem, and he gives special consideration to the narrative theme of temple and divine presence (similar to Beale).[58] In keeping with a two-age (Pauline) eschatology, Alexander demonstrates that the age to come was inaugurated in Christ's resurrection, though it remains to be consummated in his return (the second coming). Therefore, the age to come is both realized (presently experienced) and future, a concept that Alexander explains as an eschatological progression of the Jewish conception of the *already* and *not-yet*.[59] Following Christ's first coming, God's glory is victoriously extended into creation as believers operate as the new temple, fulfilling the Edenic task of vice-regency by glorifying God as his examples amid creation.[60]

Satan's authority in this age is a product of Adam's failed vice-regency—yet where the first Adam failed, Christ (as the new and better Adam)

---

57 Dumbrell, 341, 344–45. Dumbrell's position on John 12:31 (that Satan was cast down from heaven, not cast out from this world or eschatologically defeated) is a minority approach to that text, as he maintains that John 12:31 conveys that "the inner meaning of the cross is the possibility of freedom from Satan's rule," 253. Emphasis in original. Dumbrell also distinctively approaches the fall narrative's cosmology by viewing the serpent as a representative of all animals, while the protoevangelistic seed is said to act as the representative of all humanity. Dumbrell, 17, 26–27.

58 T. Desmond Alexander, *From Eden to the New Jerusalem: An Introduction to Biblical Theology* (Grand Rapids: Kregel, 2013), 10–11. Alexander views Eden as the first stage in a progression toward a New Jerusalem. T. Desmond Alexander, The City of God and the Goal of Creation (Wheaton, IL: Crossway, 2018), 20; cf. Alexander's discussion of Dumbrell's view; contra Beale, who conceives of a proto-sanctuary environment or an original "temple" in Eden and, oppositely, Block's paradigm of a pristine Edenic garden (i.e., non-temple) upon which subsequent temples or sanctuaries act as restorations. Alexander, *City of God and the Goal of Creation*, 20n6, 19n4, 19n5.

59 Alexander, *From Eden to the New Jerusalem*, 156. Alexander maintains that Paul develops Jewish eschatological conceptions by showing that the Davidic Messiah has appeared in Christ, in a time of overlap between this present evil age and the coming new age. Alexander, 158.

60 On Adamic vice-regency, see Alexander, 61–77, 89ff.

has victoriously succeeded by freeing his children from the domain of Satan.[61] Alexander shows that the biblical narrative sheds light on Satan's story, beginning with his shadowy emergence in Eden, continuing through the time of his defeat in Christ, and forecasting his ultimate defeat in the advent of the victorious New Jerusalem.[62] Alexander describes Scripture as a story of anticipation for what Christ has done and will do, a story that gives us only occasional glimpses into the spiritual victories that are present behind our earthly experiences. In the Gospel narratives, Jesus's demonic exorcisms function as a revelation of the advance of the kingdom of God in this age, giving credence to his ministry while also foreshadowing the global exorcism in which Christ casts out Satan, sin, and death.[63] Due to Christ's defeat of Satan, a measure of satanic dominion in this world has been removed, while believers are still being freed from Satan's challenge to God's sovereignty (1 John 5:18–19).[64]

Though there remains a paucity of scholarship in the area of satanic exorcism, several modern eschatological works, notably those from the Reformed or amillennial camps, have observed many of the accompanying features of satanic exorcism within their eschatological framework. A robust doctrine of satanic exorcism involves addressing the New Testament development through the lens of eschatological inauguration—the *already* and the *not-yet*, more precisely referred to in the biblical language of *this age* and *the age to come*. It is to the New Testament paradigm of two-age eschatology that the next section will now turn.

---

61 Alexander, 102ff.

62 Alexander suggests caution with possible Old Testament references to Satan (e.g., Isa 14) outside the clear, immediate context—though he previously allows for a measure of "proleptic ambiguity" in the Gen 1–3 account. Alexander, 112, 18.

63 Alexander, 155. Alexander uses the language of exorcisms "foreshadowing" the kingdom instead of "proving" or validating the kingdom. Satan's defeat also fulfills the protoevangelium. Alexander, 189, 191.

64 Alexander notes that believers are "being wrested" away from the evil one. Alexander, 75, 100.

Satanic Exorcism in the Overlap of This Age and the Age to Come

Geerhardus J. Vos

Satanic exorcism is a distinguishing consequence of the inbreaking into *this age* by *the age to come*. *This age* is the time that experiences the effects of the Fall (sin, death, and suffering), while *the age to come* is the experience of God's victorious reign and lasting freedom from the fallen state of this age. Satanic exorcism is a significant eschatological event in the inauguration of this period, and the restraint that characterizes satanic exorcism is a defining characteristic of the current overlap of *this age* and *the age to come*. To already live in *the age to come* is to experience satanic defeat, while concurrently living in the last days of *this age* entails suffering from satanic assaults directed against God and his church (see Figure 3).

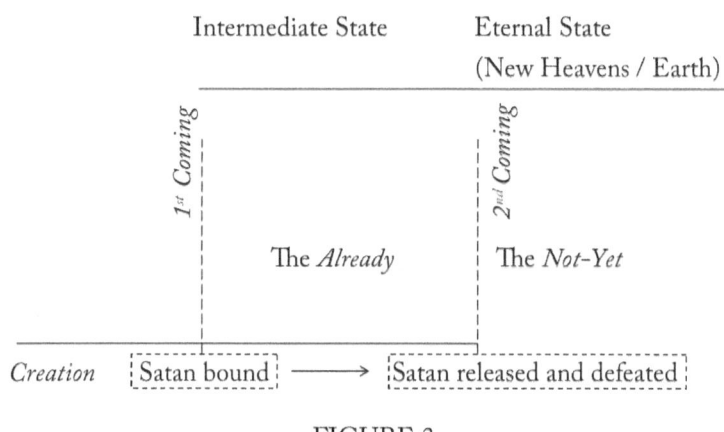

FIGURE 3

Geerhardus Vos gives a foundational understanding of this overlap of the ages through his description of a two-age paradigm—a schema of understanding the eschatology of *this age* and *the age to come* replicated in the subsequent work of many theologians.[65] Vos explains the two-age para-

---

65 Vos's two-age construct is evident in the work of Storms, who refers to the paradigm as a "binary configuration" or "recapitulation eschatology." Storms, *Kingdom Come*, 29, 34–35.

digm through the illustration of "womb and birth"—*this age* is in the process of generating *the age to come* (see Figure 4).

		This Age		
			The Age to Come >>	
<< Eden		1ˢᵗ Coming		2ⁿᵈ Coming
<< Fall		Exorcism from this World		Final Defeat

FIGURE 4

The first coming of Christ has conclusively inaugurated *the age to come*, even while *this age* will remain until the second coming. The eschatology of the New Testament is mainly developed and expounded upon by the apostle Paul, whom Vos describes as "the father of Christian eschatology."[66]

Vos satisfactorily describes eschatology as an understanding of historical movement within redemptive history, a movement that is directed toward a final goal (*telos*). The redemptive movement in history has been clarified and fulfilled by the work of Christ, as Vos observes: "Through the appearance or resurrection of Christ the eschatological process has been set in motion."[67] Eschatology flows throughout Scripture as a movement containing a "note of epochal finality" that is not solely found in the book of Revelation but is present in a consistent progression across the biblical narrative.[68]

Vos contends that the Pauline writings are frequently ignored (or at least undervalued) in modern eschatology, while instead, much attention and focus are given to Revelation (especially, and often solely, to chapter 20). Vos correctly observes that sound principles of biblical theology (and biblical interpretation in general) require recognizing eschatological development

---

66 Vos, *Pauline Eschatology*, 36–38.
67 Vos, 1, 39.
68 Vos, 5. Vos characterizes this progression (movement) by two main "streams" (or "woes") of resurrection and judgment that give birth to the age to come. He observes: "Resurrection and Judgment are the two correlated acts of the final consummation of things. They are like twin-woes in the travail by which the age to come is brought to birth." Vos, 72, 261.

as it is progressively revealed in Scripture, rather than abandoning or ignoring previous revelation to focus exclusively on latter development. A robust eschatology will recognize the significant level of continuity from the Old Testament to the New Testament concerning final things while also recognizing the radical escalation of eschatological development involved in Christ's first coming.[69] Vos observes that human life itself bears an "eschatological stamp" since God has revealed his redemptive plan to mankind as history approaches the eternal state of "life" and "glory."[70]

Satan enters into Vos's two-age paradigm as the evil "god of this age" (ὁ θεὸς τοῦ αἰῶνος τούτου; 2 Cor 4:4), though satanic personification is likewise found in the "enemies," "powers," and "death" that is opposed to Christ (Col 2:15).[71] Referring to Colossians 2 and the spiritual battle that is taking place behind the veil of this world, Vos observes:

> In the various passages dealing with this subject [spiritual warfare] one gains the impression that the Apostle [Paul] was conscious of a mysterious drama being enacted behind the scenes of this visible world in the world of spirits, and that not a drama bearing significance in itself; it is something pregnant with the supreme solution of the world-drama at the close of history.[72]

In Jesus's first coming, judgment visited the evil spirits of this world, making the truth of Christ plain against the powers of deception in this age.[73] Due to the work of Christ, Vos's eschatological assessment is that the conflict between Satan and God has been replaced largely by the conflict between the First and Second Adam. That is to say, Vos recognizes that the work of Christ results in Paul (if not the rest of the New Testament writers, with the notable exception of John's Revelation) speaking far less about

---

69 Vos, 226. Vos appeals to the "analogy of faith" for interpreting Revelation 20 only after grasping Paul's sweeping view of eschatology, at the risk of being otherwise "hermeneutically unmethodical." Vos, 226.
70 Geerhardus Vos, *Biblical Theology: Old and New Testaments* (Grand Rapids: Eerdmans, 1988), 71, 307. Vos also elaborates on the concept of "prophetic foreshadowing" in eschatological literature. Vos, *Pauline Eschatology*, 95.
71 Vos, *Pauline Eschatology*, 12–13, 92. Vos's main discussion of Pauline satanology can be found on pp. 279–283.
72 Vos, 281.
73 Vos, 282–83.

Satan as the antithesis to God, and far more about the contrast between the first Adam's failure contrasted with the second Adam's (Christ's) victory.[74]

Christ has defeated Satan through the work of his first coming, and the New Testament focus subsequently shifts to the anthropological theme of Christ redeeming man through his work as the new and better Adam (Rom 5:14; 1 Cor 15:22, 45–47). The victorious reign of Christ and defeat of all satanic adversaries precedes his final victory over death—imminent in the long-expected final coming of Christ.[75]

Michael S. Horton

Contributing to and building upon the two-age eschatology of Geerhardus Vos is the more recent work of Michael Horton. Horton develops the concept of eschatological dualism as it appears within the Gospels and Pauline epistles, upholding the two-age model against the contention that Paul based his eschatological framework on comparable pagan Greek abstractions.[76] The dualism that Horton addresses is the Pauline eschatological distinction between that which is above and that which is below—a dualism that recognizes the godly, heavenly kingdom operating amid the sinful, earthly realm. Biblical eschatological dualism is a theme in both the Gospels and the later Pauline writings: Horton notes: "Ontological dualism is replaced with eschatological dualism. Instead of the 'true world' of eternal perfection versus the 'apparent world' of temporal change we find 'this present age' and 'the age to come.'"[77]

---

74 Vos, 280.
75 Vos, 73, 245. Vos thus rejects chiliasm, something he refers to as occupying "a peculiar place in the scheme of Biblical Eschatology." Vos, 226. Referring to 1 Cor 15:24, Vos observes that Christ's abolition of all rule, authority, and power "is not confined to the last crisis strictly so called; it belongs, with the exception of the abolishment of death, the last enemy, to the period intervening between the resurrection of Christ and the Parousia." Vos, 280.
76 Horton notes that biblical (and especially Pauline) eschatology is different from a Platonist two-world model since Paul specifically employs the concept of *sarx* and its relationship to the "eschatologized" (not ontological) dimensions of "above/heavenly" and "below/earthly" in a manner apart from Greek abstractions. Horton, "Eschatology after Nietzsche," 41–42.
77 Horton, 45.

This eschatological dualism appears not only in the Pauline corpus but in the Gospels as well."[78] Horton observes that a critical component of eschatological dualism is the instructive paradox of the *already/not-yet*—God in Christ has already brought about the inauguration of heavenly realities. At the same time, these spiritual realities are not yet experienced to the consummative extent they one day will be. This *already/not-yet* paradox also provides biblical continuity by uniting the garden commission given to Adam and Eve (Gen 1:28–30) to the latter escalated Great Commission of God's people in the new covenant (Matt 28:18–20).[79]

By combating views that over-realize the eschatological victory Christians experience in this age (such as the prosperity-plagued "theology of glory"), Horton clarifies that the apostles affirm a theology of the cross—a cruciform and suffering-minded theology.[80] We experience the blessings and victory of *the age to come*, while we experience these victories alongside the lasting effects of evil at work in *this age*. Horton clarifies the dynamic of the present victory that believers experience in Christ's victory:

> It is clear in Paul's writings that the "new" which has come is not merely anticipatory or revelatory, but effective. The resurrection of Jesus Christ has begun to make all things new – not simply to return creation to a pristine origin, but to take a redeemed people and a redeemed creation into a newness which has continuity with the past but is clearly different from anything in the past.[81]

The overlap of *this age* and *the age to come* has brought real, substantive victory experienced in believers' lives, even while suffering and persecution are extant hallmarks of this age that is passing away. Horton correctly observes that believers presently enjoy the fruits of Christ's victory over satanic deception, even while suffering and evil persist in this world.[82]

Geerhardus Vos and Michael Horton are not alone in recognizing the eschatological overlap of *this age* and *the age to come*. However, their analyses

---

78 Horton, 45.
79 Horton, *Christian Faith*, 935, 959.
80 Horton, "Eschatology After Nietzsche," 46–47, 49. Horton terms an intersection between the kingdom of grace (now) and the kingdom of glory (not-yet); Horton, *Christian Faith*, 940–42.
81 Horton, "Eschatology After Nietzsche," 52.
82 Horton, *Christian Faith*, 940–42.

are particularly instructive for engaging an eschatological theme within our present experience—namely, the doctrine of inaugurated satanic exorcism. The two-age paradigm shows the biblical progression of satanic work before Christ (*this age*), his restrained mechanisms following Christ's first coming (the eschatological overlap), and the impending hope of Satan's final defeat (the consummation of *the age to come*).[83] The next section will discuss a methodological focus that is appropriate to biblically tracing the development of satanic exorcism.

The Theological Deficit Concerning the Effects of Satanic Exorcism

There are relatively few theologians who speak about Christ's defeat of Satan using cosmic exorcism language, and fewer still that engage satanic exorcism seeking systematic-theological conclusions, recognizing the truthfulness of the biblical accounts and seeking practical application of theological principles. Relatively few scholarly works approach this area of eschatological thought with the expectation that the biblical narratives of satanic exorcism reflect actual occurrences, events that are accurately reflected in the inspired text and applicable for shaping contemporary Christian praxis. While recognizing the shortage of theological scholarship regarding satanic exorcism, there are a few scholars that have set a substantial precedent for identifying satanic defeat in Christ's first coming as a genuine and tangible defeat that has brought about discernible eschatological consequences.

J. Ramsey Michaels

One scholar who has expressly recognized the exorcism motif present in satanic defeat is J. Ramsey Michaels. Michaels observes that Satan is referred to in the Gospels as the ruler of this world (John 12:31, 14:30, 16:11)—he is the "strong man" who exercised a measure of power and authority before Christ's first coming (Matt 12:29, cf. 12:24), though Christ has now cast Satan out from his previous place of power (Luke 10:18).[84] Michaels points

---

83 Recker similarly maintains that there can be no real element of Christological rule "in a world which is dominated by Satan and where he has not met his master." Recker, "Satan," 136.

84 Similar expressions are found in 1 Corinthians 2:6, Ephesians 2:2, and (per Michaels) 2 Corinthians 4:4. J. Ramsey Michaels, *The Gospel of John*, NICNT (Grand Rapids:

out the language found in John 12:31: "Now is the judgment of this world; now will the ruler of this world be cast out (ἐκβληθήσεται ἔξω)." Michaels observes that the language used in John's satanic exorcism passage "can easily be read as the language of exorcism, especially with 'the ruler of this world' as its object."[85] Though ἐκβάλλω/ἐκβληθήσεται has other New Testament uses, Michaels observes that it is used over thirty times "in connection with exorcisms in the synoptic Gospels,"[86] showing strong parallels to exorcistic language used in the Johannine ἄρχων passages. Michaels's recognition of satanic exorcism in the eschatological flow of the New Testament is an important contribution since most comparable studies recognize demonic exorcism as a hallmark of Christ's kingdom advance, but they do not move beyond this observation to the category of satanic exorcism.

William F. Cook and Charles E. Lawless

Exorcism was a foundational component of Christ's public ministry, as Cook and Lawless explore in a recent study on spiritual warfare.[87] Cook and Lawless observe that Christ's first coming is the decisive, inaugurated victory in a cosmic conflict between God and Satan—a spiritual war that runs throughout the biblical storyline.[88] Christ has redeemed believers from the grip of this present evil age (Gal 1:4; Col 1:14) along with its rulers and authorities (Gal 4:3), though the inaugurated nature between Christ's first and second comings entails the continuing presence of satanic influence in this age.[89] Christ has defeated the satanic forces of this world (Col 2:15; Heb 2:14–15; 1 John 3:8–12), and the church shares in his victory (Col 1:13; 1 John 2:13–14)—yet the church experiences this victory amid satanic persecution and suffering (John 10:10; Eph 6:10–12).[90] Believers are thus called to be defensively minded in spiritual matters—relentlessly on guard against satanic assault (Acts 4:23–31; 2 Cor 11:3–4, 11:12–14; Eph 6:16,18–20; 1 Thess 3:3; 1 Pet 5:8–9; 1 John 3:8–12) even though their victory in Christ is certain (1 John 4:1–6).[91] Cook and Lawless maintain

---

Eerdmans, 2010), 696n44.
85 Michaels, *Gospel of John*, 695.
86 Michaels, 695n41.
87 Cook and Lawless, *Spiritual Warfare*.
88 Cook and Lawless, 7.
89 Cook and Lawless, 105, 108, 96.
90 Cook and Lawless, 197.
91 Cook and Lawless, 197–98.

that believers are engaged in a spiritual battle, yet it is a battle that is already decisively won in Christ, resulting in the believer's deliverance from this present evil age (Gal 1:4; cf. Col 1:14).[92]

In their study, Cook and Lawless examine the public exorcism ministry of Christ, focusing on four major "casting out" episodes in the Gospels to assemble narrative characteristics of exorcisms in the work of Christ. These episodes include the exorcism in the Capernaum synagogue and that of the Gadarene demoniac, the Syrophoenician woman's daughter, and the demonized boy.[93]

Cook and Lawless observe that scholarly literature widely recognizes that Christ accomplished exorcistic work in his ministry, yet Christ's exorcisms were conducted with a pronounced level of power and authority that set them apart from any analogous exorcisms in the surrounding culture.[94] There are other biblical examples of demonic exorcism and confrontation with the satanic realm that could be included with these four examples. Nevertheless, these selected passages are reported with clarity and detail in the Gospel accounts, serving as a characteristic template of Christ's entire exorcism ministry.[95]

These four exorcism narratives share commonalities with the Johannine ἄρχων passage (John 12:31), indicating that a satanic exorcism is in view in Christ's expulsion of Satan.[96] Christ's exorcism of demonic spirits shows his power and authority over the forces of darkness and his unmatched eschatological freedom in exorcising those forces in the work of

---

92 Cook and Lawless, 105.
93 Cook and Lawless, 50, 61–62.
94 Cook and Lawless, 50. Cook and Lawless notably reference the works of Graham H. Twelftree at this point (see the following section for a summary of Twelftree).
95 Cook and Lawless, 51.
96 Cook and Lawless, 77. Cook and Lawless show that Satan's name develops into the form of a proper name through the biblical narrative (25) and demonstrate that Satan himself is only mentioned in three Old Testament books (39). They further recognize the figure of Job 1–2 only as a member of the divine council, while not necessarily Satan (25). Eamonn M. Ferguson's related study surveys satanic interactions with individuals within the Gospel passion narratives, including Peter's rebuke (Matt 16:22), Satan's request to sift Peter like wheat (Luke 22:31), Judas's possession (John 6:70), Judas's covenant with Satan (Luke 22:31), the disciples' abandonment of Jesus (Matt 26:31), Jesus's prayer in the garden (Matt 26:39), and the crucifixion (Matt 27:18). See Eamonn M. Ferguson, "The Devil in the Details: Satan in the Passion Narratives," *Logia* 28.1 (2019): 19–24.

his first coming. These four exorcisms expose key eschatological dynamics such as the conflict of God's kingdom with the kingdom of darkness, universal spiritual recognition of Christ's identity, and the absolute eschatological power that Christ employs in *this age* and *the age to come*.[97] Cook and Lawless significantly advance scholarship concerning satanic exorcism by delineating typical features in the demonic exorcism ministry of Christ and consequently making an application to the later development of satanic exorcism that shares many linguistic and eschatological characteristics.

Graham H. Twelftree

A thorough investigation of the theme of exorcism in the work of Christ's first coming is found in Graham Twelftree's extensive work on demonic expulsion in the ministry of Christ.[98] Twelftree identifies and examines the theme of exorcism present in Christ's ministry, though his examination generally does not seek systematic or eschatological conclusions.[99] The development of exorcism in Christ's ministry is examined in light of the surrounding context of first-century Palestinian exorcism, which Twelftree describes as "a form of healing used when demons or evil spirits were thought to have entered a person and to be responsible for sickness."[100]

Twelftree examines the appearance of Satan in Christ's first coming as a demonstration of the overlapping of the ages—particularly, as an outworking of the extant evil remaining in this world during the eschatological overlap.[101] Twelftree observes that in the Gospels, the Satan of the Synoptic Gospels emerges as the same evil figure as the ἄρχων of John (12:31, 14:30, 16:11)—one linked with the emergence of end-time

---

97 Cook and Lawless, *Spiritual Warfare*, 61–62.
98 Graham H. Twelftree, *Jesus the Exorcist: A Contribution to the Study of the historical Jesus* (Eugene, OR: Wipf & Stock, 2011); *Jesus the Miracle Worker: A Historical and Theological Study* (Downers Grove, IL: InterVarsity Press, 1999); "The Miracles of Jesus: Marginal or Mainstream?," *JSHJ* 1.1 (2003): 104; "Paul's Experience of the Miraculous," *EvQ* 87.3 (2015): 195–206. Twelftree sets the pursuit of "historical" understanding as distinct from faith and doctrine. Twelftree, *Jesus the Exorcist*, 9, 3n10.
99 Twelftree's study methodologically operates as an assessment of the "historical Jesus" and contributes to that field.
100 Twelftree, *Jesus the Exorcist*, 13.
101 Timothy J. Geddert, "Apocalyptic Teaching," in *DJG*, 24; see also Graham H. Twelftree, "Demon, Devil, Satan," in *DJG*, 171.

matters, who is judged and exorcised from this world by Christ's work.[102] Satan thus plays a significant role in the spiritual conflict that takes place in Christ's first coming. Twelftree examines exorcisms as a subcategory within the broader context of miracles, which he regards as the dominating feature of Christ's public ministry.[103]

Twelftree makes the thought-provoking distinction that exorcisms were neither a result nor a testimony of the kingdom of God (which he generally defines as God's operative presence), but rather that exorcisms *were* the kingdom of God itself, manifested in the lived-experience of the beneficiaries of these episodes.[104] The regular occurrence of exorcisms in Christ's ministry is closely connected to the kingdom's inbreaking—demonstrating the already-present reality of the kingdom in Jesus's first coming.[105]

Twelftree observes that in his exorcism ministry, Christ was "endowed with the eschatological Spirit and therefore an eschatological figure himself."[106] Twelftree shows that the demonic exorcisms performed by Christ were inherently eschatological since they were miracles that gave definitive visual evidence that the time of the end had come in the person and work of Jesus.[107] Twelftree also notes that John's exorcism language explains the phenomenon of casting out in a unique way distinct from what is found in the Synoptic Gospels. The Synoptics convey demonic exorcisms in a way that reveals Christ's exercise of divine power. In contrast, the Johannine satanic exorcism passages illuminate Christ's broader work in the cosmic victory of light over darkness that was achieved in the first coming—the period when Christ overcame "both the world (John 16:33) and its 'prince' (John 12:31)."[108]

The exorcism of John 12:31 reveals a spiritual conflict (see John 14:30) that will result in judgment upon the ἄρχων ("ruler") being rendered (John

---

102 Twelftree, "Demon, Devil, Satan," 164, 171.
103 Twelftree, "The Miracles of Jesus," 105, 108.
104 Twelftree, 118, 120. Twelftree's view contrasts with that of other authors, who define the kingdom of God as the rule or reign of God and the sphere of its experience (Ladd, *Presence of the Future*, 262), and alternately, as the church (Vos).
105 Twelftree, *Jesus the Exorcist*, 108–9, 218.
106 Twelftree, "The Miracles of Jesus," 119.
107 Twelftree, *Jesus the Exorcist*, 122. Twelftree, however, appears to subsume exorcisms under the broader heading of "miracles." See Twelftree, *§16, 136*.-
108 Twelftree, "Demon, Devil, Satan," 171.

16:11) and applied (John 12:31), while the outworking of evil will yet remain in the world in the overlapping period between the ages.[109] In terms of the narrative of cosmic spiritual warfare, Christ's exorcism of Satan is the high point of the eschatological drama of demonic exorcisms. Twelftree observes that satanic defeat bears the common first-century Palestinian mark of bifurcating the eschatological stages—a widely-expected two-stage defeat of Satan that would begin with binding (that was later recognized in Christ's exorcisms) and conclude with the judgment at the advent of the *eschaton*.[110] Twelftree concludes that satanic exorcism demonstrates the eschatological transition between the ages, representing an early Christian modification of Jewish apocalyptic eschatology that is clarified in light of Christ's first coming.[111]

Regarding the timing of Satan's exorcism in the biblical narrative, Twelftree notes that the totality of the ministry of Christ is the high mark of God's victory over evil (and Satan) in this world.[112] Twelftree observes: "That Jesus chose [demonic] exorcisms in particular to engage and destroy Satan may have been because, for practical purposes, he was obliged to translate the cosmic theatre of war of the apocalyptic literature into the mundane theatre of human existence and conflict with the devil and his minions."[113] Both demonic and satanic exorcism share the similar language of "binding" and "loosing" of the evil one, something that is observable in the passage of the synagogue demoniac (Mark 1:23 // Luke 4:33) when compared with the controversy of the "strong man" (i.e., the Beelzebul controversy; Matt 12:29 // Mark 3:27 // Luke 11:21).[114] Demonic exorcisms employ the dynamics of "power" and "authority" in the accounts found in both biblical and extra-biblical literature—God's enemies are

---

109 Twelftree, 171.
110 Twelftree, *Jesus the Exorcist*, 222–23, 227–28. Twelftree appeals to the *Isaiah Apocalypse* (Isa 24:22) and similar writings in *1 Enoch* and *Jubilees* to show that a common Jewish apocalyptic conception included territorial angelic spirits restrained in a first stage, while final judgment comes with the second coming of the Messiah.
111 A similar conclusion is reached in Geddert, "Apocalyptic Teaching," 24.
112 Such an observation is without parallel in Judaism. Twelftree, *Jesus the Exorcist*, 114–15, 127 (§11).
113 Twelftree, "The Miracles of Jesus," 122.
114 Twelftree, *Jesus the Exorcist*, 70–71, 98, 219. Twelftree argues that the language of the Beelzebul controversy suggests the presence of a satanic exorcism. Twelftree, 112.

cast out (ἐκβάλλω) "so that God's purpose can be fulfilled."[115] A transfer, or reclamation, of power and authority is an eschatological consequence of exorcisms, both demonic and satanic. Satan has been brought down, judged, and defeated—and yet he still exercises sufficient power to the extent that Christ's prayer for his disciples is that they be kept from the evil one (John 17:15).[116]

Gregory A. Boyd

The theme of satanic defeat is at the forefront of Gregory Boyd's work. Boyd writes on the broad themes of God's role as divine warrior and the Christological victory achieved through the atonement (Christus Victor). However, his work allows significant possibility for further development in the area of satanic exorcism.[117] Operating from the perspective of a "warfare worldview" that illuminates the spiritual conflict that rages in the unseen realm, Boyd discusses themes such as the origin of Satan, the restraint and binding of the "strong man" in the Gospels, and the component of spiritual warfare in Christ's Gospel exorcisms.[118]

The "warfare worldview" that Boyd advances describes spiritual warfare from the perspective of a cosmic war between God and Satan, wherein messianic exorcisms play a role in the conquering-warfare motif (again, exemplifying themes of the Christus Victor perspective). Boyd discusses the advent of Satan as the spiritual opponent who is engaged in open warlike rebellion against God (Yahweh); however, Boyd contends that the figure of Satan receives very little Old Testament development prior to his more

---

115 Twelftree, 20, 51.
116 Geddert, "Apocalyptic Teaching," 24; Twelftree, "Demon, Devil, Satan," 171.
117 Gregory A. Boyd, *God at War: The Bible & Spiritual Conflict* (Downers Grove: InterVarsity Press, 1997); *Satan and the Problem of Evil: Constructing a Trinitarian Warfare Theodicy* (Downers Grove, IL: InterVarsity Press, 2001); *The Crucifixion of the Warrior God: Volumes 1 & 2*, Combined ed. (Minneapolis: Fortress,) Boyd's conclusions regarding open theism and "free will dualism" are problematic and clearly leave space for refutation. See Boyd, *God of the Possible: A Biblical Introduction To The Open View Of God* (Grand Rapids: Baker Books, 2000).
118 These themes are explicated in Boyd, *God at War*, chapters 5, 6, and 7 (respectively). Boyd's presentation of the "warfare worldview" contends that "myth anticipates reality," frequently focusing on territorial spirits and demonic geographic assignments (similar to C. Peter Wagner's work). Boyd, 17–19, 195.

visible New Testament emergence.[119] Boyd's depiction of "God at war" is commendable in its description of the cosmic conflict that surrounds Christ's defeat of Satan. However, Boyd troublingly contends that Satan's ongoing presence is a temporary defeat of Yahweh in this age—something he refers to as a necessary outgrowth of "modified dualism" or "free will dualism."[120] This "modified dualism" leads to Boyd's unfortunate conclusion that God himself (notably in the person and work of Christ) is "revolting" against the satanic powers of this age, stemming from Boyd's consistent interpretive effort to free God of any meticulous control in this age, thus eliminating the divine will from lying behind any evil act.[121]

Boyd's work is commendable in its presentation of the conquering aspect of Christ's first coming and the connections it draws between Christus Victor and the divine warrior motif of both the Old Testament and the New Testament. However, Boyd's conclusions leave significant room for necessary correctives, particularly in an affirmation of the doctrine of divine sovereignty and in a recognition of the Creator-creature distinction which Boyd neglects.[122]

Richard H. Hiers

Though many (perhaps most) scholars subsume Christ's exorcisms under the broader category of "miracles and signs," Richard Hiers maintains that Jesus never described his miracles in such categories. Conversely, Hiers argues that Christ even warned against seeking such signs as evidence of the

---

119 Boyd, 164. Boyd references 1 Chron 21:1 as the only explicit mention of Satan in the Old Testament.
120 Boyd, 176, 179–80.
121 Boyd troublingly relates the incarnation (as "revolt") to Adam's revolt against YHWH. Boyd, 22, 154, 201. Boyd presupposes that God's controlling desire is love (contra glory) and that creaturely freedom is a dominant theme within Scripture.
122 God as Creator brings creatures (including Satan) out of non-being. See Herman Bavinck, *Reformed Dogmatics, Vol. 2: God and Creation*, ed. John Bolt, trans. John Vriend (Grand Rapids: Baker Academic, 2004), 416. For further discussion of the Creator/creature distinction between God (Creator) and Satan (creature), see Cornelius Van Til, *Introduction to Systematic Theology: Prolegomena and the Doctrines of Revelation, Scripture, and God*, ed. William Edgar, 2nd ed. (Phillipsburg, NJ: P&R, 2007), 200; Robert Letham, *Systematic Theology* (Wheaton, IL: Crossway, 2019), 598–99.

kingdom (cf. Luke 17).[123] While Hiers maintains that exorcisms are distinct from miracles and signs, the proliferation of exorcisms in the Gospel narratives is directly related to the expansion of the kingdom that is accomplished in the public ministry of Christ. Thus, exorcisms are a consequence and exhibition of the kingdom.

Hiers describes the spiritual implications of exorcism: "Satan is being bound. The world is being wrested from his control: the victories Christ and his disciples gain over the demons should therefore be a clue to the fact that Satan is being defeated, and that, consequently, the establishment of God's Kingdom on earth is near" (see Matt 12:28 // Luke 11:20).[124] Hiers observes that as the kingdom advances in the work of Christ, the evil forces that hold power in this world are exorcised as a result of the triumphant kingdom advance. Christ's exorcisms of demons are a "fundamentally eschatological activity" that prepare the path for kingdom expansion, leading to and including the binding and restraint of Satan.[125] The kingdom invades territory previously held by satanic powers, and Christ casts out the satanic inhabitants that previously exercised authority and power in this world.[126]

Hiers perceptively observes that the kingdom described in the Gospels (so often portrayed in close narrative proximity with exorcism passages) cannot be assumed as appearing in its full and final manifestation since

---

123 Hiers, "Satan, Demons, and the Kingdom of God," 37. Hiers contends that one of the most characteristic features of Jesus's earthly work—yet one that has received scant attention—is the exorcisms and spiritual warfare against the satanic. Hiers, 35.

124 Hiers, 42. Similar to Craig Evans' work on the theme of eschatological conquest—the conquest of a divine warrior God who was (and is presently) establishing his kingdom through the progressive defeat of evil in this age—Evans contends that Jesus's proclamations in the aftermath of demonic exorcisms function as proclamations of kingdom advance (Mark 1:15, 23–27, 32–34, 6:7; Luke 11:20; Matt 10:7–8). Craig A. Evans, "Inaugurating the Kingdom of God and Defeating the Kingdom of Satan," *BBR* 15.1 (2005): 49.

125 Hiers, "Satan, Demons, and the Kingdom of God," 47. Hiers also surveys extant Second Temple literature, studying the historical development of belief.

126 Patrick Schreiner helpfully defines the kingdom as "the King's power over the King's people in the King's place" and uses the analogy of the kingdom as a growing tree (Gen 2:9; Rev 22:2; cf. Isa 11:1; Ps 1:3; Matt 13:31; Mark 4:31–32; Gal 3:13) that communicates 1) sovereignty, 2) relationship, and 3) place. Patrick Schreiner, *The Kingdom of God & the Glory of the Cross*, Short Studies in Biblical Theology (Wheaton, IL: Crossway, 2018), 29–30; cf. Patrick Schreiner, *The Body of Jesus: A Spatial Analysis of the Kingdom in Matthew*, Library of New Testament Studies 555 (New York: Bloomsbury, 2016).

there is an element of satanic rule yet present in this age. Hiers clarifies: "Synoptic tradition presupposes that Satan holds sway (*exousia*) over the kingdoms of the world ... and attempts to retain and exercise that power over men through his household, the demons."[127] The kingdom is advancing by divine decree, though its advance entails expelling the evil powers that stand in its way. The timing of satanic eviction in the Gospel narratives remains a difficulty; however, Hiers contests the contention made by some that Christ initially bound Satan as a result of Satan's failed temptations in the wilderness (Matt 4:1–2 // Mark 1:12–13 // Luke 4:1–2). Hiers instead states that Christ's victory over satanic temptation in the wilderness initiated the eschatological progression of Satan's binding, something that would be evidenced by Christ's subsequent vision of Satan falling in the wake of the disciples' mission (Luke 10:18).[128]

Toward Building a Doctrine of Satanic Exorcism

Christ has achieved victory over Satan in the work of his first coming, whether this victory is understood as occurring in the entirety of his first coming (from the wilderness temptation to his post-resurrection ascension) or occurring specifically in his work through the cross (i.e., his death, burial, and resurrection). Though some of the authors surveyed in this chapter differ in their approach at this juncture, it is apparent that the redemptive work of Christ's death, burial, and resurrection is the capstone of the first coming. This study further contends that, when all relevant matters are considered, the victory over Satan achieved through Christ's work is likely reflected in progressive development through the entirety of his earthly ministry. The place of power and authority that Satan held before the first coming has been curtailed—he has suffered a decisive defeat that has produced enduring consequences in this world.[129]

---

127 Hiers, "Satan, Demons, and the Kingdom of God," 41.

128 Hiers, 43–44. Similar is John Stott's conception of the six-fold victory of Christ over Satan which was completed in the cross: (1) the conquest predicted (protoevangelium; Gen 3:15); (2) the conquest begun (Gospels exorcisms and the kingdom of God; cf. Luke 10:18); (3) the conquest achieved (at the cross; John 12; 14; 16; Col 2); (4) the conquest confirmed and announced (all enemies subjected underfoot); (5) the conquest extended (the mission to the nations; Rev 20:1–3; Matt 28:18–20); and (6) the conquest consummated (the *parousia* and the last enemy destroyed; 1 Cor 15:26). See John R. W. Stott, *The Cross of Christ* (Downers Grove: InterVarsity Press, 2006), 227–32.

129 Such curtailment is most obvious in Satan's prosecutorial role. See Canoy, "Time and Space, Satan," 264.

In past scholarship, Satanic deception often has been regarded as a purely soteriological concept—one that entails satanic prevention of mankind from seeking salvation.[130] However, more recent theological studies describe satanic deception primarily in its eschatological sense, noting the role that deception plays in humanity's revolt against God—and the destruction through judgment that invariably follows such creaturely rebellion. Satanic deception and the resultant destruction that accompanies it are integrated concepts in eschatology, and this concept will be further explored in the following chapters. In the work of satanic exorcism, there is an evident degree of authority (ἐξουσία) that has been taken away from Satan and rightly delivered to the conquering Christ. The dynamic of ἐξουσία continues in the subsequent commissioning of the disciples (Luke 10), who, through union with Christ, exercise authority over "all people of all nations" (πάντα τὰ ἔθνη) because Christ has been given "all authority" (πᾶσα ἐξουσία; Matt 28:18–20; cf. Mark 16:14–18*, Luke 24:44–49, and John 20:19–23).[131] Christ now exerts authority over and against the power that Satan has lost in this world, alongside the authority that was similarly wrested from all satanic powers and authorities.[132] The transfer of authority that has occurred describes a monumental shift in the spiritual power at work in this age—an eschatological change that is brought about by the first coming of Christ.

In the wake of Christ's victory and atoning work, Satan has suffered a decisive defeat that is subsequently explicated across the New Testament narrative. The precise consequences of satanic defeat are often debated, but many scholars recognize the tension in the New Testament between present inaugurated victory and future consummation.[133]

Remaining Questions

Even from the brief preceding survey of relevant works, it is apparent that few works of eschatology discuss the theological effects of satanic

---

130 So Harris, "Satan's Work as a Deceiver," 190–202.
131 Paul Hertig, "The Great Commission Revisited: The Role of God's Reign in Disciple Making," *Missiology* 29.3 (2001): 345–46.
132 Clinton E. Arnold, *Ephesians*, Zondervan Exegetical Commentary on the New Testament 10 (Grand Rapids: Zondervan, 2011), 130, 497.
133 Especially so within Reformed works on Pauline eschatology; see Horton, "Eschatology After Nietzsche," 45.

restraint. Even fewer studies focus on the theme of satanic exorcism as a New Testament theme—one that is occurring in its inaugurated state in the present eschatological overlap of *this age* and *the age to come*. There is room in this facet of eschatology to illuminate the nature and effects of satanic defeat, especially regarding the context of the intersection of the ages. Through Christ's first coming, Satan's defeat bears the mark of a cosmic exorcism—Christ has cast out Satan in this age, forcibly throwing him from this world and enforcing limitations on the remaining power he is permitted to exercise. Satan's defeat follows an initial fall that is only indistinctly referred to in the biblical narrative, and it precedes his final defeat that will come when Christ returns in glory to judge the living and the dead (1 Thess 4:16; 2 Tim 4:1).

Approaching a cross-canonical eschatological theme (and focusing on its expression in the New Testament) is a challenging task, and this approach requires a methodology that is both prudently balanced and sufficiently focused. As an inquiry of systematic theology, this study recognizes that the interpreter of Scripture must ultimately be reliant on the Holy Spirit's illuminating guidance.[134]

In the theological subcategory of satanic exorcism, seemingly disconnected passages scattered across the biblical narrative serve to fill in the various pieces of this thematic puzzle, eventually giving way to a clearer overall picture once these passages are analyzed in conjunction with one another. Each passage must be examined initially within its particular narrative context, with interpretive attention given to its location in its immediate and broad setting in Scripture. This interpretive approach primarily focuses on theological examination of the relevant passages in their biblical context, as opposed to relying primarily upon the surrounding extra-biblical backgrounds of extant literature to clarify or define meaning.[135] This focus on the biblical text may be referred to as a "canonical hermeneutic"

---

134 Andreas J. Köstenberger and Richard Duane Patterson, *Invitation to Biblical Interpretation: Exploring the Hermeneutical Triad of history, Literature, and Theology* (Grand Rapids: Kregel Publications, 2011), 61, 64–65. See also Beale's discussion of progressive divine revelation and spiritually aided understanding, in G. K. Beale, "A Surrejoinder to Peter Enns," *Themelios* 32.3 (2007): 20.

135 "Discourse meaning" in our usage reflects the meaning of the author as it was initially delivered to its recipient. See Peter Cotterell and Max Turner, *Linguistics and Biblical Interpretation* (Downers Grove, IL: InterVarsity Press, 1989), 69, 230; Köstenberger and Patterson, *Invitation to Biblical Interpretation*, 576–77.

that evaluates the greater flow of the biblical narrative, focusing primarily on the content of the biblical passages as they are preserved in the canon of Scripture.[136] Extra-biblical literature is considered and not ignored, but primary interpretive weight is sought within the biblical text itself.[137]

There is a paucity of contemporary scholarship in eschatology that makes theological application to the church's contemporary lived experience, and the theme of satanic exorcism can be particularly helpful in developing the eschatological experience of the church. As a result of the victory that Christ secured through the work of his first coming, the church currently experiences victory over the forces of darkness while simultaneously experiencing persecution and suffering in this age. Here the theme of a truly Christological eschatology becomes clear—the church experiences victory through suffering in a manner that reflects Christ's victory. Just as Christ conquered through the avenue of suffering in his first coming, his church likewise presently conquers through suffering and persecution through the persistent witness of their faith—"And they have conquered [Satan] by the blood of the Lamb and by the word of their testimony, for they loved not their lives even unto death" (Rev 12:11; cf. 1 John 5:4).

Just as Christ has defeated Satan, the church enjoys the current experience of a defeated enemy even as this age is passing away. Understanding the role of satanic exorcism in the theology of the church is a relevant doctrine for these last days (Rev 1:9), one that gives immeasurable hope for the final victory that is to come (Rom 16:20). The next chapter will begin to build a doctrine of satanic exorcism by briefly examining satanic activity prior to the first coming, followed by an examination of exorcisms (both demonic and satanic) that appear in the Gospels in the ministry of Christ.

---

136 Jason P. Kees, "At the End of All Things: Identifying the Ideal-Reader of the Revelation" (PhD diss., Midwestern Baptist Theological Seminary, 2018), 6–9. Kees observes: "this [canonical] approach highlights the text, its canonical section, and the message from that passage contributes to the canon as a whole and what the latter's consequent larger message would therefore be;" Kees, 9.

137 This approach was markedly shaped by Graham Cole's recent theological work on angelology, Charles Scobie's cross-canon biblical eschatology, and Keith Mathison's narrative eschatology; Graham A. Cole, *Against the Darkness: The Doctrine of Angels, Satan, and Demons*, Foundations of Evangelical Theology (Wheaton, IL: Crossway, 2019); Scobie, *Ways of Our God*; Mathison, *From Age to Age*.

Chapter 3

Satanic Exorcism in the First Coming

To properly understand the dynamic of satanic exorcism as it develops in the pages of the New Testament, it is important to first gain a fundamental grasp of Satan's activity and authority prior to the first coming of Christ. Although Old Testament references to Satan are relatively few, and there is often a noticeable lack of interpretive consensus regarding these texts, an understanding of satanic activity in the Old Testament theologically grounds one's understanding of similar activity in the New Testament.[1] The results of Satan's exorcism in the first coming of Christ are clarified when they are compared with the Old Testament testimony of his previous activity, sparse though these accounts may be. Satanic activity in the Old Testament will be viewed through the lens of canonical eschatology—recognizing that eschatology embraces all the events in redemptive history that God has worked to establish his kingdom on earth.[2] This section will address a few key passages that impact satanic activity in the Old Testament while also briefly addressing other passages that certain interpreters have considered applicable.

---

1 The thematic "parts" of the canon are best interpreted in light of the "whole." See Köstenberger and Patterson, *Invitation to Biblical Interpretation*, 58. In affirming a unified canon, Köstenberger and Patterson thus observe: "The goal and end of interpretation is theology" (66). On applying both a "canonical" and "theological" approach, see Jeremy M. Kimble and Ched Spellman, *Invitation to Biblical Theology: Exploring the Shape, Storyline, and Themes of Scripture*, Invitation to Theological Studies (Grand Rapids: Kregel, 2020), 42; cf. Brevard S. Childs, *Biblical Theology of the Old and New Testaments: Theological Reflection on the Christian Bible*, (Minneapolis: Fortress, 1993); Scobie, *Ways of Our God*, 81ff.

2 Mathison, *From Age to Age*, 699.

Satanic Authority Prior to the First Coming

Satan's role in the Old Testament has a substantial eschatological impact on one's understanding of New Testament satanic exorcism, though his presence in the Old Testament is relatively sparse. Satan is a spiritual being opposed to God, yet the origin of his rebellion and opposition to God is shrouded in mystery. Some scholars have considered certain New Testament passages as referring to a post-creational originating fall (such as Luke 10:18; John 12:31; Rev 12:9), though these passages, in context, speak to the satanic defeat that was definitively accomplished in Christ's first coming.[3] The Old Testament scarcity of detailed reflection on satanic themes should not imply that Hebrew writings are void of an awareness of spiritual adversaries, but such a reality reveals that robust recognition of Satan's character and work is most evident with the revelation of the New Testament writings.[4] Especially within the later writings of the Old Testament, a personified force of evil gains clarification—the Satan, the adversary of God and his people.[5]

How did "Satan" become the proper name of the evil spiritual being we recognize so clearly in the pages of the New Testament? As observed previously, the proper name Satan (Σατανάς / *Sātānās*) is essentially a transliteration of the Hebrew noun שָׂטָן, variously rendered both with and without the definite article (הַשָּׂטָן / *haśśātān*).[6] The use of שָׂטָן can denote an accu-

---

3 See Scobie, *Ways of Our God*, 268.
4 Stokes similarly contends: "Satan as he appears in the book of Revelation is a prince of evil, the main adversary of God and Christ in the end time. It may come as a surprise to Christian readers that no such figure is known in the Hebrew Bible;" Ryan E. Stokes and John J. Collins, *The Satan: How God's Executioner Became the Enemy* (Grand Rapids: Eerdmans, 2019), ix. Stokes bases this conclusion on the reasoning that Satan is anachronistically read back into the Old Testament by New Testament editorial processes—his contention encourages careful exegesis, though his overall argument leaves significant room for further discussion; see Stokes and Collins, 7. Cf. Elaine H. Pagels, "The Social history of Satan, the 'Intimate Enemy': A Preliminary Sketch," *HTR* 84.2 (1991): 106.
5 Scobie, *Ways of Our God*, 243. Stokes also recognizes a common strain of a שָׂטָן figure in the Hebrew Scriptures that has interrelated commonalities between passages, though Stokes interprets this as a sort of progressive reinterpretation and reapplication by the biblical authors; in Stokes and Collins, *Satan*, 5–7.
6 The Old Testament uses of the name שָׂטָן are relatively few; Breitenbach finds only nine uses of the noun שָׂטָן in the Old Testament, with five contextually referring to humans and the remaining four passages referring to angelic beings.; See Breytenbach and Day, "Satan," 726.

sational or adversarial role or office, using language that is evocative of a prosecutorial position in a heavenly courtroom setting. However, the usage of שָׂטָן has a semantic range that is dependent on the particular context.[7] The etymology of the title שָׂטָן / שָׂטָן yields some degree of clarity with possible allusions of Aramaic origin conveying the idea of "envy" or being "despised." However, the referent of the individual passage must rely more strongly on contextual usage of the title, rather than on a diachronic analysis of possible semantic origins.[8] Though there are ongoing disagreements concerning the exegetical occurrences of specific references to Satan within the Old Testament, the most sensible conclusion is that there are few direct references to Satan in the Old Testament accounts, while most other incidences of שָׂטָן refer to human beings.[9]

When considered from a theological-canonical standpoint, the name "Satan" is often used interchangeably (both within the New Testament and the LXX) with titles such as "devil" (διάβολος / *diabolos*, owing to an LXX translation), "Beelzebul" (Βεελζεβούλ / *beelzeboul*, related to "Strong One"; Matt 10:25), "the Evil One" (ὁ πονηρὸς / adjectival *pōneros*; Matt 13:19; John 17:5; Eph 6:16; 2 Thess 3:3), "the Tempter" (ὁ πειράζων / *ho peirazōn*; Matt 4:3, 1 Thess 3:5), and "the Prince" or "the Ruler" (ὁ ἄρχων / *ho archōn*; John 12:31, 14:30, 16:11).[10] There is a majority opinion within theological scholarship that Satan occupies the role of an accuser, both in

---

7 Ryan Stokes contends: "שָׂטָן in Biblical Hebrew can be used with reference either to a human or to a superhuman being, and its particular nuance can vary depending on the context in which it occurs. Generally speaking, the translation of שָׂטָן as 'adversary' or 'opponent' is not altogether incorrect. This translation does, however, lack precision." Ryan E. Stokes, "Satan, Yhwh's Executioner," *JBL* 133.2 (2014): 253.

8 The Hebrew שָׂטָן (Gk. Σατανᾶς) is related to the older Aramaic form שִׂטְנָא—the root שׂטם includes the semantic range "to envy, despise," etymologically related to "enmity" (Sitnah, שִׂטְנָה; Gen 26:18, 26:21; cf. (Prince) Mastemā and שָׂטָן, *Sātān* in *Jubilees* 17:15–18), *Sātān* takes the form of a proper noun in Job 1:7; 2:3–5; Zech 3:1–2; see Daniel F Gershenson, "The Name Satan," *Zeitschrift für die alttestamentliche Wissenschaft* 114.3 (2002): 443. For a differing approach of diachronic contra synchronic examination of שָׂטָן, see Stokes and Collins, *Satan*, xv. There are twenty-six occurrences of שָׂטָן in its noun form in the Old Testament, with most seeming to refer to a heavenly/angelic being—see exegetical groundwork (though his conclusions are lacking) in a study by Johnny Awwad, "Satan in Biblical Imagination," *TR* 26.2 (2005): 112.

9 Ryan E. Stokes, "The Devil Made David Do It . . . or 'Did' He? The Nature, Identity, and Literary Origins of the 'Satan' in 1 Chronicles 21:1," *JBL* 128.1 (2009): 93–94.

10 Breytenbach and Day, "Satan," 726–27. Stokes perceives: "*Diabolos*, 'adversary' or 'devil,' is the word with which the Greek translators of the Hebrew scriptures chose to render the

the Old Testament and the New Testament alike as the office of accusation (presumably in a heavenly setting) is regarded as his primary role.[11] Though certain Old Testament passages (including some reviewed in this section) are difficult to ascertain as to whether שׂטן refers to an individual, a general position, or a generalized type, the New Testament reveals a great deal more about the designation שׂטן—including a consistent recognition that the New Testament personal figure, Satan, is synonymous with the שׂטן found in various Old Testament passages (such as Job and Zechariah).[12]

The following sections will observe the description and actions of שׂטן in the respective Old Testament contexts while preserving a canonical-theological approach, before briefly considering a few other relevant biblical texts that are often considered to speak of the personal שׂטן.[13]

The Garden Serpent (Genesis 3:1–15)

> NOW THE SERPENT WAS MORE CRAFTY THAN ANY OTHER BEAST OF THE FIELD THAT THE LORD GOD HAD MADE. (GEN 3:1)

The first biblical passage to be considered may prove to be one of the most significant due to the eschatological position of its Old Testament context.

---

noun *sātān* in Zech 3:1–2, 1 Chr 21:1, and Job 1–2. This word and related terms (*diabolē*, *diaballein*) can refer to opposition of various sorts." Stokes and Collins, *Satan*, 201.

11 See William Caldwell, "The Doctrine of Satan I: In the Old Testament," *Biblical World* 41.1 (1913): 32. Stokes offers the contrasting opinion that the written development of Satan in a prosecutorial role prior to the second century is scant. See Stokes and Collins, *Satan*, 211.

12 Stokes contends that the New Testament usages of ὁ Σατανᾶς are titles and not proper names, reflecting the Old Testament usage in Zech 3 and Job 1–2 (exceptions in Luke 22:3; 2 Cor 12:7), though Stokes views these differentiations difficult if not impossible; Stokes and Collins, *Satan*, 200. Stokes advances the minority view that the assumed *modus operandi* of שׂטן /לשׂטן is accusation, while its translation should denote physical attack as an "attacker" or "executioner;" Stokes and Collins, *Satan*, 252. Stokes seems to ground his argument in a narrow Old Testament-theological perspective, as later texts such as Rev 12:10 function to clarify and balance his conclusions.

13 The canonical approach recognizes that the Dragon of Revelation that John later identifies is the same as the accuser of Job (Job 1–2) and adversary of Joshua (Zech 3); however, Satan's Old Testament depiction is not as thorough without considering subsequent New Testament explanation. Stokes and Collins observe that John "no doubt intends to speak of the same figure whom one encounters in these earlier Hebrew texts," though thhe incorrectly explains this as "creative" communal theological development. See Stokes and Collins, *Satan*, xiv.

In the book of Genesis, the opening two chapters describe God's creation of the world and the creatures that inhabit it. These two opening chapters are followed by an equally foundational third chapter that contains Adam and Eve's commission of sin and their subsequent expulsion from the Garden. The narrative of Genesis 3 begins with the abrupt introduction of a serpent (נָחָשׁ / *nāḥāš* MT; ὁ ὄφις / *ho ophis* LXX), one who is described as a uniquely "crafty" (עָרוּם / *ārûm*) animal. The serpent proceeds to speak to Eve, questioning God's prohibition against eating the fruit of the tree in the middle of the Garden, and is subsequently cursed by God after his actions contribute to man's sin and punishment (Gen 3:14–15).

Although Satan has historically been identified with the serpent in this narrative, a sizeable interpretive challenge must be recognized from the outset: שָׂטָן is not openly mentioned in this passage. Taken at face value, the text of Genesis 3 only refers to a נָחָשׁ, a relatively common Hebrew expression for a serpent.[14] The serpent's identity is not explained, but it is identified as a creature that "the Lord God had made" (3:1). Therefore, although the serpent's origin is not explained, it is clear that the נָחָשׁ is a created being and not any sort of dualistic divine or pre-existent spiritual being.[15] Dietrich Bonhoeffer exemplifies those who recognize the serpent's inherent evil character while yet questioning its identification with Satan: "It is not simply said that the serpent is the devil. The serpent is a creature of God, but it is more subtle than all the others. In the entire story the devil incarnate is never introduced. And yet evil does take place: through man, through the serpent, through the tree."[16] Identifying the Garden serpent with the biblical character of Satan is an interpretive challenge that warrants caution, yet this challenge is surely not insurmountable.

---

14 Victor P. Hamilton, *The Book of Genesis: Chapters 1–17*, NICOT (Grand Rapids: Eerdmans, 1990), 187. Hamilton observes thirty-one Old Testament uses of נָחָשׁ, along with the possible wordplay between נָחָשׁ and נְחֹשֶׁת.
15 "There is no room here for any dualistic ideas about the origins of good and evil. Clearly Gen. 1–3 makes no room for the idea that in the beginning there were two." Hamilton, *Book of Genesis: Chapters 1–17*, 188.
16 Dietrich Bonhoeffer, *Creation and Fall; Temptation: Two Biblical Studies*, First Touchstone ed. (New York: SCM, 1959), 72. Though he does not identify the serpent with the Devil (contra man's ability to claim satanic victimhood for sin), Bonhoeffer appears to acquiesce to the serpent's satanic identity by suggesting invoking Matt 4:10 ("begone Satan") as the appropriate Christian response; 75, cf. 70.

What is to be made of this serpent in Genesis 3? Was this creature Satan in serpent form, or was the serpent being used by Satan for his nefarious purposes? Martin Luther, who often spoke of the Devil and his machinations, held the opinion that the serpent was an animal inhabited by Satan for his deceptive means: "The devil was permitted to enter beasts, as he here entered the serpent."[17] Luther thus held, along with John Calvin, that the serpent was an earthly animal that was inhabited by Satan to accomplish his destructive purposes against humanity.[18]

Though described as a unique creature that was especially "crafty" (i.e., shrewd, subtle), the serpent is explicitly said to be one of God's creatures, lending substantial credence to the identification of the serpent as an ordinary creature that was used as an earthly vehicle for satanic intentions.[19] Reading the narrative of Genesis 3 in view of the broader lens of the Pentateuch reveals that there is far more in view than just a serpent, or an allegory, or a psychological event—there is a perceptible element of satanic involvement.[20] Though the narrative in Genesis 3 does not explicitly draw out the spiritual identity of the serpent, later biblical reflection will speak of the serpent (ὁ ὄφις) who deceived Eve (2 Cor 11:3), the serpent who is now being crushed underfoot in the work of Christ (Luke 10:19), and the one who "soon" will be crushed underfoot with finality (Rom 16:20). This serpent is the one whom John clearly identifies as "the great dragon . . . that ancient serpent, who is called the devil and Satan, the deceiver of the whole world" (Rev 12:9, cf. 20:2).

---

17 Martin Luther, *Luther's Works, Volume 1 (Genesis chs. 1-5)*, ed. Jaroslav Pelikan (St. Louis: Concordia, 1958), 1.151, cited in Kenneth Mathews, *Genesis 1–11:26*, NAC 1A (Nashville: Broadman & Holman, 1996), 233.

18 John Calvin, *Commentary on the First Book of Moses Called Genesis*, ed. and trans. John King (Bellingham, WA: Logos Bible Software, 2010), 1:140.

19 Kidner observes, "The chapter [Genesis 3] speaks not of evil invading, as though it had its own existence, but of creatures rebelling;" *Genesis: An Introduction & Commentary*. TOTC 1 (Downers Grove, IL: Inter-Varsity Press, 1967), 67.

20 Caldwell, "The Doctrine of Satan I: In the Old Testament," 31. The Pentateuch context also connects the serpent to ceremonially unclean animals that were associated with God's judgment (Lev 11:41–45); see Mathews, *Genesis 1–11:26*, 233–34. Mathews observes, "Although the snake is never identified as Satan in the Old Testament, more than the principle of evil must have been intended by the serpent's presence since 3:15 describes an ongoing war between the serpent and the seed of the woman. "All the days of your life" (3:14) shows that the serpent is treated as a personal being. The serpent's role is consistent with the adversary (*haśśātan*) depicted in Job 1–2. Although not identified as a serpent, he impugns the character of God and attempts to destroy Job."

Evaluating the Garden narrative of Genesis 3 with a canonical-theological perspective in view, the primary actors involved in the story are the two people created by God (Adam and Eve) along with the serpent whom biblical revelation later clarifies is Satan (Rom 16:20, cf. Gen 3:15; Rev 12:9, cf. 2 Cor 11:3). The interaction between these three actors leads to the introduction of creaturely rebellion by the serpent, the subsequent sin of both Adam and Eve, and the resultant prophecy concerning the oppositional "seeds" (Gen 3:15).[21] Scobie observes,

> Historically, what we see throughout the Bible as a whole is a growing awareness of the existence of a personal power of evil in the world. Canonically, it is legitimate and indeed necessary to read Gen 3 in the light of that later development and to recognize that here at the outset of human history battle is joined between the forces of good and the forces of evil.[22]

What is still not clear is the origin of satanic evil, though it must be recognized that this is not the narrative focus of Genesis 3. What does seem clear, and indeed has been the pervasive Christian belief through the history of the church, is that the serpent of Eden is to be identified with Satan—Satan having been created good as one of God's creatures and yet one whose sinful actions precipitated the judgment rendered in Genesis 3:14–15.[23]

That the serpent is described as "crafty" (מוּרָע) gives the impression that Satan is an intelligent, cunning adversary. Though מוּרָע has positive uses in Scripture (notably in the Proverbs), מוּרָע also has negative connotations that range from murderous intentions (Exod 21:14) to rebellion against God (Ps 83:3). Here, the serpent's craftiness seems decidedly negative (as opposed to being wise or discerning, which meanings are in the semantic range of מוּרָע), as the serpent is connected with deception and creaturely rebellion. There is also an observable similarity in the Hebrew between the serpent's craftiness (מוּרָע) and Adam and Eve's nakedness (מוּרָמִים / *ᵃrûmim*, Gen 2:25),[24] again drawing the biblical reader to assign a malicious, evil

---

21 See Douglas Mangum, Miles Custis, and Wendy Widder, Lexham Research Commentary: *Genesis 1–11*, (Bellingham, WA: Lexham, 2012), Gen 3:1–24.
22 Scobie, *Ways of Our God*, 244.
23 "The Fall," in *ODCC*, 600.
24 Mathews, *Genesis 1–11:26*, 232; Hamilton, *Book of Genesis: Chapters 1–17*, 187.

connotation with the serpent's craftiness—craftiness that led to rebellion and subsequent destruction.

The biblical text offers no origin of the serpent's craftiness, yet the description עָרוּם encourages an understanding that the serpent's evil intentions are planned and calculated, which is certainly an intrusive and unprecedented invasion into the Garden narrative. Eve did not seem to find the serpent's behavior suspicious enough to warrant caution. However, this fact only further draws attention to the deceptive and duplicitous nature of the serpent's activity. The serpent proceeded to question the woman and misrepresent God's divine commands, in what Bonhoeffer memorably referred to as "the first conversation about God, the first religious, theological conversation."[25] This satanic activity inexorably led to Eve's (and subsequently Adam's) disobedience against God's command and the ensuing destruction it brought.[26] From this first passage that introduces Satan's work, there is a pattern of Satanic deception leading to human destruction. Later New Testament reflection clarifies that although Adam sinned, Eve was distinctive in being deceived by the satanic serpent (1 Tim 2:14; 2 Cor 11:3)—a deception that led to the destruction that Christians frequently refer to as "the Fall."[27]

As a result of the serpent's sin ("because you have done this," Gen 3:14), the serpent is cursed beyond any animal, cursed to eat the dust of the ground, and cursed with the result that its "seed" would be in conflict with the woman's "seed" (Gen 3:14–15). Syntactical irony is implied in the text as the serpent is first described as being "crafty" (*arum*) before eventually being characterized as "cursed" (*arur*).[28] The author of Genesis provides no

---

25 Bonhoeffer, *Creation and Fall; Temptation: Two Biblical Studies*, 76.
26 Though it was Eve and not Adam who was deceived (1 Tim 2:14), Adam failed his initial instruction to watch over ("keep," Gen 2:15) the garden, which would include Eve (cf. Rom 5:12). See Owen Strachan, *Reenchanting Humanity: A Theology of Mankind* (Fearn: Mentor, 2019), 71–72, cf. 133–34.
27 Mangum, Custis, and Widder note, "Genesis 3 is recognized for its narration of the introduction of sin into the world. By eating from the tree of the knowledge of good and evil, Adam and Eve brought the world into a fallen state [...] commonly referred to as "the fall." Mangum, Custis, and Widder, *Lexham Research Commentary: Genesis 1–11*, 24.
28 Collins observes the zoomorphic language in use: "A reader [of Genesis 3] will conclude that the serpent acts as a tool of an Evil Power (called "Satan" in later writings). The expressions "go on the belly" and "eat dust" convey an image of defeat and humiliation—the serpent will not have the final victory." C. John Collins, "The Place of the

additional explanation of satanic origins (or motivations therein), nor is there a reference to Satan's prior position in the spiritual realm.[29] An early spiritual conflict has taken place, and eschatological promises and curses have been levied in its wake.

There is an integral eschatological content to the serpent's defeat in Genesis 3. The serpent initially enjoyed apparently unrestricted access to both the Garden and humanity, exercising a great measure of freedom of influence. What follows the serpent's initial introduction in Genesis 3 is a pattern that is consistent with satanic influence found in later biblical passages—the serpent deceived Eve with the object of destroying both Adam and Eve, and the serpent was subsequently brought under judgment by having his power and authority curtailed (through the judgment levied in Gen 3:14–15). The serpent's initial denial of God's judgment (Gen 3:4) leads to the promise of deliverance that is offered alongside a pronouncement of judgment and victory over the serpent (Gen 3:15), a passage that frequently is understood to be the first articulation of the gospel (*protoevangelium*) in the biblical story. Concerning Genesis 3:15, Kidner observes: "Redemption is about God's rule as much as about man's need (*cf.* Ezk. 36:22, 'not . . . for your sake')."[30] The promise of Genesis 3:14–15 is about redemption for man, yet it is also about God re-establishing dominion over rebellious creatures. Along with the pronouncement concerning the seeds of both the serpent and the woman, the serpent is cursed, and his eventual defeat is prophesied by the words of the conquering God (cf. Isa 42:13).[31] The serpent is revealed to be a created being, one who only operates within God's permission—such that, as Luther noted, even the Devil is "God's Devil."[32]

'Fall' in the Overall Vision of the Hebrew Bible," *TJ* 40.2 (2019): 171n20, cited in C. John Collins, *Did Adam and Eve Really Exist? Who They Were and Why You Should Care* (Wheaton, IL: Crossway, 2011), 63–64.

29 Bonhoeffer pontificates: "How does this happen? The Bible does not give an answer, at any rate not a direct or an unequivocal one; characteristically it answers indirectly." Bonhoeffer, *Creation and Fall; Temptation: Two Biblical Studies*, 71.

30 Kidner, *Genesis*, 70.

31 See the divine warrior theme in Tremper Longman and Daniel G. Reid, *God Is a Warrior*, Studies in Old Testament Biblical Theology (Grand Rapids: Zondervan, 1995).

32 Timothy George, "Where Are the Nail Prints? The Devil and Dr. Luther," *JETS* 61.2 (2018): 253. Cf. Erwin W. Lutzer and R. C. Sproul, *God's Devil: The Incredible Story of How Satan's Rebellion Serves God's Purposes* (Chicago: Moody, 2015).

The Accuser of Job (Job chs. 1–2)

> NOW THERE WAS A DAY WHEN THE SONS OF GOD
> CAME TO PRESENT THEMSELVES BEFORE THE LORD,
> AND SATAN ALSO CAME AMONG THEM. (JOB 1:6)

The book of Job opens with an introductory section in chapters 1 and 2 that describes וְהַשָּׂטָן entering the presence of God after some activity of roaming about on the earth. The role of וְהַשָּׂטָן in this narrative involves וְהַשָּׂטָן speaking directly with יהוה (Yahweh) about Job, and eventually, וְהַשָּׂטָן inflicting divinely permitted harm upon both Job and his family. וְהַשָּׂטָן is mentioned several times in these introductory chapters to the saga of Job, and the setting of the interaction seems to describe וְהַשָּׂטָן as an inhabitant of the heavenly court consistently.[33] וְהַשָּׂטָן is introduced alongside a gathering of the בְּנֵי הָאֱלֹהִים ("sons of God" / *bᵉnê hāʾlōhîm*), presumably a gathering of the angels or other created celestial beings who have gathered at the command of יהוה.[34] Satan's casual presence among the "sons of God" indicates that he possessed some level of routine access to the heavenly court. Certainly, he possessed a level of heavenly familiarity that is no longer present in the New Testament narrative.[35]

Similar to the serpent's entrance in the Genesis 3 narrative, the appearance of וְהַשָּׂטָן in Job 1–2 is quite sudden and is introduced into the narrative without much background information. His position is essentially that of a tertiary character in Job's story. However, his involvement in the formative initial chapters is significant, and his activity of pursuing accusation and destruction bears the consistent markings of the actions of Satan throughout Scripture.[36] The שָׂטָן is a unique character in this narrative, contrasted

---

33 Satan is introduced with the definite article (וְהַשָּׂטָן), though this does not necessarily denote an official prosecutorial position as the referent. The use of וְהַשָּׂטָן may instead simply refer to a specified heavenly accuser who is being described, rather than indicating some official heavenly capacity or office. See Stokes, "Satan, Yhwh's Executioner," 267; Breytenbach and Day, "Satan," 728.

34 John E. Hartley, *The Book of Job*, NICOT (Grand Rapids: Eerdmans, 1988), 71. On "heavenly council" interpretation, see Hartley, *Book of Job*, 71n6.

35 Stokes concludes that this heavenly familiarity indicates that the "parting of the ways" between God and Satan had not yet occurred during the time of Job. See Stokes and Collins, *Satan*.

36 So Scobie, *Ways of Our God*, 243. Scobie favors the view that Satan is in the role of a distinct heavenly council member. John Hartley further contends that Satan's brusque

with the "sons of God," as he has power to roam the earth ("going to and fro on the earth, and from walking up and down on it"—Job 1:7). In the initial chapters of the book of Job, "the Satan" is given divine permission to attack a godly and innocent person, one who is innocent of the charge of false loyalty that is levied by הַשָּׂטָן. The actions of הַשָּׂטָן strongly suggest that he intends to seek Job's destruction and employs accusation toward that end.[37] The relationship between satanic authority and the subsequent destruction of humanity is indeed quite close.

In the Job narrative, there is danger of placing an unbalanced emphasis on the actions of הַשָּׂטָן—either by suggesting that he seemingly wields unchecked autonomy, or that he exercises an equally limited authority as is described later in the New Testament.[38] Either overemphasizing or deemphasizing the unique authority that הַשָּׂטָן exercises potentially obscures the eschatological import of the scene that is unfolding—his exercise of freedom on the earth, his access to the heavenly courts, and his ability to make accusations to God against humanity.[39] The text in Job continues the consistent Old Testament testimony that the נָחָשׁ is a created spiritual being, one who only operates in the direction of God's command and yet one who continually seeks the destruction of humanity through attack and accusation.[40]

---

responses in Job reveal a contemptuous attitude toward God and man. See Hartley, *Book of Job*, 72n8.

37 Stokes notes the lexical similarities between Job 2:6 (LXX) and 1 Cor 5:5, both of which speak of someone being "handed over" (παραδοῦναι in 1 Cor 5:5; παραδίδωμί in Job 2:6 LXX) to Satan, who then attacks or destroys their "flesh" (σάρξ). Stokes and Collins, *Satan*, 206n35, cf. 95.

38 On closely linking (even conflating) God's permission to Satan in Job with the New Testament Christian ability to resist Satan, see Erickson, *Christian Theology*, 449. Contra Caldwell, who inappropriately states: "In this passage Satan's independence of God is as complete as it ever becomes in the Old Testament." William Caldwell, "The Doctrine of Satan III: In the New Testament," *Biblical World* 41.3 (1913): 168.

39 Stokes maintains that the customary historic belief in the Christian church that the הַשָּׂטָן in Job (and in Zechariah) primarily is an "accuser" may benefit greatly from recognizing the identity of נָחָשׁ with his aims or goals: his role is one of destruction and ruin for humanity, something that extends beyond a truncated heavenly prosecutorial role. Stokes, "Satan, Yhwh's Executioner," 268. Stokes's contention is worth noting, though the canonical description of Satan emphasizes his activities of deception and accusation (Rev 12:9–10).

40 Some have also seen prophetic echoes of the serpent's/dragon's future defeat in Job 40:19. See Riddlebarger, *Man of Sin*, 103.

The Accuser of Joshua (Zechariah 3:1–5)

> THEN HE SHOWED ME JOSHUA THE HIGH PRIEST STANDING BEFORE
> THE ANGEL OF THE LORD, AND SATAN STANDING AT HIS
> RIGHT HAND TO ACCUSE HIM. (ZECH 3:1)

The scene in Zechariah 3 unfolds with the prophet receiving visions from the Lord (וַיַּרְאֵנִי), including a vision of וְהַשָּׂטָן standing in a place of prestige and power at the right hand) of the angel of the Lord (מַלְאַךְ יְהוָה / *mălăk Yahweh*) to accuse Joshua, the high priest. The figure of וְהַשָּׂטָן in Zechariah initially seems to resemble the figure from Job's opening chapters due to the similarity of their positions of accusing godly men in the heavenly court.[41] Continuing the discussion from Job 1–2, it is possible from the semantic range that וְהַשָּׂטָן primarily reflects a role or positional description in Zechariah 3 and not necessarily a proper name. Translating וְהַשָּׂטָן in this manner would entail venturing away from the LXX translation of ὁ διάβολος and instead rendering this passage closer to the translation of "the opponent standing on his right hand to oppose him" or "the accuser standing on his right hand to accuse him."[42]

The role of וְהַשָּׂטָן in Zechariah 3 appears similar to the position or role that was described in Job 1–2, namely, that of a heavenly adversary. The predominant interpretation of this passage is that the וְהַשָּׂטָן of Zechariah occupies the role of a heavenly accuser of men, indeed an "an accuser and prosecutor in the trial of the high priest Joshua."[43] Thus, many commentators view this passage as a description of a defined role in the heavenly court and not as a personification of an evil entity such as the biblical Satan.[44] Yet from the perspective of canonical eschatology, it is difficult not to see the strong parallels between the וְהַשָּׂטָן of Zechariah and the וְהַשָּׂטָן of Job—and even further similarities with the satanic activity of the Garden

---

41 Breytenbach and Day, "Satan," 729.
42 So John Calvin, *Commentaries on the Twelve Minor Prophets*, ed. and trans. John Owen (Bellingham, WA: Logos Bible Software, 2010), 81n1. The Hebrew (MT) renders Zechariah 3:1 as "standing to oppose" (לְשִׂטְנוֹ), while the LXX shows more distinction between the one who stands (ὁ διάβολος) and the nature of his opposition (ἀντικεῖσθαι / ἀντικεῖμαι).
43 Scobie, *Ways of Our God*, 243.
44 Stokes and Collins, *Satan*, 13.

serpent as well.⁴⁵ The name שָׂטָן may still function in the lexical range of a common noun ("accuser" or "adversary"), yet this figure exemplifies the consistent pattern of bringing accusation against humanity with the thinly veiled goal of achieving their destruction.⁴⁶

The vision of יְהוֹשֻׁעַ in Zechariah leads to a recognition of a spiritual reality that takes place behind the shroud of human experience: the adversary, the שָׂטָן, stands ready to levy accusations that are meant to lead to man's destruction. Yet the שָׂטָן does not operate beyond God's control. As Calvin rightly notes: "Though God had hitherto let loose Satan to assail the Church as to the priesthood, yet God would be the faithful guardian of his Church, and would check Satan, that he might not execute what he intended."⁴⁷ Though Joshua stands before the Lord in spiritually filthy garments (representing the sins of Israel), the Lord sternly rebukes the accusations of שָׂטָן—not because they lack validity, but because of the eschatological plan of God for redeeming his people (Zech 3:2). The שָׂטָן seeks to accuse the people of God and thereby bring about their devastation, yet his plans do not come to fruition.

Unclear Passages (Isaiah 14:12; 1 Chronicles 21:1; Ezekiel 28:14)

Isaiah 14:12, 1 Chronicles 21:1, and Ezekiel 28:14 seem to be the clearest Old Testament referents to Satan, describing a sinister figure who appears only through the form of a serpent in the garden (Gen 3), while later appearing to occupy a role of prosecutor or destroyer in the heavenly court (Job 1–2; Zech 3). In all three passages surveyed, the activity of the שָׂטָן shares distinct similarities: the occupation of a place of power, the accusation of humanity before God, and the desire to bring about men's destruction.

---

45 Carl Friedrich Keil and Franz Delitzsch, *Commentary on the Old Testament*, vol. 10 (Peabody, MA: Hendrickson, 1996), 524. Keil and Delitzsch also reference Rev 12:10 as a further parallel of the "accuser." Stokes opposes the standard translation of "accuser," and maintains that there is nothing accusatory or legal in this passage. See Stokes and Collins, *Satan*, 14. It is worth noting that Satan's accusatory role does not negate his ability to seek mankind's destruction (the two functions are not mutually exclusive), nor should the absence of accusatory activity in one depiction negate the larger canonical testimony as a whole.

46 Joyce G. Baldwin, *Haggai, Zechariah, Malachi: An Introduction & Commentary*, TOTC 24 (Downers Grove, IL: Inter-Varsity Press, 1972), 113.

47 Calvin, *Commentaries on the Twelve Minor Prophets*, 84.

There are other Old Testament passages that may refer to Satan, though these remaining Old Testament passages are far less clear in their referent than the three passages previously examined. One such passage is found in the taunt pericope against the king of Babylon found in Isaiah 14: "How you are fallen from heaven, O Day Star, son of Dawn!" (Isa 14:12). The clearly identified referent of the passage is the king of Babylon, though some interpreters[48] have maintained that there is a spiritual figure prophetically referred to that exists beyond the immediate scope of the text.[49] This interpretation is partially due to the powerful language of the passage which seems too substantial to refer to a human king.[50] Isaiah records that this "Day Star" is said to have desired to ascend to heaven and be seated even above God (Isa 14:13), making himself "like the Most High" (Isa 14:14).[51] In the interpretive history of this passage, the Latin Vulgate trans-

---

48 The early church fathers Tertullian and Origen, and later Jerome, interpreted Isaiah's reference to the "Daystar"/"Lucifer" as Satan . This interpretation is held in the present day by many in the King James Only movement due to the fact that the KJV preserves the nomenclature of "Lucifer." See "Lucifer," in , *The Westminster Bible Dictionary*, ed. Thomas J. Shepherd (Philadelphia: Presbyterian Board of Publication, 1880), 323–24; "Lucifer," in *ODCC*, 1008; ; "Lucifer," in *LBD The Eerdmans Bible Dictionary*, ed. Allen C. Myers (Grand Rapids: Eerdmans, 1987), 267.

49 In examining this phenomenon in Danielic eschatological prophecies, Riddlebarger describes it as the "prophetic perspective" and notes that some prophecies "are fulfilled more than once." He goes on to assert, "Such prophecies are usually connected to an immediate or imminent fulfillment in the lifetime of the prophet and again to a more distant fulfillment in the messianic age (at our Lord's first or second advent). This phenomenon is also known as 'prophetic perspective.'" Riddlebarger, *Man of Sin*, 68.

50 Proposals for the king's specific identity range from Tiglath-pileser III to Nebuchadnezzar to Merodach-baladan. See the discussion in Brevard S. Childs, *Isaiah: A Commentary*, 1st ed., Old Testament Library (Louisville: Westminster John Knox, 2001), 127; Gary V. Smith and E. Ray Clendenen, *Isaiah 1–39*, NAC (Nashville: Broadman & Holman, 2007), 310.

51 Motyer observes, "*Morning star* (*hêlēl*) alludes to the Canaanite myth of Helal/Ishtar who attempted a heavenly coup that failed. The Old Testament uses allusions like this without attributing reality to the characters concerned. The king had, mentally at least, made his own bid for the heights—but look at him!" J. Alec Motyer, *Isaiah: An Introduction and Commentary*, TOTC (Downers Grove, IL: InterVarsity Press, 1999), 136. Smith similarly observes: "The 'morning star' (lit. 'shining one,' *hîlēl*) probably refers to Venus, which is the 'son of the dawn,' the morning star that was sometimes used to represent divinity in ancient Near Eastern religion. This analogy indicates how high this Babylonian king had raised himself up and how far he would fall." Smith and Clendenen, *Isaiah 1–39*, 315. Similarly, see John Goldingay, *Isaiah*, Understanding the Bible Commentary (Grand Rapids: Baker Books, 2012), 103.

lation of "Day Star" was rendered using *lucifer* ("light-bearer"), a translation that some early church fathers believed to be a description of Satan that depicted his pre-mundane fall from heaven. Yet Scobie is likely correct in observing that there is precious little in the text to support this claim and assigning such a lofty status to Satan likely misses the point that the true "Day Star," in eschatological terms, is Christ.[52]

Another unclear text that could refer to Satan is found in the account of David's census of Israel (1 Chr 21:1 // 2 Sam 24:1) in what may be "the most debated of the satan [*sic*] passages in the Hebrew scriptures."[53] In the account in Chronicles, שטן incited David to take a census of the nation of Israel, while the parallel account in 2 Samuel conversely highlights the initiative of the action of יהוה.[54] The action being taken by שטן initially seems similar to that seen of the figure in in Job 1–2, as a heavenly being incites God to act with judgment and destruction against humanity. The role of שטן in instigating human action in this narrative indicates the involvement of a spiritual creature. If this passage is, in fact, a reference to a heavenly being, this passage would be one of only two Old Testament uses of שטן that refers to a heavenly creature that occurs without the use of the definite article.[55] A difficulty with the narrative of David's census is ascertaining how the spiritual being of Chronicles should be understood concerning the divine operations revealed in 2 Samuel. God is not unable

---

52 Scobie, *Ways of Our God*, 264. Scobie maintains, "The reference to the king as 'Day Star' or 'Morning Star' may reflect a Canaanite myth of a minor deity who sought to become equal with the High God. The Vulgate translated 'Day Star' as 'Lucifer' (lit. 'light-bearer'), and certain church fathers linked this figure with Satan, regarded as a rebellious angel cast out of heaven before creation. However, there is no hint of a connection with Satan in the biblical text, and such patristic speculations fall outside the province of BT [biblical theology]." Scobie, *Ways of Our God*, 244–245. Scobie is echoed by Alexander, *From Eden to the New Jerusalem*, 112.

53 In their discussion, Stokes and Collins specifically reference 1 Chron 21:1. Stokes and Collins, *Satan*, 17. Thompson considers this one of three explicit satanic Old Testament references (along with Job 1–2 and Zech 3). J. A. Thompson, *1, 2 Chronicles*, NAC 9 (Nashville: Broadman & Holman, 1994), 161.

54 For similar uses of the verb "incite" (תוּס) in addition to 2 Samuel 24:1 and 1 Chronicles 21:1, see Deut 13:6; Josh 15:18; Judg 1:14; 1 Sam 26:19; 1 Kgs 21:25; 2 Kgs 18:32; 2 Chr 18:2, 31; 32:11, 15; Job 2:3; 36:16, 18; Isa 36:18; Jer 38:22; 43:3, 36. For many of these references, see Stokes and Collins, *Satan*, 20n35.

55 Stokes finds four passages of שטן as a heavenly adversary: Num 22, Job 1–2, Zech 3, and 1 Chron 21 (which he finds may be a proper noun usage). See Stokes, "The Devil Made David Do It . . . or 'Did' He?," 94, cf. 104.

to make use of Satan for his purposes, yet it is also plausible that the שטן of Chronicles is simply a heavenly being that is referenced using שטן as a descriptive title.[56] Stokes recognizes this possibility: "The satan of 1 Chr 21 is very likely a divine [heavenly] attacker or executioner like the one who comes against Balaam in Num 22. Several impressive similarities between the Chronicles and Numbers pericopes make this by far the most plausible interpretation of the Chronicles passage."[57] If Chronicles is referring to the spiritual being known as Satan, the activity described is consistent with his Old Testament pattern—the provocation of humanity through deception with his aim being their eventual destruction.

One final passage that warrants mention in a discussion of the Old Testament's view of Satan is the prophecy/lament passage concerning the king of Tyre found in Ezekiel 28. The passage's structure and genre produce some unique interpretive challenges, as the text contains elements of prose and poetry that appear to blend in the narrative. Though it is a lament passage, Ezekiel 28 lacks the typical expressions of grief that one may expect from a text in this genre, as Block observes: "The oracle sounds more like a divine judgment speech than a lament."[58] Though this passage (similar to Isaiah 14) has a clear earthly referent, many interpreters have viewed its language as a prophetic reference to someone more than a mere man. In Ezekiel's description, the king is said to be the very "signet of perfection, full of wisdom and perfect in beauty" (Ezek 28:12), having been "in Eden, the garden of God" (v. 13), an "anointed guardian cherub ... on the holy mountain of God" (v. 14), yet one who was "proud because of your beauty" who was subsequently "cast . . . to the ground" (v. 17). The language that refers to Eden and a fall from grace is unmistakable, as Taylor observes: "These verses [Ezek 28:11–19] abound in allusions to Genesis 2; 3 and the Paradise story. The connecting link is doubtless in the sin of

---

56   In support of the שטן in this passage as an unnamed heavenly being, see Stokes, 94ff. For the conclusion that this passage is a proper name for Satan used without the definite article, see Breytenbach and Day, "Satan," 729. Thompson notes that this passage's focus is men's actions and not Satan's identity. Thompson, *1, 2 Chronicles*, 161.
57   Stokes and Collins, *Satan*, 21.
58   Daniel I. Block, *The Book of Ezekiel: Chapters 25–48* (Grand Rapids: Eerdmans, 1998), 102. Block further points out that the language in 28:14a (no verbs used) is unusual. See Block, *Book of Ezekiel*, 112ff.

pride which both Adam and Tyre were guilty of, but it is not always clear what picture is in Ezekiel's mind."[59]

Several church fathers understand the background of Ezekiel 28 (and Isa 14 as well) as referring to an account of Satan's fall not found in Scripture.[60] Though these descriptions may, in fact, be using a form of "prophetic perspective" to use a lesser earthly event to speak of a more significant spiritual event, the same caution from Isaiah 14 is likely the best approach in Ezekiel 28 as well.[61] The passage uses the eschatological language of Eden, yet its relationship to cosmic spiritual warfare is tenuous at best.

The above survey of Old Testament satanic passages is cursory by necessity, and it is not designed to satisfy every interpretive question surrounding questionable referents (e.g., Isa 14; 1 Chron 21; Ezek 28). Nevertheless, even a cursory review of satanic passages in their Old Testament contexts is of great value for building a New Testament eschatology concerning satanic exorcism. After surveying the Old Testament texts with the clearest attestation to Satan as a personal figure (Gen 3; Job 1–2; Zech 3), a discernable pattern of satanic activity emerges that should support the following discussion of the dynamic of New Testament satanic exorcism.

In the Old Testament passages surveyed, it is apparent that Satan exercised a significant measure of autonomy and authority in this world—he emerged through the serpent in the pristine Garden of Eden, and he proceeded to interact freely with the only two human characters present (Gen 3). He was later found presenting himself before God, accusing humanity while he stood in the very presence of Yahweh (Job 1–2).[62] He was found exercising a substantial measure of authority, standing in a heavenly courtroom setting to make formal accusations against God's people (Zech 3). Satan's method of intervention varied through the three passages surveyed, yet all three passages showed a consistent attempt to divide humanity from God through accusation, lies, and outright destruction. The resultant response to Satan from God was pronouncing a curse (Gen 3), advancing a

---

59 John B. Taylor, *Ezekiel: An Introduction & Commentary*, TOTC22 (Downers Grove, IL: Inter-Varsity Press, 1969), 196.
60 Lamar E. Cooper, *Ezekiel*, NAC 17 (Nashville: Broadman & Holman, 1994), 264.
61 Hoekema, *Bible and the Future*, 9, 29, 156.
62 The Old Testament role of accusation is clarified by Rev 12:10; see Stokes and Collins, *Satan*, 210, and their interaction with the positions of Beale, *Book of Revelation*, and David Aune, *Revelation 6–16*, WBC 52B (Grand Rapids: Zondervan, 2014).

challenge (Job 1–2), and finally levying an open rebuke of him (Zech 3). Satan's consistent assaults share a common objective–the destruction of God's people, whether of an individual (Job 1–2), the covenant people in general (Zech 3), or even humanity at large (Gen 3). This common theme of satanic assault seeking destruction will surface again later in this chapter after the following section observes some commonalities of demonic exorcisms that will inform an eschatological understanding of satanic exorcism.

Demonic Exorcisms as Proleptic Victory

Four Major Gospel Exorcisms

With the impending manifestation of cosmic satanic exorcism at hand, the Gospel accounts of the public ministry of Christ place particular emphasis on Christ's exorcism of demons. Demonic exorcism (and later, satanic restraint) function as hallmarks of Jesus's reign and the advance of his kingdom, while demonic exorcisms function as a means of precursory victory in the advent of kingdom advance.[63] Later in the Gospel accounts, Christ makes clear that "if it is by the Spirit of God that I cast out demons, then the kingdom of God has come upon you" (Matt 12:28; see Luke 11:20). Thielman succinctly observes: "One of the most important elements in the vocation of Jesus, the apostles, and other evangelists is the deliverance of Satan's victims from his power (Acts 10:38; 26:18)."[64] Demonic exorcisms are intimately connected to the conquering advance of the kingdom of God and the reclamation of authority that accompanies that kingdom advance.

Demonic exorcisms also function as a type of proleptic victory, exhibiting the constant New Testament tension between the *already* and the *not-yet* while also foreshadowing a greater satanic exorcism that is accomplished in the work of Christ.[65] Following the pattern developed by Cook

---

63 Ladd, *Presence of the Future*, 151; Hoekema, *Bible and the Future*, 46. Sproul notes, "Demon-exorcism is almost totally unheard of in Old Testament times, and rarely mentioned even in the New Testament after the [G]ospels" (see 1 Sam 16; Acts 16:16–18)." R. C. Sproul, *A Walk with God: An Exposition of Luke* (Fearn, Scotland: Christian Focus, 1999), 73.

64 Frank Thielman, *Theology of the New Testament: A Canonical and Synthetic Approach* (Grand Rapids: Zondervan, 2005), 126.

65 "All of New Testament theology is qualified by the tension between the already and the not yet." Hoekema, *Bible and the Future*, 52.

and Lawless, this section will observe some common features shared in four of the major Gospel exorcisms to develop a general understanding of demonic casting out prior to examining the satanic casting out that follows.[66]

The Capernaum Synagogue (Mark 1:21–28 // Luke 4:31–37)

> BUT JESUS REBUKED HIM, SAYING, "BE SILENT AND COME OUT OF HIM!" AND WHEN THE DEMON HAD THROWN HIM DOWN IN THEIR MIDST, HE CAME OUT OF HIM, HAVING DONE HIM NO HARM. (LUKE 4:35)

Only Mark and Luke record the demonic exorcism that occurs in the Capernaum synagogue, and the two accounts share many distinctive similarities.[67] The Lucan account of this passage highlights the liberating themes referred to earlier in Luke's Isaiah reference (Luke 4:18–19; cf. Isa 61:1–2, 58:6).[68] The passage takes place in Capernaum on the northwest shore of the Sea of Galilee, a prominent Jewish center in the region.[69] Christ is found in the synagogue, and He is said to be preaching on the Sabbath day. The Gospel accounts record several similar healing miracles that Christ performed on the Sabbath (Luke 4:38; 6:6; 13:14; 14:1–4; John 4:8–9; 9:14), though this particular exorcism does not engender the Sabbath-related opposition that is experienced later.[70] Both accounts note that Christ's teaching is unlike that of men, because it possesses unique authority (ἐξουσία), while Mark's account emphasizes that Jesus's teaching is "not as the scribes" (Mark 1:22; see Matt 7:28–29).[71] Luke's inclusion of ἐξουσία provides a fascinating chiastic structure to the passage, emphasizing the dynamics of power (Luke 4:14), authority (4:32), authority (4:36), and power (4:36) in

---

66 Cook and Lawless, *Spiritual Warfare*, 50–62.
67 There is a wide-ranging discussion of the Synoptic issues raised by the texts in this section (not the least, issues of chronology and identification of parallel events) that lie outside the parameters of the present study.; See Darrell L. Bock, *Luke 1:1–9:50*, BECNT (Grand Rapids: Baker Books, 1994), 423n1.
   68 Liefield, "Luke," 871.
69 Bock, *Luke 1:1–9:50*, 428; Robert H. Stein, *Luke*, NAC (Nashville: Broadman & Holman, 1992), 162.
70 R. C. Sproul, ed., *The Reformation Study Bible: English Standard Version*, 2015 ed. (Orlando: Reformation Trust, 2015), 1792.
71 John Calvin, *Commentary on a Harmony of the Gospels* 45:153, cited in Beth Kreitzer et al., eds., *Luke*, RCS 3 (Downers Grove, IL: InterVarsity Press, 2015).

an ABBA pattern.[72] In the context of Christ's authority manifesting among the crowds, his authority is manifested by the works of kingdom advance—the healing of the sick (4:39) and the casting out of demons (4:35–36, 41).[73] The manifestation of Christ's ἐξουσία is an eschatological event that is manifested in the spiritual conquest over the forces of darkness.

With the surrounding context of Christ teaching with authority, a man abruptly enters the scene who is demon possessed. Mark's description of the event is similar to Luke's account but is also characteristically shorter. Mark reports the man as having an "unclean spirit" (πνεύματι ἀκαθάρτῳ; Mark 1:23), comparable to Luke's description of a man with an "unclean demon" (πνεῦμα δαιμονίου ἀκαθάρτου; Luke 4:33).[74] Though it is unpopular to many modern Western minds to accept the possibility of demonization, the Capernaum synagogue account is an account of a foreign spiritual entity exercising authority and power over an individual. Hendriksen notes: "[The] fact is that demon-possession describes a condition in which a *distinct* and *evil* being (Mark: 'an unclean spirit'; Luke 4:33, 'the spirit of an unclean demon'), foreign to the person possessed, has taken control of that person."[75]

The demon responds to Christ's presence by crying out: "Ha![76] What have you to do with us, Jesus of Nazareth? Have you come to destroy us? I know who you are—the Holy One of God" (Luke 4:34 // Mark 1:24). The demon's response is instructive on several levels. First, it shows a tangible fear of the power of Christ as the demon asks, "What have you to do with

---

72 Whether this narrative structure is by design is unclear, though the relationship between ἐξουσία and δύναμις is still present nonetheless. See Stein, *Luke*, 163–64.
73 Stein, *Luke*, 162–63. Stein observes that ἐξουσία is used more than 20 times in Luke and Acts without connection to teaching, while Liefeld notes the Lucan inclusion of λόγος in emphasizing ἐξουσία. See Gaebelein et al., *The Expositor's Bible Commentary: Matthew, Mark, Luke*, 871.
74 See Bock, *Luke 1:1–9:50*, 431. Stokes notes: "the notions of 'evil spirit' (*riah raa*) and 'demons' (*sedim*) are distinct in the Hebrew scriptures. In later literature, 'demons' and 'evil spirits' come to be more or less synonymous." Stokes and Collins, *Satan*, 70; see also semantic range discussion on 49.
75 Though Hendriksen prefers the perspective of complete control in demonic possession as opposed to a more nuanced element of demonization. William Hendriksen, *Mark: New Testament Commentary* (Grand Rapids: Baker Books, 1975), 64. Emphasis in original.
76 The Greek expression here, ἔα, can also be translated, "ah!" BDAG, s.v. "ἔα."

us?"[77] The demon's fear of destruction demonstrates his recognition of the advent of the kingdom (Luke 4:21), the defeat of demonic forces like him in Christ's wake (10:17–18; 11:20), and the specter of the abyss that awaits him (11:20; see Rev 20:9–10).[78] This confrontation in the Capernaum synagogue illustrates the Christocentric victory that is being achieved over the forces of evil. Luke especially makes clear that Christ's demonic exorcisms represent a demonstration of kingdom advance (Luke 9:27, 60, 62), and it is in the context of spiritual warfare and kingdom advance that Christ commissions his followers (9:1–3; 10:8–9, 17).[79]

In the ensuing response, Christ exercises a commanding measure of power and authority over the demonic forces, elevating the work of Christ to something far more significant than merely that of a good teacher or moral leader.[80] The demon recognizes the authority that Christ possesses, recognizing Him as "the Holy One of God" (ὁ ἅγιος τοῦ θεοῦ)—holiness that is in distinct contrast with the "uncleanliness" (ἀκαθάρτου) of the demon.[81] Demonic exorcism highlights the eschatological mission of Christ's first coming, and it gives important context to this first miracle recorded in both Mark and Luke's gospels: "That it is a battle with demonic forces is appropriate, for it is evil and Satan that Jesus seeks to overcome through his ministry."[82] Christ's confrontation with the evil forces of this age shows the spiritual warfare inherent in the overlap of *this age* and *the age to come*—conflict erupts as the kingdom of God engages in battle with the kingdom of darkness.

Christ's response to the demon is both concise and effective: He commands the demon, "Be silent (Φιμώθητι) and come out (ἔξελθε) of him!" (Mark 1:25 // Luke 4:35). After a violent reaction from the demonized host, the demon immediately leaves his victim in obedience to Christ. Bock colorfully asserts,

---

77 Cf. Luke 8:28; John 2:4; Jdg 11:12; 2 Sam 16:10; 19:22; 1 Kgs 17:18; 2 Kgs 3:13. See Stein, *Luke*, 163.
78 Stein, *Luke*, 163. It should be noted that Stein here references Revelation 20:1–3 in a chiliastic fashion.
79 Walter L. Liefield, "Luke," in *EBC* 8, ed. Frank E. Gabelein (Grand Rapids: Zondervan, 1984), 872.
80 Bock, *Luke 1:1–9:50*, 427.
81 Liefield, "Luke," 872. Liefield puzzlingly concludes here that this account is not an exorcism due to the absence of an incantation or invocation of authority.
82 Bock, *Luke 1:1–9:50*, 430. See also Sproul, *Walk with God*, 73.

God's power manifested in the anointed Jesus and the power of evil face off. The spiritual nature of this conflict is highlighted in 1 John 3:8, but in Luke the conflict is put in terms of personal confrontation. Judaism knew that demonic power would be crushed in the messianic age (T. Zeb. 9.8; T. Moses 10.1; Luke 7:22; SB 4:527). The die of cosmic confrontation is cast. The nature of the times and the victor are revealed by the battle.[83]

The crowd's response is poignant—they are "amazed," though their amazement is not indicative of either understanding or belief (see 2:48; 4:22; 9:43).[84] The exorcism of a demon leaves the crowd amazed, while Christ commands silence to preserve the timing of his work (cf. John 7:30; 8:20; 13:1).[85] The exorcism in the Capernaum synagogue gives a strong testimony of the authority that Christ possesses and the power with which He quickly dispatches demons—demons who often leave with much violence, and yet, who leave immediately.[86]

The Gadarene/Gerasene Demoniac (Matt 8:28–34 // Mark 5:1–20 // Luke 8:26–39)

> MATTHEW 8:32 "AND HE SAID TO THEM, 'GO.' SO THEY CAME OUT AND WENT INTO THE PIGS, AND BEHOLD, THE WHOLE HERD RUSHED DOWN THE STEEP BANK INTO THE SEA AND DROWNED IN THE WATERS."

Matthew's description of a demonic exorcism takes place amid the Gadarene tombs (Matt 8), which Mark and Luke both refer to as the "Gerasene" tombs in their descriptions of the event (Mark 5; Luke 8).[87] Following a turbulent boat passage that included Christ's calming of the storm (Matt 8:23–27 // Mark 4:35–41 // Luke 8:22–25), he and his followers arrive at the far shore of the Sea of Galilee near the area of the tombs. Upon reaching the shore, Matthew portrays an immediate confrontation

---

83 Bock, *Luke 1:1–9:50*, 431.
84 Stein, *Luke*, 162.
85 Sproul, *Reformation Study Bible: English Standard Version*, 1792.
86 Extra-biblical sources show close similarities, with power/authority being fundamental dynamics. See Twelftree, *Jesus the Exorcist*, 20, 51.
87 The location was most likely a district of Gentile territory controlled by the large city of Gadara, east of the Sea of Galilee and near the town of Gadara. Daniel M. Doriani, *Matthew*, 2 vols., REC (Phillipsburg, NJ: P&R, 2008), 1:356.

with two "demon-possessed men", though Mark and Luke focus on one of the men in particular who is "with an unclean spirit" (Mark) and "who had demons" (Luke).[88] This man is described as "fierce" and obstructing the way (Matthew), such that the disciples are unable to bind or shackle him (Mark), and the man's demonization reduces him to living unclothed and homeless (Luke) in an unclean area of the country. Living among the tombs was considered ceremonially unclean (Num 19:11–16; Ezek 39:11–15) and would have separated this man from both Jewish and Gentile societies, exemplifying the "holy" confrontation theme from the Capernaum Synagogue exorcism (Luke 4:33, ἀκαθάρτου; 4:34, ἅγιος).[89]

The demonization of this man even had led him to harm himself (Matt). The man "was always crying out and cutting himself with stones" (Mark 5:5), as the demonizing oppression seemingly had driven him to determined self-destruction.[90] His destructive tendencies are so fierce that no one could "subdue" (δαμάσαι/ δαμάζω; Mark 5:4) him—a semantic range that includes taming wild animals, indicating that no one could "tame" the demonized man.[91] The demonizing influence was so intense (before the encounter with Christ) that the man is headed toward imminent destruction with seemingly no one who can help. When the man confronts Christ, there is an immediate recognition of Christ by the demon, along with a fear of judgment and subsequent torment. The demon recognizes his opponent as "Jesus, Son of the Most High God" (Mark 5:7 // Luke 8:28; cf. Luke 1:32)[92] in two of the accounts, while Matthew conveys the abbreviated "O Son of God" (Matt 8:29). The demon, who actually turns out to be demons (i.e., in the plural), unmistakably recognizes Christ at first sight. Christ asks for the demon's name, to which the demon responds with the

---

88 In the ensuing discussion, elements in the text described by only one or two Synoptic Gospel writers will be denoted in parentheses; when all three writers describe the element in the passage, there will be no annotation. In his analysis of Matthew's account, D. A. Carson writes, "The best explanation is that Matthew had independent knowledge of the second man. Mention of only one [man] by the other Gospel writers is not problematic." "Matthew," in *EBC* 8, ed. Frank E. Gabelein (Grand Rapids: Zondervan, 1984), 217.
89 Doriani, *Matthew*, 1:356–57.
90 Doriani, 1:357.
91 David E. Garland, *Mark*, NIVAC (Grand Rapids: Zondervan Publishing House, 1996), 202–3; BDAG, s.v. "δαμάζω."
92 Doriani, *Matthew*, 1:359.

designation "Legion"—denoting a significant number of demonizing influences (Mark; Luke).[93]

Recognizing that a confrontation is imminent, the demons resist being sent away completely and instead request to inhabit a herd of pigs nearby. The swine's presence serves as a reminder of the locale of this confrontation, away from Jewish customs and well into Gentile territory.[94] Beyond the borders of Israel, Christ is here pictured encountering and defeating the demonic in Gentile lands, giving visible testimony to the advance of the kingdom. Doriani observes the content of the demonic request: "Oddly, they do not plead for mercy; they plead for delay. They seem to think Jesus has no right to trouble them *now*, before the judgment day, and no right to trouble them '*here*.'"[95] The demonic host appears to have prior knowledge that confrontation with Christ will eventually bring definitive judgment in the abyss (see Matt 25:41; 2 Pet 2:4; Jude 6; Rev 20:10), while their only hope of complaint is that it is not yet time (καιροῦ; Matt 8:29) for this to take place.[96] Christ's judgment is sure, and the kingdom advance is at hand (Matt 12:28), while the demonic host lobbies for a delay of the inevitable.

Once Christ grants their request to inhabit the pigs, the demons apparently move on to the swine and subsequently drive them over the cliff to immediate destruction and death. Why the demons choose the swine and why they immediately drive them to their deaths is unclear, but it follows a consistent demonic pattern of causing destruction to God's creatures and inciting animosity against God's kingdom.[97] This incident is followed by great fear among the observers and an impassioned public testimony given by the previously demonized man (Mark; Luke).

The Syrophoenician (Matt 15:21–28 // Mark 7:24–30)

> Then Jesus answered her, "O woman, great is your faith! Be it done for you as you desire." And her daughter was healed instantly. (Matt 15:28)

---

93 A Roman legion included over six thousand soldiers. Doriani, *Matthew*, 1:357.
94 Carson, "Matthew," 217.
95 Doriani, *Matthew*, 1:359. Emphasis in original.
96 Carson, "Matthew," 218; Doriani, *Matthew*, 1:360.
97 A desire for an abiding earthly home does not seem a likely motivating factor. See Carson, "Matthew," 218.

In a passage recorded only by Matthew and Mark, this third passage under consideration takes place in the areas of Tyre and Sidon—geographic areas of noteworthy spiritual import. Matthew's account, in particular, includes the name of both cities (Mark lists only Tyre), likely evoking these cities' negative connotations to God's people and highlighting the spiritual gulf that this incursion represents (see Matt 11:21–22 // Luke 10:13–14).[98] The cities of Tyre and Sidon were often associated with Israel's enemies in the Old Testament narrative (such as the Philistines and the Canaanites; see 2 Sam 24:7; Jer 47:4; Joel 3:4).[99] The account begins with Christ being sought out by a Canaanite woman (Matt), one whom Mark further specifies to be a Gentile Syrophoenician woman (Ἑλληνίς, "Greek;" Mark 7:26); Matthew's designation of "Canaanite" (Χαναναία; Matt 15:22) likely further emphasizes the spiritual gulf that existed between her people and the Jewish nation.[100] As shocking as this experience was on social, geographic, and spiritual-spatial grounds, it is consistent with the larger theme of Christ's work among the Gentile nations in the Gospel accounts. Christ had previously worked among the Gentile people (Matt 8:5–13, 28–34) and had subsequently commissioned his disciples in a similar fashion (Matt 10:18; 28:19–20).[101]

Despite the social gulf that existed, the woman approaches Christ with apparent confidence and correctly recognizes Christ, crying out "O Lord, Son of David" (Matt 15:22). This exclamation is nearly as shocking as the demonic recognition of Christ in the passage of the Gadarene demoniac (Matt 8:28–34 // Mark 5:1–20 // Luke 8:26–39)—the Syrophoenician woman, in the pagan land of Tyre and Sidon, both recognizes Christ and

---

98 Craig A. Evans, *The Bible Knowledge Background Commentary: Matthew–Luke*, ed. Craig A. Evans and Craig A. Bubeck (Colorado Springs: Cook, 2003), 309. "Was it only a coincidence that, just as Jerusalem had furnished such sorry specimens of dead formalism, the distant borders of heathen Tyre and Sidon should immediately thereafter furnish one of the very noblest examples of living faith?" John M. Gibson, "The Gospel of St. Matthew," in *The Expositor's Bible* 4 (Hartford: Scranton, 1903), 748.
99 Evans, *Bible Knowledge Background Commentary: Matthew–Luke*, 309.
100 Evans, 309; Craig L. Blomberg, *Matthew: An Exegetical and Theological Exposition of Holy Scripture*, NAC 22 (Nashville: Broadman & Holman, 1992), 242; J. Knox Chamblin, *Matthew: A Mentor Commentary*, 2 vols. (Fearn: Mentor, 2010), 2:793.
101 Doriani, *Matthew*, 1:53–54. The Markan account is shorter on details of Gentile mission (cf. Mark 4:24–24, 8:5–13). On this point, see Wessel, "Mark," 354.

appeals to his power and authority.[102] The woman pleads with Christ for mercy upon her daughter and gives a report that her daughter is "severely oppressed by a demon" (Matt). Although this Syrophoenician woman is from a culture and people group well outside the typical scope of Jewish life, during her encounter with Christ, she repeatedly pleads for her daughter's deliverance after Christ initially rejects her request. Christ's initial rebuff of the woman's request leads to a lesson in faith—faith that is rewarded through her daughter's deliverance from demonic oppression.

In response to her persistence, Christ lauds the woman for her faith and immediately speaks a word of healing over her daughter, echoing the Gospel theme of God's power and the faith of those delivered (see Matt 8:13).[103] Though the woman's daughter is not even physically present in the episode, she experienced instant healing (Matthew; Mark), and a report is given that the demon had subsequently departed (Mark). Though Christ was not even physically present alongside the girl, He assured the Syrophoenician that the demon "had gone" (Mark 7:29) as the girl was now "healed instantly" (ἀπὸ τῆς ὥρας ἐκείνης—"from that hour;" Matt 15:28).

The Demonized Boy
(Matt 17:14–20 // Mark 9:14–29 // Luke 9:37–43)

> AND JESUS REBUKED THE DEMON, AND IT CAME OUT OF HIM, AND THE BOY WAS HEALED INSTANTLY. (MATT 17:18)

The final passage under consideration takes place in the wake of the events on the Mount of Transfiguration, as Christ and his disciples leave the mountain outside of Jerusalem to journey toward Galilee.[104] Jesus, Peter, James, and John descend from the mountain, and a loud debate ensues between the disciples and the religious teachers, one that draws a great

---

102 Doriani, *Matthew*, 1:48. "On this woman's lips, "Lord" (most recently used by the disciples during the Christophany of 14:28, 30) will again call Jesus' divinity to Matthew's readers' minds. "Son of David" (cf. 1:1; 9:27; 12:23) is the distinctively Jewish designation for the Messiah and proves equally striking on this pagan woman's lips." Blomberg, *Matthew*, 243.
103 Chamblin, *Matthew*, 2:797–98. Mark's Gospel account mentions the demon (δαιμόνιον) four times, likely in emphasis.
104 Carson, "Matthew," 390.

crowd to gather.¹⁰⁵ At the center of the debate are the circumstances surrounding a boy, one who was oppressed by a demon (δαιμόνιον, Matt and Luke; πνεῦμα, Mark) that caused him physical harm. During the argument, a nameless man petitions Christ loudly about his son's demonized state, begging for his healing. The man reports that his son suffers terrible seizures (Matt), with a spirit that seizes him (Luke) and makes him mute as well (Mark). The demonic attacks cause frequent physical harm to the boy, as he had fallen into both fire and water (Matt) after having seizures and convulsions due to the demonization (Mark; Luke).¹⁰⁶ The demon was reported to have "thrown down" the boy, denoting a violent act of dashing him to pieces (ῥήσσω) on the ground.¹⁰⁷ The effects of the demonization are so strong that the disciples, whom the father had initially approached for a healing, are unable to cast this demonic presence away from the young man.

This incident is made even more unique by the disciples' inability to effectively cast out the demon (Mark 9:14–18), something they bring to Christ's attention (9:28–29).¹⁰⁸ The disciples' confusion is understandable—they had previously been empowered to heal disease and cast out demons and had already been successful in these efforts (efforts directly tied to kingdom advance—Matt 10:8; Luke 9:6; 10:17; Mark 3:15; 6:7, 13).¹⁰⁹ Judging from the content of Christ's subsequent rebuke, the disciples are unsuccessful due to their lack of faith ("little-faith," ὀλιγοπιστίαν; Matt 17:20)—either lacking faith in Christ, relying on their own abilities to produce results, or both.¹¹⁰ Christ responds by giving a stern rebuke of a

---

105 Walter W. Wessel, "Mark," in *EBC* 8, ed. Frank E. Gabelein (Grand Rapids: Zondervan, 1984), 702.
106 The term "waters" (ὕδατα, plural; Mark 9:22) likely denotes pools or streams. Wessel, "Mark," 703. Though the boy's symptoms resemble epilepsy, France is correct in maintaining: "All three evangelists, however, narrate it [the episode] unambiguously as an exorcism, and Mark and Luke offer no term comparable to our 'epilepsy.'" R. T. France, *The Gospel of Mark: A Commentary on the Greek Text*, NIGTC (Grand Rapids: Eerdmans, 2002), 362.
107 France, *Gospel of Mark*, 365; BDAG, s.v. "ῥήσσω."
108 France, *Gospel of Mark*, 361.
109 Kim H. Tan, *Mark*, NCC (Eugene, OR: Cascade, 2015), 124; France, *Gospel of Mark*, 362; Doriani, *Matthew*, 1:117.
110 Doriani, *Matthew*, 1:117–18; Evans, *Bible Knowledge Background Commentary: Matthew–Luke*, 335. On the disciples' "little faith" (ὀλιγοπιστίαν), see also Matt 6:30; 8:26; 14:3; 16:8.

"faithless and twisted generation" (Luke 9:41) before summoning the man to bring his boy into Christ's presence. When the boy comes to Christ, Mark records an immediate recognition of Christ by the demon, while both Mark and Luke describe the violent reaction by the demon in throwing the boy to the ground. Mark's account further details the moving plea for faith on the part of the boy's father: "I believe; help my unbelief!" (Mark 9:24). All three Gospels record Christ's authoritative rebuke of the demonic entity, an entity that is analogously described as a "demon" (δαιμόνιον; Matt; Luke) or a "spirit" (πνεῦμα; Mark). There is a violent reaction by the boy as the demon is cast away, so violent that the boy first appears to be a corpse (νεκρὸς; Mark 9:26) to all those who witness the exorcism.[111]

Though the exorcism is exceptionally violent and frightening to the crowd, Christ's rebuke of the demonic spirit brings instant healing to the demonized boy. Christ subsequently rebukes the disciples' lack of faith (Matt; Mark; Luke) and discloses that this kind of demon can only be dealt with through prayer (Mark). As with the other Gospel exorcism narratives, this passage maintains a close correlation between physical healing and demonic exorcism, as the work of Christ continues visibly to overcome the curse of sin in the world.[112] Christ's exorcisms and the visible advance of the kingdom serve to give glory to God, as Luke notes that "all were astonished at the majesty of God" (9:43).[113]

Five Common Features in Gospel Exorcisms

Though the above overview of the four major demonic exorcisms in the Gospels is necessarily succinct, its substance is sufficient to highlight some important commonalities. Demonic exorcism plays a foundational role in understanding the focal subject of satanic exorcism, since some of these commonly shared characteristics will resurface (though in greater form) in

---

111 Wessel, "Mark," 703–4. France observes, "The simple form of the verb, while originally used for such violent action as a dog tearing up a carcass (and thus closer to the meaning of ῥήγνυμι; see on v. 18), came to be used medically for retching or convulsion, and this seems the most likely sense here. The description of the boy rolling around on the ground foaming at the mouth is more dramatic than ξηραίνεται in v. 18." France, *Gospel of Mark*, 366.

112 D. A. Carson, *When Jesus Confronts the World: An Exposition of Matthew 8–10* (Grand Rapids: Baker Books, 1987), 31–32.

113 Evans, *The Bible Knowledge Background Commentary: Matthew–Luke*, 335.

the satanic exorcism that follows. There are five common elements of the demonic exorcisms surveyed that are of note.[114]

First, the advance of God's kingdom leads to spiritual conflict with the kingdom of darkness. There is a demonic and satanic presence in this world, a palpable presence in the Old Testament and described in the New Testament as a characteristic of this age that is yet extant. The power of Satan and his demonic forces are at work in this age, forming the spiritual backdrop of the narrative of this world. As Christ establishes his kingdom through the realization of his first coming (Matt 3:2, 4:17; Mark 1:15), the kingdom of darkness is forcibly pushed back by his work—something made visible as demons, and later Satan, are cast out by Christ. Demonic exorcisms are the spiritual battles that erupt in the conflict between light and dark, as Christ ministers to both Jew and Gentile, subsequently commissioning his disciples to do the same.

Second, demonic exorcisms commonly show both a demonic ability to exercise influence over people and an immediate recognition of Christ by the demonic spirit. The extent of demonic control over a human victim is something that is often overemphasized in popular culture—the biblical depiction of demonization or demon-possession (δαιμονίζω) exhibits a level of demonic authority and power over an individual, without unduly suggesting that the demon exerts complete and autonomous control over its victim.[115] Thus far, the passages surveyed show that demons could inflict harm and exercise a measure of control over a person, though the demon's power and influence had divinely regulated limits. The human victim can be driven away from society, brought to physical harm, and even led to attack others, yet the demonic presence always responds in submission when confronted by Christ. The limitations of demonization are evident in their immediate and fearful recognition of Christ, a recognition that clarifies the true dynamic of authority operational in spiritual warfare.

Third, demons are able to demonize an individual in a combined effort, and they often exhibit territorial tendencies both in terms of the human victim and spatial geography. There are examples of more than one demon plaguing a single human victim, even responding of their great

---

[114] These five common elements are summarized from the conclusions of Cook and Lawless, *Spiritual Warfare*, 61.
[115] Hendriksen, *Mark: New Testament Commentary*, 64–65.

numbers with terms appropriate to that time and culture ("legion"; Mark 5:9 // Luke 8:30). Those demonic influences that are encountered are also adamantly resistant to spiritual incursions into the areas they occupy. Demonization includes specific territorial qualities—demonic influences existing in certain regional *spaces* that seem reflective of a more expansive spiritual conflict. While the demonic influences are numerous and their resistance fierce, they encounter defeat in Christ's eschatological proclamation of the kingdom.

Fourth, demons resist leaving their victim, and there is often a violent reaction that accompanies the demonic exorcism. There is an evident demonic desire to continue demonizing an individual, but it is significant to recognize that demons do not appear to harm or kill their host once exorcised. There is often a palpable struggle involved in their forcible exit, but the demonic spirit is ultimately subject to the divine power and authority involved in the exorcism. Demonization often exhibits destructive intentions toward the victim, though those destructive intentions are curtailed in the event of demonic exorcism. Once the destructive influence is removed, the victim is restored and often responds with words of praise to God.

Fifth, demons show a debilitating fear of Christ. Following a demon's recognition of Christ is their fear of destruction and judgment—though the source of their knowledge is unclear, the demonic forces seem well-informed both of Christ's identity and his ability to judge and punish them. The demons are not ignorant of where authority and power lay in the realm of spiritual warfare, and this recognition of authority extends to those whom Christ commissions in his name. Christ accomplishes eschatological victory over demonic forces in his very presence in his first coming, and the desperate plea of demons is only a delay of the inevitable judgment that awaits them.

Satanic Exorcism in the Gospels

There was an escalation of spiritual warfare in Christ's first coming as the initial demonic exorcisms gave way to a cosmic satanic exorcism, one that shares many characteristics with the former but is a powerful attestation of the dawning of the blessings of the age to come. The contention offered in this section is that the New Testament describes a cosmic satanic exorcism that took place in the first coming of Christ and that the Gospels began describing that satanic exorcism as a spiritual reality that was already occurring in Christ's public ministry. This discussion of satanic exorcism will show certain parallels with the conclusions of significant demonic exorcisms listed above, though satanic exorcism is, in many ways, an escalation (or consummation) of the spiritual conquest that Christ displayed in the exorcisms of demons. There is also a developing understanding offered of the dynamics of power and authority present throughout these passages—a theme that will be explored in greater detail later.[116]

The Strong Man (Matt 12:22–30 // Mark 3:22–27 // Luke 11:14–23)

The "strong man" passage recorded in all three Synoptics (sometimes referred to as the Beelzebul controversy) describes a "strong man" (τὸν ἰσχυρόν) who had lost authority and power over the "house" he had once occupied—more accurately, someone had "bound" him and taken that authority away from him.[117] This passage is vital in clarifying both demonic and satanic exorcism since it directly addresses both. The "strong man" passage also links the connection of exorcism(s) to the inbreaking of the kingdom, and it does so by describing a healing occurrence with no direct Old Testament precursor (blind and mute; cf. Isa 29:18, 33:5, 42:7–20, 43:8, 61:1).[118]

From the perspective of the Gospel narratives, the binding of the "strong man" is furtherance of eschatological anticipation that began quite early in the Gospels—the description of Christ overcoming Satan's temptations in the wilderness (Matt 4:1–11 // Mark 1:12–13 // Luke 4:1–13). Satan boasted of exercising authority and power in this age, which is consistent

---

116 Portions of the following passage analysis sections rely on previous work by the present author, including: "An Evaluation of the Great Commission and the Church," a paper presented for DR37337 Biblical Ecclesiology, Midwestern Baptist Theological Seminary, November 2018; "The Eviction of the Ruler: An Exegetical Examination Of John 12:31," a paper presented for DR35090 Advanced Biblical Hermeneutics, Midwestern Baptist Theological Seminary, August 2019; "Conquest, Dominion, And The Nations: A Trinitarian Eschatology," a paper presented for DR 37395 Advanced Systematic Theology, Midwestern Baptist Theological Seminary, February 2020; and "Satan's Defeat In This Age: A Systematic Eschatology of Satanic Defeat," a paper presented for DR39011 Eschatology Directed Study, Midwestern Baptist Theological Seminary, November 2019.
117 Twelftree accurately observes that the language and context of this passage refer to a Satanic exorcism. Twelftree, *Jesus the Exorcist*, 112.
118 Twelftree, 98, 108–9.

with the power and authority he seems to have held in the Old Testament. Hiers notes, "However it had come about, synoptic tradition presupposes that Satan holds sway (ἐξουσία) over the kingdoms of the world ... and attempts to retain and exercise that power over men through his household, the demons."[119] The eschatological setting of the Gospels describes Satan and the demons at work in the world, having a measure of enduring power and authority that exorcisms (both demonic and satanic) forcibly removed in this age.

Adam had sinned in the Garden and failed in his temptation by the serpent, a failure that subsequently led to the curse upon the serpent and the proliferation of sin in this age (Gen 3:14–15). Yet while Adam was tempted and failed, the Gospel accounts now describe success in resisting satanic temptation and an eschatological reversal of satanic power in this world (cf. Rom 5:12–21).[120] The narrative of Christ overcoming Satan in the wilderness employs the contextual language of Psalm 91:11–12, as Beale observes: "Jesus's refusal to follow Satan's advice during the wilderness temptations was the beginning victory over Satan prophesied in the psalm [91]. [This] further reveals the theme of Jesus's victory over opposition."[121] Christ's first coming brought triumph in contradistinction to Adam's failures, and a significant means of Christ's victory was manifested in his resistance to satanic temptation. Christ's triumph is also a reminder of the paradox of victory-through-suffering—just as he emerged victorious through the satanic attack to exercise the demonic (and satanic), so Christ calls his followers to triumph through suffering.[122] The eschatological victory was achieved amid trials and suffering.

The Old Testament background of the "strong man" passage finds common language that is expressed in Isaiah 49:25:

> For thus says the LORD:
>
> "Even the captives of the mighty shall be taken,
> and the prey of the tyrant [עָרִיץ] be rescued,

---

119 Hiers, "Satan, Demons, and the Kingdom of God," 41. Hiers expands on the biblical development of Satan as "ruler of this world," alongside Old Testament connections.

120 "Exorcisms anticipate God removing sin from his people;" Carson, *When Jesus Confronts the World*, 33.

121 Beale refers here to Matthew's depiction of Jesus's wilderness temptation (Matt 4:6). Beale, *New Testament Biblical Theology*, 420.

122 Carson, *When Jesus Confronts the World*, 98, 137.

for I will contend with those who contend with you,
and I will save your children."

The context of Isaiah 49 is a description of Yahweh (יהוה) exercising the function of divine warrior, promising the liberation of his people and the defeat of those who hold them captive.[123] It is the language that invokes the recognition of God's warlike conquest against the forces of evil and the liberation that this conquest brings in deliverance for his people.

From this background understanding of the psalm, the Gospel narrative proceeds into a confrontation between Christ and the crowds, a confrontation that erupted due to a demonic exorcism. Christ was confronted by those who opposed his work, opponents who raised concerns about the proper observance of the Sabbath (Matt 12:1–14), and those who especially opposed Christ performing an exorcism on a "demon-oppressed man who was blind and mute" (Matt 12:22).[124] The Pharisees, united in their opposition to Christ and to this exorcism, responded by accusing Christ of surreptitiously operating in league with "Beelzebul, the prince of demons" (τῷ Βεελζεβοὺλ ἄρχοντι τῶν δαιμονίων; Matt 12:24).[125] Christ's response to this accusation was to point out the absurdity of Satan working against himself (vv. 26–27). Christ explained that it was by the power and authority of God that he had come, and by this divine power, Christ exorcised demons in the completion of his ministry (v. 28a). It is in this context that Christ compared his first coming and works to the home invasion of a "strong man" (τὸν ἰσχυρόν; 12:29, cf. Mark 3:27 and Luke 11:22), explaining that if a strong man's abode is to be entered and plundered, the strong

---

123 Beale and Gladd, *Story Retold*, 85. See also J. Lyle Story, "Jesus' 'Enemy' in the Gospels," *American Theological Inquiry* 6.1 (2013): 52.

124 Blomberg, *Matthew*, 195.

125 In this passage, the comparable terms Βεελζεβοὺλ and Σατανᾶς are both used for Satan, though it is uncertain how the former term ("lord of flies" used in 2 Kgs 1) came to be synonymous with Satan in first-century Galilee. See "Be-Elzebul, Beelzebub," in *BEB*, 273. On alternative roots of the term, see Charles Meeks, "Beelzebul" in *LBD*. The term "Satan" itself is inconsistently used within Second Temple Judaism; however, the New Testament shows a more consolidated usage, including reference to Satan in 74 percent (20/27) of New Testament books (137 probable references to Satan from 149 possible references) according to a study by Farrar and Williams, "Talk of the Devil," 72–96.

man must first be restrained so that he cannot defend his home against the invader.¹²⁶

In making this surprising comparison, Christ is not associating himself with the wicked activity of a burglar (a criminal or evildoer), nor is he associating his works with evil deeds. The focus of the passage rests on the necessary restraint of Satan that must take place in order for the demonic exorcisms to be accomplished. In the immediate context of a demonic exorcism, it may be tempting to assign the identity of the "strong man" (τὸν ἰσχυρόν) to a demon, or even to the demonic realm at large—which would seem to connect Christ's explanation directly with the demonic exorcism in question.¹²⁷ Nevertheless, the "strong man" passage has a singular referent in mind that is far larger and more eschatologically significant than a mere demon and its victim. This "strong man" narrative entails Christ defending his exorcism of demonic spirits by referencing his conquering invasion of this world and the concomitant defeat of this world's prince of darkness—Satan himself. Christ cast out demons in the power of the Holy Spirit (πνεύματι θεοῦ; Matt 12:28 // Mark 3:28–30)—certainly not by the unclean, demonic spirits of this world.¹²⁸ The Holy Spirit is given to Christ's commissioned disciples as the eschatological application of Christ's victory in this age (John 14:16; 14:26; 15:26; cf. 17:18). Following Christ's ascension, the Holy Spirit who had rested on Him (John 1:33–34; Matt 3:16–17) was sent to dwell in his followers (Acts 2:4; Rom 8:11) for the task of proclaiming the gospel to the nations (Matt 28:19).¹²⁹ Christ's exorcistic conquest was evidenced by demonic exorcisms, and the reclamation of his rightful authority was finally brought to bear in the restraint and exorcism of Satan himself.

Christ's possession of authority was not something new, nor something curiously gained, since authority in this world was rightfully possessed by Christ (see Matt 28:18).¹³⁰ The illustration of the "strong man" is shocking

---

126 The term ἰσχυρός is used in Matthew 12:29 and Luke 11:21, 22; cf. also Matt 3:11 ("mighty").
127 Similar exorcistic equivalents of demon-binding may be found in *Tobit* 8:3 and *Jubilees* 10:7ff.; See Hiers, "Satan, Demons, and the Kingdom of God," 43.
128 Hiers, "Satan, Demons, and the Kingdom of God," 43.
129 Andreas J. Köstenberger and Scott R. Swain, *Father, Son and Spirit: The Trinity and John's Gospel*, NSBT (Downers Grove: InterVarsity Press, 2008), 146, 93–96.
130 Carson, *When Jesus Confronts the World*, 21.

because the eschatological reality it describes is likewise shocking. Just as a burglar would bind a strong homeowner (effectively restricting his power and limiting his activity), so Christ in the work of his first coming has bound Satan, eschatologically restricting satanic powers that were previously held by evil elements. Beale is undoubtedly correct to observe that this passage describes "Jesus's beginning rule over Satan's kingdom."[131]

Physically restraining a strong man to enter his home is a powerful metaphor, but what is the extent of Satan's restraint that is described in this passage? Perhaps the most apparent restraint concerns Satan's inability to prevent or halt the work of Christ in his first coming.[132] From the context given in the synoptic passage of the "strong man," the binding of Satan occurred attendant to Christ's exorcism of demonic powers and his subsequent delegation of his disciples. Satan was bound (δέω; see Matt 13:30; 16:19; 18:18) because Christ was accomplishing victory over the satanic forces of this world—eschatological victory that is both accomplished and yet ongoing. Matthew described this binding (δήσῃ / δέω) using language similar to that used to describe: (1) Herod's binding of John the Baptist (ἔδησεν / δέω; 14:3); (2) the account of the disciples finding the donkey bound by a rope (δεδεμένην / δέω; 21:2); and (3) the binding of Christ when he was brought before Herod (δήσαντες / δέω; 27:2).[133] Luke described this satanic binding with the verb νικήσῃ—its singular usage in Luke's gospel, but a word reflecting triumphant victory that is far more common in the Apocalypse of John.[134] This same reference to binding

---

131 Beale, *New Testament Biblical Theology*, 435. Though Satan's specific category within the angelic realm is not clear, he is described as the prince of demons (Mark 3:22–30; Luke 13:10–17) and the leader of certain angelic beings (Matt 25:41; 2 Cor 12:7; Rev 12:7–9). See Stokes and Collins, *Satan*, 197.

132 Höhne notes, "The Gospel narratives are quite explicit about the presence of various agents that seek to thwart or oppose the mission of the royal and eternal Son and . . . are encapsulated in the 'strong man' parable that Jesus himself tells (Matt. 12:25–31; Mark 3:23–30; Luke 11:17–23). The most obvious is, of course, Satan and the various demons or evil/unclean spirits that confront the Messiah directly." David A Höhne, *The Last Things, Contours of Christian Theology* (Downers Grove, IL: InterVarsity Press, 2019), 230–31. Höhne also observes the ongoing satanic opposition to the Spirit's work in the New Testament (cf. 1 Cor 7:5; 2 Cor 2:11; 11:14; 12:7; Eph 4:27; 6:11; 1 Thess 2:18; 1 Tim 3:6; 5:15; Jas 4:7; 1 Pet 5:8; Rev 2:10).

133 See also Matthew 16:19 and Jesus's similar language to his disciples of "whatever you bind [δήσῃς] on earth."

134 Νικήσῃ (*nikēsē*) / νικάω (*nikaō*)—see esp. Rev 6:2; 12:11; 17:4.

(νικήσῃ / δέω) will surface again later in the present work's discussion of Revelation 20, where similar reference is made to Satan having been bound (δέω) in this age to prevent him from deceiving the nations to unite in rebellion against Christ.[135]

Christ explained the exorcism of demons and the binding of the "strong man" (satanic restraint/exorcism) in close proximity with the advance of the kingdom of God (Matt 12:28b).[136] The spread of demonic and satanic exorcisms in the Gospels were the very hallmarks of the reign of Christ, and exorcisms notably served as assurances of the advance of Christ's kingdom and the furtherance of God's plans in this world.[137] In the "strong man" passage, Christ explained (Matt 12:28 // Luke 11:20) that the kingdom of God was present if it was by the Spirit of God that He cast out (ἐκβάλλω) demons.[138] Kingdom advance and exorcisms subsequently became interwoven eschatological threads in the Gospel narratives:

> A double process of preparation for the Kingdom of God takes place through the exorcisms. In the first place, Satan is being bound. The world is being wrested from his control: the victories Jesus and his disciples gain over the demons should therefore be a clue to the fact that Satan is being defeated, and that, consequently, the establishment of God's Kingdom on earth is near.[139]

Satanic exorcism is indicative of the eschatological reclamation that Christ's work represents.

Though Satan sought to lead humanity into deception and eventual destruction, Christ's first coming was characterized by a restraint and binding of Satan's previous authority—restraint that eventually led

---

135   Hoekema, *Bible and the Future*, 229.
136   For further discussion of the inaugurated kingdom of God, see Horton, *The Christian Faith*; Herman N. Ridderbos, *The Coming of the Kingdom*, ed. Raymond O Zorn, trans. H. de Jongste (Phillipsburg, NJ: P&R, 1962); George Eldon Ladd, *The Gospel of the Kingdom: Scriptural Studies in the Kingdom of God* (Grand Rapids: Eerdmans, 2011).
137   Hoekema, *Bible and the Future*, 46. Hoekema ties this reality to similar themes in Matt 12, Luke 10, John 12, and Rev 20. See Hoekema, *Bible and the Future*, 229.
138   Matthew 12:28 is the first use of ἐκβάλλω in reference to exorcisms in the New Testament. The typical LXX usage of this verb occurs when an enemy of God is cast out "so that God's purpose can be fulfilled." Twelftree, *Jesus the Exorcist*, 109–10.
139   Hiers, "Satan, Demons, and the Kingdom of God," 42.

to a subsequent gospel-commissioning of his disciples in the world.[140] Demonic exorcisms and the binding of the strong man (i.e., satanic exorcism) are inherently eschatological events. Hiers concludes: "Nevertheless, exorcism of demons, who are understood to represent Satan's household if not Satan himself, is a fundamentally eschatological activity: one of preparation for the coming of the Kingdom of God."[141] Demonic exorcisms functioned as a foreshadowing of an even greater satanic exorcism, and the freedom granted to victims of demonization foreshadowed an even greater spiritual freedom granted to a world liberated of Satan's previously held authority and power in this age.[142]

Exorcisms played a significant role in the ministry of Christ's first coming, as Thielman observes: "One of the most important elements in the vocation of Jesus, the apostles, and other evangelists is the deliverance of Satan's victims from his power."[143] It is worth noting that the object of faith and joy in these passages is deliverance and salvation for the believer, not necessarily Satan's defeat as such (Luke 10:20)[144]—yet the passage of the "strong man" shows that eschatological victory in Christ is biblically framed alongside the exorcism of demonic forces and the exorcism of Satan himself. The "strong man" passage demonstrates that demonic exorcisms helped define the satanic exorcism that Christ accomplished, communicated within a robust narrative context.[145] The strong man's binding remains an inaugurated reality—a curtailment of power and authority, but not yet a complete cessation of all activity. As Story observes, "Strangely enough, the Strong Man, though bound, still exercises power."[146] Though his attacks and influence remain present in *this age*, the "strong man" has been bound with the advent of *the age to come*.

---

140 Thielman, *Theology of the New Testament*, 634.
141 Hiers, "Satan, Demons, and the Kingdom of God," 47.
142 Story contends that there are two aspects of the defeat of the strong man, both cosmological (this age) and personal (salvific/redemptive). Story, "Jesus' 'Enemy' in the Gospels," 46. See also John Stott's six-fold Christological victory paradigm, especially stage four, and his reference to "the conquest confirmed and announced" as designating all enemies being subjected underfoot by Christ. Stott, *Cross of Christ*, 227–232.
143 Thielman, *Theology of the New Testament*, 126. Thielman additionally gives several related examples.
144 Hoekema, *Bible and the Future*, 47.
145 Twelftree, *Jesus the Exorcist*, 219.
146 Story, "Jesus' 'Enemy' in the Gospels," 51.

The Ruler (John 12:31)

> Now is the judgment of this world; now will the ruler of this world be cast out. (John 12:31)

Readers of John's Gospel may recognize a relative scarcity of language describing spiritual warfare, demonic exorcisms, and satanic dealings compared to what is observable in the Synoptic Gospels.[147] However, John's gospel provides a unique introduction of spiritual conflict with a figure he refers to as the "ruler of this world" (ὁ ἄρχων τοῦ κόσμου τούτου)—one whose defeat is set in the shadow of the cross.[148]

Though the title of ὁ ἄρχων τοῦ κόσμου occurs only in John (John 12:31; 14:30; 16:11), this figure seems consistent with the canonical figure of Satan—the spiritual adversary to the work of Christ who seeks the destruction of humanity.[149] John's first declaration of Satan's defeat occurs in 12:31, as the theological setting of John begins to shift from Christ's public ministry into the passion narrative that imminently leads to the cross.[150] Raymond Brown observes that in the latter part of his ministry, Jesus brings condemnatory judgment to the prince of this world [ὁ ἄρχων τοῦ κόσμου τούτου] but life to those who are drawn by Jesus ... [yet] the last few hours of the light that is Jesus emphasize the surrounding darkness that is closing in."[151]

---

147 John does once refer to Satan (ὁ Σατανᾶς) in 13:27. See Gerald L. Borchert, *John 12–21*, NAC 25B (Nashville: Broadman & Holman, 2002), 58.

148 Herman N. Ridderbos, *The Gospel according to John: A Theological Commentary*, trans. John Vriend (Grand Rapids: Eerdmans, 1997), 438n194. The English translation of "ruler" for the Greek term "ἄρχων" is relatively common (ESV, NASB, NRSV, CSB, NKJV, NET), while the translation "prince" is at least possible (so NIV, KJV).

149 Michaels, *Gospel of John*, 696, 696n44. The phrase ὁ ἄρχων τοῦ κόσμου τούτου is used here by John to refer to Satan, a phrase that is closely related to John's use of "the evil one" (John 17:15, "τοῦ πονηροῦ"). See also R. V. G. Tasker, *The Gospel According to St. John: A Concise, Workable Tool for Laymen, Teachers and Ministers*, TNTC 4 (Grand Rapids: Eerdmans, 1960), 153n31; Twelftree, "Demon, Devil, Satan," 164.

150 T. Desmond Alexander observes: "We catch but occasional glimpses of this shadowy opponent. This should not surprise us. As divine revelation, the Bible exists to give us a deeper understanding of God. It is not designed to promote knowledge of the enemy, beyond what is necessary for comprehending the world in which we live and our own experience of it. Consequently, many questions remain unanswered when we collate what the Bible says about the devil or Satan." Alexander, *From Eden to the New Jerusalem*, 100.

151 Raymond E. Brown, *The Gospel According to John I–XII*, AB 29 (New York: Doubleday, 1966), 477.

In John's Gospel, Satan primarily appears during times of conflict between the Jews and Christ's followers—more precisely, during conflicts between Christ and the world. By the time John 12 takes place, the tension between the world and Christ has reached "the point of almost a transitory dualism," with Satan seemingly exercising pervasive influence over the evil world.[152] Satan's title ὁ ἄρχων semantically suggests a sort of kingly or mediatorial status in the world, yet this status is revoked in the light of Christ, the true Mediator and King.[153] Satan is portrayed as patently evil in the same way John speaks of the world Satan rules as evil. Satan's presence is likewise indicative of the cosmic conflict between light and dark, and his position and power are being cast down and defeated in the work of Christ.[154] The casting out of Satan takes on the distinctive characteristic of Johannine exorcism language, and it does so in direct proximity to Christ's work. As Shogren helpfully asserts, "Despite the absence of exorcism accounts in John's gospel, the authority of Satan's kingdom also comes into sharp relief. Jesus is said to have overcome both the world (John 16:33) and its 'prince' (John 12:31)."[155]

It is within this eschatological hour of Christ's ministry that he announces, "Now will the ruler of this world be cast out" (John 12:31). The setting of the eviction of Satan is framed within the eschatological force of Christ's first coming and the impending work of his death and resurrection.[156] Satan's defeat is clearly realized in its Johannine context in the

---

152 Gerhard Delling, "ἄρχων," in *TDNT* 1:488–89.
153 Though again, linguistically, this exact title for Satan occurs nowhere else in the New Testament. Alan F. Segal, "Ruler of This World: Attitudes about Mediator Figures and the Importance of Sociology for Self-Definition," in *Jewish and Christian Self-Definition, Vol. 2: Aspects of Judaism in the Greco-Roman Period*, ed. E. P. Sanders with A. I. Baumgarten and Alan Mendelson (Philadelphia: Fortress, 1981), 252, 404n4.
154 Segal, "Ruler of This World," 258–59.
155 G. S. Shogren, "Authority and Power," in *DJG*, 53. Hendriksen notes, "This prince (or *ruler*) is clearly satan [*sic*]. Elsewhere the author of the Fourth Gospel and of the book of Revelation describes him symbolically as being the 'red dragon, having seven heads and ten horns, and upon his heads seven diadems' (Rev. 12:3). Cf. also Luke 4:5, II Cor. 4:4; Eph. 2:2; 6:12." William Hendriksen, *John: New Testament Commentary*, 2 (Grand Rapids: Baker Books, 2002), 2:202.
156 Dale C. Allison Jr. rightly observes: "John, like Mark and Matthew, associated the end of Jesus with end-time themes. In his gospel the death of Jesus is 'the judgment of this world' (12:31). The crucifixion brings about the casting out of the devil (16:11) . . . and is associated with the destruction of 'the son of perdition' (17:12; cf. 2 Thess 2:3). . . .

inaugurated context of Christ's victory through the cross (John 12:33).[157] This relationship between satanic defeat and Christological victory is established with the temporal language associated with the ἄρχων passage—it has *now* (νῦν) occurred, while it remains yet to be consummated. Satan's exorcism is a sentence of divine judgment, a judgment rendered even as the evil of the surrounding world sought to pass its judgment on Christ.[158] In the hour of Christ's work, Satan is evicted from this world, while his final judgment remains yet to come.[159]

The language John uses to describe Satan's defeat bears strong similarities to the exorcism language found in other passages in the New Testament, painting the portrait of Satan's eviction in John with words and phrases elsewhere reserved to depict demonic exorcism (e.g., ἐκβάλλω; ὁ ἄρχων). John's use of exorcism language describes a sort of global satanic exorcism from the world itself (τοῦ κόσμου τούτου; cf. "the cosmic powers over this present darkness" in Eph 6:12), "by virtue of the 'throwing out' of its ruler."[160] The Synoptic Gospels convey exorcisms in the ministry of Christ as a manner in which his divine power is revealed, while John especially illuminates the work of Christ as God's cosmic victory of light over darkness. Twelftree astutely remarks, "In the Synoptic Gospels the defeat of Satan is linked with Jesus's exorcisms. In John the defeat of Satan is linked with the cross (John 14:30; 16:11)."[161] The Synoptics portray a series of lesser exorcisms showing the progressive victory of Christ at work, as the demonic exorcisms foreshadow the greater satanic exorcism to come.[162] Each demonic exorcism functions to portray visibly the establishment of

---

One is tempted to say that in John, Jesus himself is the eschaton, its real content. When Jesus came, the end came." Dale C. Allison Jr., "Eschatology," in *DJG*, 209.

157 Brown asserts: "To suggest that the Fourth Gospel is so much in the atmosphere of realized eschatology that the writer expects no further victory over evil than that won in the victorious hour of Jesus' life is to reduce him to a hopeless romantic who cannot recognize existing evil in the world." Brown, *Gospel according to John I–XII*, 477.

158 F. F. Bruce, *The Gospel of John: Introduction, Exposition, and Notes* (Grand Rapids: Eerdmans, 1994), 266–67. Bruce casts the judgment of the ἄρχων as a cosmic reversal, one that is brought by the world's self-judgment in its rejection of Jesus.

159 Arthur W. Pink, *Exposition of the Gospel of John* (Grand Rapids: Zondervan, 1982), 272.

160 Michaels, *Gospel of John*, 695–96.

161 Twelftree, "Demon, Devil, Satan," 171.

162 In this way, demonic exorcism functions as a type of "inaugurated" satanic expulsion. See Storms, *Kingdom Come*, 339; Ladd, *Presence of the Future*, 151, 165.

God's sovereignty in the world, in anticipation of the final and decisive exorcism of this world's false ἄρχων. Alexander notes, "In the Gospels the life-restoring activities of Jesus and the exorcisms of unclean or evil spirits are both associated with the coming of God's presence to the earth."[163]

John remains relatively silent on exorcisms until Christ's decisive victory and Satan's defeat are pronounced—in the work of the cross and the exorcism of Satan. The eviction of the ἄρχων depicts the great satanic exorcism to which demonic exorcisms are but adumbrations, exorcisms which not only testify to Christ's power but also manifest the content of Christ's redemptive work. The exorcism of John 12:31 reveals a spiritual conflict (14:30) that will result in judgment upon Satan being rendered (16:11) and applied (12:31), even while evil will yet remain in the present age.[164] Ridderbos maintains that the glorification of Christ entails the triumphant reclamation of spiritual power and eviction of Satan, through "the reversal thus announced in eschatological and cosmic terms" wherein John is "using the familiar distinction in Jewish eschatology between 'this' world/aeon and the 'coming' world/aeon."[165] The early Christians recognized this theme of two ages as the beginning fulfillment of the last days. Geddert states, "The earliest Christians were under the conviction that even though the old age had not ended, the new age had already dawned. It was as though the two ages of Jewish apocalyptic eschatology had overlapped."[166] The timing of the devil's defeat reflects the overlapping of *this age* and the *age to come*, an event that the New Testament writers present as a historical occurrence whose effects are ongoing.[167]

---

163 Alexander, *From Eden to the New Jerusalem*, 155.
164 Twelftree observes, "In the death and resurrection, or 'hour' (12:23-36) of Jesus, the Devil, or Ruler of this World, is judged and brought down (12:31; 14:30; 16:11). However, the Devil remains sufficiently robust for Jesus to pray that his followers would be kept from *tou ponērou* ("the evil," 17:15), probably meaning the Evil One (cf. 1 Jn 2:13, 14; 3:12; 5:18, 19) until the judgment on the last day (12:48)." Twelftree, "Demon, Devil, Satan," 171. Ladd agrees that John 12 is connected with John 14 and John 16 in describing Satan's defeat, yet (possibly due to his historic premillennial position) insists that these passages need not be understood chronologically. Ladd, *Presence of the Future*, 153.
165 These two designations approximate the language of the present work when it distinguishes between *this age* and *the age to come*. Ridderbos, *Gospel according to John*, 437–38, 437n192.
166 Geddert, "Apocalyptic Teaching," 24.
167 For example, Thielman recognizes in his work that the New Testament authors are mostly unconcerned with the timing of the defeat of the *archōn*, though its substance

John presents Satan's current defeated state alongside the promise of Christological redemption through the cross: "And I, when I am lifted up from the earth, will draw all people to myself" (John 12:32). Evil is still present, and Satan remains active, yet he is limited. Nevertheless, the context of Satan's exorcism presents real and substantial eschatological consequences. An actual spiritual defeat of Satan has taken place, and his previous access to and power over the things of this world have been drastically curtailed. There is also a progressive sense to the ongoing victory through the work of Christ achieved over Satan, one in which the Adamic chains of sin and death have been irreparably damaged in Satan's defeat (see Rom 5).[168] Though evil still exists in this world, power has been (and is being) wrested away from its false ἄρχων (cf. also 1 John 5:18–19).[169]

The restraint and expulsion of Satan in John is substantial, as Ridderbos indicates: "It is the hour for the expulsion of the ruler of this world because he has no grounds for an appeal against Jesus (see [John] 14:30); in Jesus's exaltation he loses his claim on the world and is thus driven from the center of his power."[170] The connection of the casting out of Satan and Christ's salvific drawing indicates a close relationship between the two—Satan is rendered spiritually impotent in regards to deceiving the elect, preventing the spread of the gospel, and successfully destroying the people of God. He is prevented from accusing the brethren (Rev 12:7), though he is still active in the work of persecution. In D. A. Carson's work on John's Gospel,

---

is tied inextricably to the cross. Ladd observes a temporal element within John 12, yet he maintains: "Here is an essential fact in the Gospel [of John]: the suprahistorical and the historical are inseparably wedded in Heilsgeschichte." Romanowsky correctly asserts that the defeat of the *archōn* and Christ's victory must be read within the Johannine discourse context, one that maintains a present and achieved (i.e., in part)triumph. Thielman, *Theology of the New Testament*, 690; Ladd, *Presence of the Future*, 155; John W. Romanowsky, "'When the Son of Man Is Lifted up': The Redemptive Power of the Crucifixion in the Gospel of John," *Hor* 32.1 (2005): 114.

168 Cf. Bruce Milne, *The Message of John*, BST (Downers Grove, IL: InterVarsity Press, 1993), 190; Brown, *Gospel according to John I–XII*, 477. Milne views this as part of a fourfold exposition of the cross in John 12:30–32: (1) the judgment of the world; (2) the defeat of sin; (3) the exaltation of Jesus; and (4) the drawing of men. T. Desmond Alexander highlights that in his defeat of Satan, Jesus perfectly fulfills the eschatological vice-regency in which Adam failed. See Alexander, *From Eden to the New Jerusalem*, 92–95 & 92n32.

169 Alexander, *From Eden to the New Jerusalem*, 75, 100.

170 Ridderbos, *Gospel According to John*, 439.

he similarly recognizes that judgment on the world (and by extension, its ἄρχων) is resolved in Christ's passion and subsequent resurrection.[171] Carson recognizes that in John 12, the events of the *eschaton* have already begun: "The judgment of the world, the destruction of Satan, the exaltation of the Son of Man, the drawing of men and women from the ends of the earth—these might all be reserved for the end times. But the end times have begun already."[172] In the Johannine discourse context, the defeat of Satan is associated with the subsequent spread of the gospel to all the world (beginning with the "Greeks"), a gospel spread that is empowered and protected by Christ's eschatological victory over Satan.

The defeat of the satanic ἄρχων in John may be summarized by his eviction from a place of power previously held (12:31), his lack of claim on Christ (14:30), and his judgment being rendered because of the cross (16:11).[173] Despite John's lack of spiritual warfare language similar to that found in the Synoptics, John presents Christ's paradoxical victory through the lens of his work on the cross as he transforms the very evil intended into an epoch-changing defeat of Satan. Christ's death and resurrection purchased human redemption and also brought actual defeat to Satan and to his rule on earth.[174] Within John's account, Satan's defeat may be summarized by his eviction from a place of power previously held (12:31), by his lack of any claim on Christ (14:30), and by his present condemnation (16:11).[175] Tellingly, John's latter application of *archōn* to Christ himself occurs in Revelation 1:5, denoting the victory achieved, as Jesus Christ is declared to be "the faithful witness, the firstborn of the dead, and the ruler of kings on earth" (ὁ ἄρχων τῶν βασιλέων τῆς γῆς).[176] Christ emerges in eschatological consummation

---

171 D. A. Carson, *Gospel According to John* (Grand Rapids: Eerdmans, 1991), 442.
172 Michaels, *Gospel of John*, 443.
173 Ladd, *Gospel of the Kingdom*, 192; cf. 118–19, 157.
174 Thielman, *Theology of the New Testament*, 689–90.
175 George Eldon Ladd, *A Theology of the New Testament*, rev. ed (Grand Rapids: Eerdmans, 1993), 192; cf. 118–19, 157. Many who study the dynamic of satanic exorcism disagree on properly defining the dynamics of satanic defeat. See John F. Walvoord, "Is Satan Bound?," *BibSac* 100.400 (1943): 502. For example, Walvoord reflects a heavily dispensational understanding that recognizes a "limiting" of Satan and his activities yet pragmatically rejects any real power inherent in this curtailment or expulsion.
176 Thielman, *Theology of the New Testament*, 489.

as the true ruler, the ἄρχων *par excellence*—victorious after the initial eviction and subsequent final judgment of the evil ἄρχων.[177]

Satan Falling (Luke 10:18–19)

> AND HE SAID TO THEM, "I SAW SATAN FALL LIKE LIGHTNING FROM HEAVEN. BEHOLD, I HAVE GIVEN YOU AUTHORITY TO TREAD ON SERPENTS AND SCORPIONS, AND OVER ALL THE POWER OF THE ENEMY, AND NOTHING SHALL HURT YOU." (LUKE 10:18–19)

A final important example of satanic exorcism in the Gospels is described in Luke 10. Though this passage is often associated with a prelapsarian (or even pre-creation) satanic fall from heaven, a thorough examination of its language and context reveals a depiction of the satanic exorcism that occurred in the first coming of Christ.[178] In this passage, Christ commissions and sends out the disciples two-by-two in a wide-reaching missional endeavor. Upon their return, the disciples remark in wonder at the spiritual power they now possess over demonic forces: "Lord, even the demons are subject to us in your name!" (Luke 10:17). Christ reminds them, however, that their real joy lies in salvation (10:20), yet he also explains the nature of their power over the demonic forces. The reason that Christ gives for his disciples' unexpected power over these demonic forces is the revelation that he had witnessed Satan fall from heaven (10:18) and had given the disciples power over the enemy (10:19).

Christ explained the recent victory of his disciples over demonic forces by explaining that he had witnessed Satan (τὸν Σατανᾶν) falling (πεσόντα).[179] In Luke's narrative flow, there has been a theme of redemptive spiritual victory developing, a victory that operates alongside the concomitant defeat of demonic spiritual forces. As the spiritual light shines more brightly, the darkness fades away (to borrow a metaphor more prevalent in John's gospel). As the disciples return from their mission in wonder, Christ responds with an enigmatic statement—yet a statement that clarified the

---

177 For lexical parallels in the New Testament with the words *archōn*, *ballō*, and *deō*, see appendix 1.

178 Luke 10 will be addressed later in this work in terms of power and authority (Chapter 5), though here it is important that Jesus has witnessed Satan's fall resultant from his ministry.

179 Luke 10:18–19's use of πεσόντα is fairly rare in Luke's Gospel; cf. also 14:5 ("that has fallen") and 16:17 ("to become void").

spiritual consequences of his earthly work: "I saw Satan fall like lightning from heaven" (Luke 10:18).[180] It is theologically tempting to draw a premature connection to an originating fall of Satan, yet the context here is undoubtedly tied to the demonic exorcisms that are in close proximity.[181]

Luke's use of exorcism language is consistent with that of John (John 12:31) and reflects an ongoing theme of exorcism in the first coming of Christ—one in which Christ's triumph leads to him observing "Satan fall like lightning from heaven" (Luke 10:18).[182] The return of the seventy depicts a satanic enemy whose defeat has begun, yet the process of defeat has not yet reached its decisive conclusion.[183] Luke's depiction of Christ successfully defeating temptation in the wilderness and the ongoing defeat of Satan through the exorcism of Luke 10 is an eschatological event "without parallel in contemporary Judaism."[184]

The subject of exorcism is so prominent in the Gospel narratives that Christ is even falsely accused of being in league with the devil due to his frequent engagement with the demonic realm (Matt 12:22–30 // Mark 3:20–27 // Luke 11:14–23). Within John's account, Christ at one point is even falsely accused of being demon-possessed himself (John 7:20).[185] Luke's narrative continues the spiritual theme that is so substantial in John—a developing New Testament theme that Christ has brought about a decisive victory over Satan, one that involves satanic defeat in this age.[186] This victory is present now in *this age*, but it will reach full consummation in *the age to come*.[187] Following the direction of this narrative illustration,

---

180 See Jon Carman, "The Falling Star and the Rising Son: Luke 10:17–24 and Second Temple 'Satan' Traditions," *Stone-Campbell Journal* 17.2 (2014): 222. Carman understands Jesus's words to be an allusion to Isaiah 14:12–15.

181 The verb "saw" in Luke 10:18 (an inceptive aorist, "I was seeing" or "I began to see") likely refers to the symbolic eschatological import of the demonic exorcisms by the 70 (or 72) disciples, exorcisms that demonstrated a greater satanic exorcism (cf. Luke 11:20–22). See Stein, *Luke*, 309. Luke's use of "see" does not suggest that he necessarily employs mythical language, as some have argued. Thielman, *Theology of the New Testament*, 634.

182 This verse likely depicts a similar scene in Rev 12:5–9, wherein the Messianic child is lifted up even as Satan is cast down. Carson, *Gospel According to John*, 443.

183 Twelftree, *Jesus the Exorcist*, 115.

184 Twelftree, *Jesus the Exorcist*, 117, 127.

185 Twelftree, "Demon, Devil, Satan," 171.

186 Ridderbos, *Gospel according to John*, 440.

187 Ridderbos contends, "On the other hand, the judgment of 'this world' and the casting out of 'this world's ruler' cannot be understood only in an anticipatory sense. The

Satan's fall from heaven (ἐκ τοῦ οὐρανοῦ) portrays his eviction from a level of spiritual access, access that he no longer enjoys.[188] Satan once was granted a measure of access into God's heavenly territory, yet this access has been decisively curtailed. The timing of Satan's fall does not seem to be the primary focus in the narrative, but the nature and result of this fall are what is significant.[189] The former place and authority of Satan have been cut off and restricted in the work of Christ. Christ then uses the imagery of witnessing Satan falling to describe his disciples' missional triumph over demonic forces.

This fall of Satan can thus be recognized as directly connected to the binding of the "strong man" depicted in Luke's ensuing chapter (Luke 11 // Matt 12 // Mark 3). Hiers illuminates the close connection between the fall of Satan in Luke 10 and the binding of the "strong man" in Luke 11:

> This [defeat of the strong-man] also seems to be the meaning of Luke 10.17f. Upon hearing the disciples' report of their successes against the demons, Jesus visualises [sic] —logically if not also by prophetic inspiration—the ultimate destruction of Satan: 'I saw Satan fall like lightning from heaven. Through the exorcisms wrought by Jesus and his disciples, Satan's power is being overcome, he is being bound, and his eventual doom is certain.[190]

hour that has now begun is also that of 'the coming of the ruler of this world' (14:30), that is, for that ruler's decisive assault on Jesus (cf. 13:12, 27; Lk. 22:31, 53). The hour that is *already* here is also the hour of the world's unbelief and hostility toward Christ (cf. 16:32f.)." Ridderbos, *Gospel According to John*, 439. Likewise, Geddert notes, "Jesus taught that the Evil One was still in control of this present world, but that in some sense he was already defeated. Jesus taught that with his own coming, judgment on the world had come, but that nevertheless a future judgment was to be expected (Jn 12:31; 16:11)." Geddert, "Apocalyptic Teaching," 24.

188 The term οὐρανός ("heaven"; "dwelling-place of God") is found in Luke 2:15; 3:21–22; 4:25; 6:23; 9:16; 9:54; 10:15; 10:18; 10:20–21; 11:13; 11:16; 12:33; 15:7; 15:18; 15:21; 16:17; 17:29; 18:13; 18:22; 19:38; 20:4–5; 21:11; 21:26; 21:33; 22:43; 24:51.

189 Carman maintains, "The reader is beset by the problem of the precise meaning of πεσόντα (*pesonta*). An aorist participle of πίπτω (*piptō*, 'to fall'), this can be interpreted as 'fallen,' conveyed in the general sense of a body moving downward in space. Yet it is possible that another meaning is at work here. Likely, πεσόντα is being used as a past form of βάλλω (*ballō*, 'to throw, hurl'), conveying the notion not of falling but of being 'thrown down.' Thus Satan is thrown or cast down from heaven." Carman, "The Falling Star and the Rising Son," 222. See the discussion of the timing of Satan's exorcism within Jesus's first coming in Twelftree, *Jesus the Exorcist*, §11.114ff.

190 Hiers, "Satan, Demons, and the Kingdom of God," 44.

Christ equips his disciples with the power of demonic exorcism (Luke 9:1; 10:1–16), describing these exorcisms as a witness of Satan's fall from heaven (10:18–19), and later setting the context of this manifestation against the backdrop of Satan's binding and restraint (Luke 11:14–22).[191]

Luke 11's recognition of Satan's binding is thus an explanation of how the gospel will advance (Luke 9) as well as how Satan is restrained (Luke 10). As Stein observes, "The themes of the coming of God's kingdom (10:9) and the defeat of Satan/demons (10:17–18) are brought together in 11:20."[192] Christ gathers and commissions the disciples to proclaim the advent of the kingdom (9:2), and their mission is safeguarded because Christ gives them his eschatological authority (10:18) to wield over the demonic forces of this age (9:2; 11:20).[193] The kingdom advances under the authority of Christ, and this advance results in the casting out of both demonic and satanic powers in this age.

Luke 11:14–22 bears a striking resemblance to a scene later described in Revelation, specifically in Revelation 12:7–12. In that subsequent Johannine passage, the great dragon (Satan) is defeated and cast down from heaven, having his powers against the elect restricted and curtailed in direct consequence to Christ's victory and the gospel's successful proclamation.[194] In Luke's passage, Christ explains the demonic exorcisms of his disciples by proclaiming the cosmic overthrow of Satan due to the spiritual victory being achieved.[195] Christ's disciples' exorcisms are a precursor to the final victory, one that is soon to be achieved on the cross. It is a victory that has already begun, even as Satan already has been overthrown. Precision with regard to the chronological timing of Satan's defeat fades as the focus

---

191 See Thielman, *Theology of the New Testament*, 126.
192 Stein, *Luke*, 309.
193 So Peter's speech summarizing Christ's ministry, which tied Christ's work to the exorcism of Satan (Acts 10:38); Carman, "The Falling Star and the Rising Son," 222.
194 Though in Revelation 12, Satan's defeat is delivered by Michael the archangel. See Canoy, "Time and Space, Satan," 254.
195 See Ladd, *Presence of the Future*, 156. Stein observes: "This passage continues the theme of the mission of the seventy(-two) and thus, by extension, the future mission of the church.... Because of his exorcisms, Jesus can assure his audience that God's kingdom has come (11:20). The exorcism of demons by Jesus's messengers is another witness to the realization of God's kingdom. Jesus saw in each one Satan's overthrow. Luke understood, as did Paul, that Jesus disarmed and conquered the powers and authorities of Satan's domain (11:21–22; cf. Col 2:15)." Stein, *Luke*, 310.

is correctly placed on the eschatological victory Christ has achieved.[196] The cause of Satan's fall from heaven is the work and victory of Christ, an achievement experienced by his disciples as they subsequently carry out his mission by the Holy Spirit.

As proof of this inaugurated victory over Satan, Christ demonstrates a significant spiritual reversal—that even while Satan tries to "give" Christ authority (Luke 4:6), Christ instead victoriously gives his disciples authority over "the enemy" (i.e., Satan himself; 10:19). In his failed temptation of Christ, Satan offers authority in this age: "To you [Jesus] I [Satan] will give all this authority [ἐξουσία] and glory, for it has been delivered [παραδίδωμι] to me, and I give [δίδωμι] it to whom I will" (Luke 4:6). In the work of his triumphant first coming, Christ later commissions his disciples with the same power that Satan had claimed to possess: "Behold, I have given you authority [ἐξουσία] to tread on serpents [ὄφεων/ὄφις; cf. Gen 3:14 LXX] and scorpions, and over all the power of the enemy, and nothing shall hurt you" (Luke 10:19). The eschatological event which brings about the victory in Luke 10:18–19 appears to be purposefully ambiguous,[197] but it is probably best to regard the entire earthly mission of Christ to be the causal factor in the defeat of Satan and his forces.[198] Beale observes:

> The basis for Jesus's followers having authority over the dominion of evil powers is Jesus's own defeat of Satan ([Luke 10] v. 18). Jesus's victory over Satan in verse 8 may have occurred at the temptation (Matt. 4; Luke 4), or it may be a proleptic vision (prophetic past) referring either to the cross or the second coming. I agree with Ladd that Jesus saw in the successful mission of the seventy evidence of the defeat of Satan and the inauguration of God's kingdom (cf.

---

196 The precise timing of Satan's fall is not as important as its referent since Luke ties Satan's fall to the exorcistic ministry of the disciples that extends from Christ's ministry. See Carman, "The Falling Star and the Rising Son," 224. See also Simon J. Gathercole, "Different Chronological Views On Lk 10: Jesus' Eschatological Vision Of The Fall Of Satan: Luke 10,18 Reconsidered," *Zeitschrift für die neutestamentliche Wissenschaft und die Kunde der älteren Kirche* 94, 3–4 (2003): 143–63.

197 The verb "have given you authority" (δέδωκα) is in the perfect tense, showing that the authority is already given to the disciples. See Stein, *Luke*, 310.

198 So also Beale, *New Testament Biblical Theology*, 421; Ladd, *Presence of the Future*, 157. This author disagrees with the experiential take that holds that Satan's fall is realized by an individual's empowerment by Christ; for this position, see Torsten Löfstedt, "Satan's Fall and the Mission of the Seventy-Two," *Svensk* SEÅ 76 (2011): 95.

Luke 10:9, 11). Probably Jesus's reference in verse 18 is to the effect of his entire ministry, culminating in the cross and resurrection as his final individual victory over Satan.[199]

It is difficult not to recognize a degree of eschatological fulfillment of the *protoevangelium* at work in Luke 10, as Christ uses the striking language of giving his disciples the authority to tread upon serpents (ὄφεων) and over "all the power of the enemy" (πᾶσαν τὴν δύναμιν τοῦ ἐχθροῦ; Luke 10:19). Christ's defeat of the serpent through his work is the eschatological restoration of God's exercise of power and authority in this age.[200] Power over the serpent has been achieved.

This chapter has traced the theological development of satanic exorcism as it is eschatologically manifested in Christ's first coming. There is a developing understanding of Satan revealed in the Old Testament, one that does not provide a great amount of detail, yet one that begins to appear from the very opening pages of Scripture. As the Gospel narratives commence with Christ's life and work, demonic exorcisms are at the forefront of Christ's public ministry. Upon examining four major demonic exorcisms in the Gospels (the Capernaum synagogue; the Gadarene/Gerasene demoniac; the Syrophoenician woman's daughter; and the demonized boy), certain common themes emerge that help to frame the concept of demonic exorcisms as proleptic victories that precede the ultimate satanic exorcism to come. After examining themes present in demonic exorcisms, the present work has examined three Gospel passages (the binding of the strong man; the ruler; and Satan falling) in order to frame the New Testament theme of satanic exorcism. The following chapter will discuss satanic exorcism as described by the New Testament epistles, illuminating how Christ in his first coming exorcised Satan from his place of power and authority in this world.

---

199 Beale, *New Testament Biblical Theology*, 436; see also Ladd, *Presence of the Future*, 157.
200 Stephen G. Dempster, *Dominion and Dynasty: A Theology of the Hebrew Bible*, NSBT (Downers Grove, IL: InterVarsity Press, 2003), 69.

Chapter 4

Satanic Exorcism in This Age

The biblical theme of satanic exorcism in this age is initially introduced in the Gospel accounts, whereas the subsequent New Testament epistles give further definition and clarification to its effects and consequences. The dynamic of satanic exorcism is an outworking of Christ's eschatological victory accomplished in his first coming—the entirety of Christ's ministry, particularly in the work of his death and resurrection—that achieved an eschatological victory in the present age.

The Conquering Christ: Christus Victor

Defining Christ's victory as eschatological is a means of emphasizing the spiritual conquest over evil that is inseparable from the salvific work accomplished through the cross and resurrection. In other words, the redemptive work of Christ provided salvation to sinners alongside the simultaneous cosmic defeat and exorcism of Satan that accompanied that redemptive work. The recognition of Satan's defeat articulated in Christ's redemptive work is a substantial component of the atonement perspective referred to as Christus Victor—a view that specifically notes humanity's liberation from the dominion of sin and death in this age alongside of satanic defeat.[1]

---

1 Gregory A. Boyd, "Christus Victor View," in *The Nature of the Atonement: Four Views*, eds. James K. Beilby and Paul R. Eddy, (Downers Grove, IL: InterVarsity Press, 2006), 23–49; Brad Harper, "Christus Victor, Postmodernism, and the Shaping of Atonement Theology," *Cultural Encounters* 2.1 (2005): 37; Gustaf Aulén and A. G. Herbert, *Christus Victor: An Historical Study of the Three Main Types of the Idea of Atonement* (London: SPCK, 1931; repr., Eugene, OR: Wipf & Stock, 2003); Stott, *Cross of Christ*, 227–53. This eschatological view of Christus Victor is not synonymous with the dualistic-transactional version of the ransom theory of the atonement or the various re-appropriations by the Word of Faith and

Christ's work in his first coming brought freedom to those previously held under the power of Satan, freedom that is attendant with the advance of the kingdom of God in this world. The eschatological freedom that was accomplished was achieved paradoxically through Christ's suffering, and it is a victory that is subsequently experienced by Christ's followers amid persecution.[2] In the letters of the New Testament, believers are warned of the satanic rulers and authorities that exist in the heavenly places (ἐπουρανίοις; Eph 6:12), even though Christ has now been raised above every ruler and authority in those heavenly places (Eph 1:20–21, 3:10).[3] Christ's victory in the first coming laid divine claim to the spiritual territory and authority in this age; further, Christ's ministry characterized that reclamation through the consistent deliverance of captives from the power of Satan (Acts 10:38; 26:18).[4] Christ's first coming accomplished eschatological victory by conquering the authority of the satanic realm and freeing believers from the power of Satan, which is a recurrent New Testament observation (see Eph 1:20–22, 2:13–18; 1 Pet 3:18a, 3:18b–22; Heb 1:3, 8:1, 10:12, 12:2; Rev 3:21, 5:5–6, 9–10, 12–13).

Christ's triumph is surprisingly achieved through suffering—the road to victory had to travel through the cross of Calvary (Eph 2:4–7), and followers of Christ are likewise called to participate in suffering in this age (John 16:33). Having achieved victory in his conquest over Satan, Christ now reigns from on high at the Father's right hand (Col 2:15; Eph 1:20–22),

---

Emergent Church movements. See Benjamin Pugh, "'Kicking the Daylights out of the Devil': The Victory Motif in Some Recent Atonement Theology," *EuroJTh* 23.1 (2014): 32.

2 See an overview of patristic support for Christus Victor (e.g., Origen, Irenaeus, Gregory of Nyssa, and Augustine) in Erickson, *Christian Theology*, 793; Harper, "Christus Victor, Postmodernism, and the Shaping of Atonement Theology," 37; and Pugh, "'Kicking the Daylights out of the Devil,'" 32.

3 See discussion on "cosmic geography" in Michael S. Heiser, *The Unseen Realm: Recovering the Supernatural Worldview of the Bible* (Bellingham, WA: Lexham, 2019), 121–22. Belief in supernatural rulers/powers/authorities was largely neglected in modern theology until the late twentieth century. See Scobie, *Ways of Our God*, 265.

4 Thielman, *Theology of the New Testament*, 126; Michael J. Vlach, "The Trinity and Eschatology," *TMSJ* 24 (2013): 207. Scobie observes: "The NT [New Testament] gives a prominent place to a personal and powerful adversary and enemy, the leader of the cosmic forces of evil. No doubt it reflects developments that had taken place within Judaism, though BT [Biblical Theology] is concerned only with the material that appears in the biblical text." Scobie, *Ways of Our God*, 251.

having expelled the previous ruler of this world by delivering freedom to its captives (John 12:31; Rev 3:21).[5]

DIVINE WARRIOR

Christ's first coming entailed the redemption of captives from the power of Satan in this age, and Christ's victory embodied the biblical theme of the eschatological warrior who vanquished the satanic enemy.[6] Scripture declares, "The LORD [יהוה] is a man of war; the LORD is his name" (Exod 15:3).[7] Scripture develops the canonical theme of divine warrior by presenting Christ as the anointed representative-conqueror, the ultimate divine warrior: "The LORD [יהוה] goes out like a mighty man, like a man of war he stirs up his zeal; he cries out, he shouts aloud, he shows himself mighty against his foes" (Isa 42:13; see Mark 1:11; cf. Ps 2:7, Isa 42:1–13).[8]

During the work of Christ's first coming, the demonic spirits immediately recognized Christ's conquering role. The demons responded to him using language that is likely evocative of the Old Testament warrior language: "What have you to do with us, Jesus of Nazareth? Have you come to destroy [ἀπολέσαι] us?" (Mark 1:24).[9] Luke similarly uses the language of the Lord's Anointed (κυρίου χριστοῦ) in recounting the prayer of the believers in Jerusalem: "Why did the Gentiles rage, and the peoples plot in vain?" (Acts 4:24–27; cf. Ps 2:1–2). The divine warrior would subdue his enemies as a footstool (Ps 110), being given dominion over all peoples and rebel nations (Dan 7) even while those nations sought to surround and

---

5 Christ's victory is inaugurated and yet not consummated. Thielman, *Theology of the New Testament*, 689–90.
6 Bethancourt observes, "Since the publication of Gustaf Aulen's *Christus Victor*, scholars have taken an interest in articulations of the divine warrior theme in church history, especially as it relates to the atonement." Phillip Ross Bethancourt, "Christ the Warrior King: A Biblical, Historical, and Theological Analysis of the Divine Warrior Theme in Christology," 2011, 7. Also see Longman and Reid, *God Is a Warrior*, 13–16. In contrast, Vlach contends that Christ's kingly role is primarily future (chiliastic). Vlach, "The Trinity and Eschatology," 208.
7 Longman and Reid correctly assert: "No one metaphor is capable of capturing the richness of God's nature or the wonder of his relationship with his creatures." Longman and Reid, *God Is a Warrior*, 15.
8 Mark 1:11's allusion to Isaiah 42:1–3 might also have in view a wider reference to the warrior language of Isaiah 42:10–13. Longman and Reid, *God Is a Warrior*, 94.
9 Also likely evocative of חרם (*ḥērĕm*). Longman and Reid, *God Is a Warrior*, 99.

persecute the righteous (Ps 118).[10] The culmination of the Old Testament divine warrior motif was realized in the coming of Christ, who came in decisive spiritual victory while surrounded by nations that persecuted him—even until death.[11] The Synoptic Gospels particularly portray Christ as a victorious invader, having bound the satanic ruler of this age to plunder his domain (Matt 12:29; Mark 3:27; Luke 11:22—similar to the Old Testament theme of "Mighty One").[12]

The New Testament describes Christ as the one who has subjected every enemy underfoot (1 Cor 15:24–28; cf. Ps 110:1) and the King who will reign forever on David's throne (Luke 1:32–33) as David's seed (Matt 1:1) in fulfillment of Old Testament promises.[13] Christ's final victory will consummate in his second coming in the gathering of all nations (Rev 15:3–4; cf. Ps 89:27), while the work of his first coming has decisively freed captives from the kingdom of Satan in this age (Heb 2:14–15; Col 2:14–15; Phil 2:10–11).[14] The outworking of Christ's victory over the forces of Satan is

---

10 On the relationship between Psalm 118 and John 12, see Köstenberger and Swain, *Father, Son and Spirit*, 81, esp. 81n23. For a discussion maintaining that Old Testament allusions can be both literal as well as archetypal, see Cole, *Against the Darkness*, 92–93. Daniel 7 speaks of "dominion" being given to and taken away from forces (beasts) prior to its being given to "one like a son of man" (Dan 7:6, 12, 13, 26, 27).

11 Walter C. Kaiser Jr., "The Promise Doctrine and Jesus," *TJ* 4 (1975): 60. Kaiser, however, presents his case with a focus on soteriology as opposed to eschatology. A sampling of Old Testament fulfillment in Christ includes Jesus's birth (Matt 1:20–23, cf. Isa 7; Matt 2:5–6, cf. Mic 5:2), his Jewish rejection (John 1:11; cf. Isa 53:3), his flight to Egypt (Matt 2:14–15; cf. Hos. 11:1), his triumphal entry into Jerusalem (Matt 21:4–5; cf. Zech 9:9), his sale for thirty silver pieces (Matt 26:15, Zech 11:12), his piercing on the cross (John 19:34; cf. Zech 12:10), lots cast for his clothing (Mark 15:24; cf. Ps 22:18), his absence of broken bones (John 19:33; cf. Ps 34:20), his burial with the rich (Matt 27:57–60; cf. Isa 53:9), his resurrection (Acts 2:24–32; cf. Ps 16:10) and his ascension (Acts 1:9; cf. Ps 68:18). See Cornelis P. Venema, *The Promise of the Future* (Carlisle, PA: Banner of Truth, 2000), 25.

12 Longman and Reid, *God Is a Warrior*, 112.

13 Vlach recognizes Christ's warrior fulfillment of the Davidic throne, though he primarily relegates this kingly role to a futurist chiliastic realization. Vlach, "The Trinity and Eschatology," 208. It should be noted that the concept of the Son's current reign as Davidic King is in opposition to classical dispensationalism. See Larry R. Helyer, "The Necessity, Problems, and Promise of Second Temple Judaism for Discussions of New Testament Eschatology," *JETS* 47.4 (2004): 598–599; Hoekema, *Bible and the Future*, 174. There is also the eschatological reality that Christ has always reigned. See Strachan, *Reenchanting Humanity*, 365.

14 Beale, *New Testament Biblical Theology*, 285, 908n25.

expounded and clarified within various New Testament letters, to which the following discussion will now turn.

Deliverance from This Present Evil Age

Galatians 1:3b–4

> Grace to you and peace from God our Father and the Lord Jesus Christ, who gave himself for our sins to deliver us from the present evil age, according to the will of our God and Father. (Galatians 1:3–4)

The New Testament people of God exist in the overlap of two ages, presently living as citizens of the kingdom of God while still surrounded by the kingdom of this world (see John 17:15).[15] The kingdom of God advances and spreads in the theological context of spiritual warfare—Christ's death provided salvation for his elect, along with decisive (yet penultimate) defeat for Satan and satanic forces.[16] Paul reflected on these elements of Christ's victory in his letter to the Galatians, observing that the work of Christ not only accomplished the redemption of sins but was also meant "to deliver us from the present evil age (τοῦ αἰῶνος τοῦ ἐνεστῶτος πονηροῦ)" (Gal 1:4).

Paul's description of Christian deliverance from this age is a triumph that is accomplished in the work of Christ, specifically in the eschatological experience of the "new creation" that results from the advance of the kingdom of God. The advancement of God's kingdom involves the inauguration of the new creation—the defeat of death and the beginning of eternal life (see Heb 2:14). In the typical usage of Pauline eschatology, the conception of this age is understood to be the evil territory into which Christ has triumphantly invaded. As George notes,

> "The present evil age" is the context in which God's purpose of salvation is now unfolding. The notion of two ages, borrowed from Jewish

---

15 Story, "Jesus' 'Enemy' in the Gospels," 63. On the kingdom of God, Ladd observes: "The Kingdom of God is his kingship, his rule, his authority." Ladd, *Gospel of the Kingdom*, 20–21.

16 Interpreters differ on whether Paul's focus in Galatians is more communal/eschatological or individual/salvific. Timothy George, *Galatians*, NAC 30 (Nashville: Broadman & Holman, 1994), 87. Kingdom advance necessarily implies spiritual warfare—see the terminology of "Christobellic" warfare in Bethancourt, "Christ the Warrior King," 4n9.

apocalyptic thought, juxtaposes a present age of sin and decay and a future age of blessing and peace. For Paul, however, the death and resurrection of Jesus has radically punctuated this traditional time line [*sic*]. The Christian now lives in profound tension between the *No Longer* and the *Not Yet*.[17]

Paul's explanation provides clarification as to the manner in which the ages relate following the work of the first coming—the ages are not mutually exclusive, but the advent of Christ has created an overlap between the ages that involves decisive deliverance from "the present evil age" (τοῦ αἰῶνος τοῦ ἐνεστῶτος πονηροῦ; Gal 1:4).[18]

The current passage under study (Gal 1:3b–4) describes liberation (ἐξέληται / ἐξαιρέω) from this age, a freedom that contains the concept of deliverance or rescue from an adverse situation.[19] Paul uses ἐξέληται here in Gal 1:4, though this is his sole use of the term, denoting a sense of rescue from the present evil age in which believers are called to live.[20] Paul's use of ἐξέληται occurs in the context of a passage that speaks of both atonement for sin ("who gave himself for our sins") and deliverance from this present evil age—the work of deliverance effectively and decisively has freed believers from the power of death in this age.[21] The physical reality of death continues just as *this age* is yet extant, while the power (ἐξουσία) of death and its eschatological finality have been undone by the advent of *the age to come*.

---

17 George, *Galatians*, 87. Emphasis in original.
18 See Figures 1 and 5.
19 Other uses infer a forcible extraction, notably so in the LXX. Alexander Souter, *A Pocket Lexicon to the Greek New Testament* (Oxford: Clarendon, 1917), s.v. "ἐξαιρέω"; *TLNT*, s.v. "ἐξαιρέω, "ἐξαιρέομαι."
20 Ben Witherington notes, "The verb ἐξέληται is found here for the only time in the Pauline corpus, but its use in Acts 7:10, 34; 12:11; 23:27; 26:17 makes it clear enough that the sense of the verb is 'rescue.' The notion here is of rescue from the evil of the age (on which cf. 4 Ezr. 6:9; 7:12–13; 2 Bar. 14:13; 15:8; CD 6:10, 14), not removal from the age itself. Christians are to live in but not of the world." Ben Witherington III, *Grace in Galatia: A Commentary on St. Paul's Letter to the Galatians* (Grand Rapids: Eerdmans, 1998), 76–77.
21 Fung notes: "The purpose of that death is further described as the believers' 'rescue … out of this present age of wickedness.'" Ronald Y. K. Fung, *The Epistle to the Galatians*, NICOT (Grand Rapids: Eerdmans, 1988), 40.

The redemption that Christ has brought is a foundational repositioning in eschatological orientation, as Beale observes: "Christ's death is the means by which people are delivered out of the old, fallen cosmos."²² Though the fallen state of *this age* continues on even after Christ's first coming, the inaugurated blessings of *the age to come* (i.e., the new creation and the kingdom of God) have already dawned and begun to bear fruit in these last days (see Rom 14:17; Gal 5:21).²³ Within the narrative flow of Galatians, Paul explains that believers are delivered from this age (1:4) because the "fullness of time" has come (τὸ πλήρωμα τοῦ χρόνου; 4:4) with the dawning of the new creation (καινὴ κτίσις; 6:15).²⁴ God's new-creational restoration is described in Scripture on both a personal and cosmic level, and the in-breaking of the new creation is a defining characteristic of the advent of the age to come.²⁵ With a narrative focus on the new-creational paradigm of salvation, Galatians highlights the outworking of the new creation in the deliverance of believers from this present evil age.

Paul's description of the current evil age (αἰών) is similar to John's use of the notion of "world" (κόσμος)—it denotes the spiritual territory of this age that stands opposed to the work of God in Christ.²⁶ Especially of note is that Paul describes this age as an "evil" [πονηρός] age with a specific evil ruler. Fung asserts: "To Paul, the present age is evil because it is subject to the sway of a wicked spiritual being (Eph. 6:16; 2 Thess. 3:3; cf. 2 Cor. 4:4; Eph. 2:2) and under the control of wicked spiritual forces (see Eph. 6:12), chief of which are the powers of sin and death (see 1 Cor. 15:55f.)."²⁷ The present age is evil because its rulers and authorities are evil, while the age to come is good because its ruler, Jesus Christ, is good. Though satanic forces have held authoritative influence within *this age*, the new-creational reign

---

22 Beale specifically refers to Galatians 1:4 and 6:14–15. Beale, *New Testament Biblical Theology*, 310.
23 Witherington, *Grace in Galatia*, 77.
24 Beale, *New Testament Biblical Theology*, 587n103. Fung identifies regeneration as the focal point of change in Galatians. Fung, *Epistle to the Galatians*, 41.
25 The difference between individual and global eschatology is addressed in Case-Winters, "The End?," 66; Grudem, *Systematic Theology*, 1091; Alan Cairns, *Dictionary of Theological Terms* (Greenville: Ambassador Emerald International, 2002), s.v. "eschatology." Also, see the distinction between individual versus general eschatology in Venema, *Promise of the Future*, 35, and individual versus cosmic eschatology in Hoekema, *Bible and the Future*, 77.
26 Fung, *Epistle to the Galatians*, 41.
27 Fung, *Epistle to the Galatians*, 40–41.

of *the age to come* brings liberation (ἐξέληται) from these satanic powers and forces, though their existence persists in anticipation of the final consummative judgment of the second coming.[28]

Authority over Rulers and Powers

Colossians 2:15

> He disarmed the rulers and authorities and put them to open shame, by triumphing over them in him. (Col 2:15)

Though Paul does not specifically refer to the figure of Satan within this passage, Colossians 2 characterizes the eschatological outcomes of satanic exorcism by referring to the defeat of the satanic "rulers" and "authorities" of this age. In the context of exhorting the Colossians to pursue Christian unity within their fellowship and to be on guard against false teaching, Paul then brings the redemptive work of Christ into the forefront of the discussion. After specifically reflecting on the work of Christ's atoning death on the cross ("this he set aside, nailing it to the cross;" Col 2:14), Paul makes mention of the "rulers and authorities" (ἀρχὰς καὶ ἐξουσίας) that Christ has "put to open shame."[29] Just as there are many "rulers" (ἀρχὰς) of this world who have served under the ultimate evil "ruler" (ἄρχων) of this world (cf. Eph 1:20–21; 3:10; 6:10ff.; Rom 8:38),[30] the identification of the rulers and authorities in this passage is clear:

> The "powers and authorities" may be either all spirit beings, good and evil, or evil spirits alone. Although the immediate context provides no clue, it would be difficult for Paul to resume a discussion which he already began without the identical words referring to the same beings (see 1:15–20). Further, it would hardly be necessary to

---

28 Beale remarks, "It is likely that most of the time when there is mention of Christ's death, included implicitly to some degree is the notion of a beginning separation from the old world, which Gal. 6:14–15 (cf. Gal 1:4) and 2 Cor. 5:14–17 formally view as an absolutely necessary element leading to the inception of new creation." Beale, *New Testament Biblical Theology*, 907.

29 Beale notes: "There is a textual problem of whether Christ triumphed through 'him' (God) or 'it' (cross or resurrection). In any case, this is an affirmation of the defeat and 'rendering powerless' of spiritual powers through the cross *and* resurrection." Beale, *New Testament Biblical Theology*, 908. Emphasis in original.

30 Sam Storms, *Biblical Studies: Colossians* (Edmond, OK: Sam Storms, 2016), Col 2:15.

disgrace (or disarm) those angels who worshiped God and contributed to his glory. This must refer to evil spirit beings.[31]

Due to the work of Christ, believers are no longer held under the authority of the satanic forces of this age. While the "elemental spirits (στοιχείων) of the world (κόσμος)" (Col 2:20) yet persist with deception and attacks, the church has been set free from such schemes through the work of Christ.

Concerning the nature of satanic defeat as expounded in Colossians 2:14–15, Paul proclaims the truth that "at the cross the principalities and powers were stripped of their power over believers by Jesus Christ."[32] These "rulers" and "authorities" are the satanic forces of evil at work in this age (Eph 1:20–21; 3:10; 6:10ff.; Rom 8:38),[33] forces which have been defeated specifically in this passage by the work of Christ's cross. The work of the cross and resurrection unseated the satanic rulers from their place of authority in this age, replacing them with the expressed authority of the triumphant Christ (cf. Matt 28:18). This victory is accomplished "at the cross"—Colossians 2:15 focuses on the atoning work of Christ in his death on the cross. Stott poetically observes: "Overcome there [at Calvary], he was himself overcoming. Crushed by the ruthless power of Rome, he was himself crushing the serpent's head (Gen 3:15)."[34] Colossians 2:15 demonstrates that it is through Christ's atoning work on the cross that he reconciles the world to himself (2 Cor 5:18–21) and achieves final victory over death (1 Cor 15:21–22), Satan (John 12:31), and all demonic and satanic powers in this world (Col 2:15).[35]

Paul thus emphasizes that the Colossian believers are united with Christ, who is Himself "the head of all rule [ἀρχή] and authority [ἐξουσία]" (Col 2:10). Because Christ has reconciled us to Himself, "making peace" (Col 1:20) under his headship (Eph 1:10, 22)—Christ reconciles, gives, appeals,

---

31 Richard R. Melick, *Philippians, Colossians, Philemon*, NAC (Nashville: Broadman & Holman, 1991), 265. Contra the view of N.T. Wright, who maintains that these rulers are "gods" of the nations. N. T. Wright, *Colossians and Philemon*, TNTC (Downers Grove, IL: InterVarsity Press, 2008), 81.
32 Mathison, *From Age to Age*, 590.
33 Storms, *Biblical Studies: Colossians*, Col 2:15.
34 Stott, *Cross of Christ*, 224. Stott then moves immediately into a helpful discussion of the Christus Victor view of the atonement.
35 Hoekema, *Bible and the Future*, 29.

and becomes sin for us (cf. "all these things," τὰ πάντα, in 2 Cor 5:18–21).[36] The rulers and authorities of this age are thereby exposed and disgraced, while Christ is honored and glorified.[37] Though it was a common Jewish expectation that God would defeat evil forces in the future, the triumph of the resurrection accomplished victory in Christ over the cosmic evil in this age.[38] This victory for believers and defeat of satanic forces has been proclaimed to all nations, as Christ has defeated the power of sin and death.[39]

Scripture makes clear that all the earth lies within the bounds of God's authority, as David observed: "The earth [יְהוָה] is the LORD's [הוהי] and the fullness thereof, the world [לְבַת] and those who dwell therein" (Ps 24:1). In the eschatological aftermath of the first coming, Scripture describes rulers (τὰς ἀρχὰς) and authorities (τὰς ἐξουσίας) that Christ has publicly humiliated in defeat. These spiritual powers are essentially imposters of the true divine ruler of this world—Paul indicates as much in his quotation of Psalm 24: "For 'the earth [γῆ] is the Lord's [κύριος], and the fullness thereof'" (1 Cor 10:26).

Yet authority over the nations was a flashpoint of the spiritual warfare in Christ's first coming, as his public ministry exposed and expelled a host of satanic rulers and authorities that were occupying positions of power in this age. The dominion mandate given to Adam and Eve (Gen 1:26–28) entailed a directive that encompassed all the "earth" (יְרָאָה)—including all the nations in its expanse.[40] God blessed Adam and Eve and then called them to rule (הָדָר, ἄρχω LXX) over all the created order on earth (אֶרֶץ). Adam and Eve's fall and subsequent expulsion from Eden inhibited the successful progress of their commission throughout the earth, and their fall and expulsion were essentially mirrored later in the rebellious gathering-together and subsequent divine dispersion of the nations in Genesis 10–11.

---

36   Stott, *Cross of Christ*, 193–94.
37   Melick, *Philippians, Colossians, Philemon*, 265–66.
38   Michael F. Bird, *Colossians and Philemon*, NCC (Eugene, OR: Cascade, 2009), 81; cf. Wright, *Colossians and Philemon*, 116–17.
39   See Philipp Melanchthon, *Colossians*, 63 (*Melancthons Werke in Auswahl*, 4:250.15–31), cited in Gregory B. Graybill, *Philippians, Colossians*, RCS 11 (Downers Grove, IL: InterVarsity Press, 2013), 196. Compare also Eph 2:15–16.
40   On Matthew 28:18–20 (cf. Mark 16:14–18* // Luke 24:44–49 // John 20:19–23) as a recommissioning of Genesis 1:26–28 (cf. Dan 7:14), see G. K. Beale, *The Temple and the Church's Mission: A Biblical Theology of the Dwelling Place of God*, NSBT 17 (Downers Grove, IL: Inter-Varsity Press, 2004), 175.

These nations [גּוֹי] geographically and religiously proceeded outward from Adam's lineage (Acts 17:26) and yet they were set in contradistinction to Israel: "When the Most High gave to the nations [גּוֹיִם] their inheritance, when he divided mankind, he fixed the borders of the peoples according to the number of the sons of God.[41] But Yahweh's (יהוה) portion is his people, Jacob his allotted heritage" (Deut 32:8–9).[42]

The theme of authority resurfaces in the presence of God's people, as God promised Abraham a "great nation [גּוֹי]" as an inheritance (Gen 12:2; 17:4).[43] The prophet Daniel spoke of the coming of "one like a son of man" (רְבַּךְ שְׁנָא; Dan 7:13) who would appear and be given "dominion [ἀρχή, LXX] and glory and a kingdom [βασιλεία, LXX], *that all peoples*, nations [אֻמַיָּא], *and languages should serve him; his dominion is an everlasting* dominion [ἐξουσία, LXX], *which shall not pass away, and his* kingdom one *that shall not be destroyed* [emphases added]" (Dan 7:14).[44] In the Old Testament context, the nations were understood to be both under God's providential jurisdiction and constituting an area that was spiritually removed from the presence and blessings of God (see Eph 2:11–12).

In reflecting on the work of Christ, the New Testament describes the eschatological victory that has been achieved over the rulers and authorities (ἀρχὰς καὶ ἐξουσίας) of this age. As a result of the victory that Christ achieved in his first coming, the prophesied Son of Man (ὁ υἱὸς τοῦ ἀνθρώπου; Matt 25:31–33, John 5:25–29) has now been given authority over all the nations (πάντα τὰ ἔθνη; Matt 28:19) by the Father. Christ has authority given to Him by the Father (Eph 1:20–22; see John 5:19–29), and that authority is now exercised in this age in the eschatological

---

41 "Nation" is typically rendered "גּוֹי" (*gōy*) in the Old Testament and "ἔθνος" (*ethnos*) in the New Testament. The English gloss "nations" is used 645 times in the ESV.

42 Michael S. Heiser, *Supernatural: What the Bible Teaches about the Unseen World and Why It Matters* (Bellingham, WA: Lexham, 2015), 81–82. Heiser's larger thesis concerning "sons of God" and the "Deuteronomy 32 worldview" is not in view in this present work, though his discussion is thought-provoking. Cf. Heiser, *Unseen Realm*, 112–13.

43 The theme of Abraham's seed blessing the nations is preserved through the line of Abraham and comes to fruition in the New Testament (Rom 4:17–18, cf. Gen 17:5; Gal 3:6–9), where it is ultimately found to be fulfilled in Christ (Matt 2:13–15; cf. Hos 11:1).

44 The conversation around the messianic content of this passage is extensive. The phrase "Son of Man" is used similarly in Matt 16:27–28; 19:28; 24:30; 25:31. See discussion in Stephen Miller, *Daniel*, NAC (Nashville: Broadman & Holman, 1994), 210.

realization of Christ's redemptive work.[45] Having been given eschatological authority in this age, Christ builds his church (Matt 16:18), restrains Satan (John 12:31) and Satan's forces (Col 2:15), and commissions his disciples (Matt 28:18–20).

Christ thus exercises authority over all things (τὰ πάντα; Heb 1:2–3), he has authority over all flesh (John 17:2), and he particularly exhibits authority over his elect people who are chosen from among the nations (John 17:6, 16).[46] In the moments leading up to his ascension, Christ sends his disciples into the world expressly due to the comprehensive authority that has been given to Him (Ἐδόθη μοι πᾶσα ἐξουσία ἐν οὐρανῷ καὶ ἐπὶ τῆς γῆς, Matt 28:18). Just as Christ gave Himself to deliver believers from this age (δόντος / δίδωμι; Gal 1:4; cf. Mark 10:45, Titus 2:14), his work likewise secures the authority that has been "given" to him (δίδωμι, Dan 7:13–14 LXX). Bruce observes: "Not only has he blotted out the record of their indebtedness, but he has subjugated those powers whose possession of that damning indictment was a means of controlling them."[47] Paul's reflection in Colossians 2 maintains this triumphant refrain, one that is in keeping with the note of divine kingly reign that is struck in so many comparable New Testament passages.[48]

Christ's victory described in Colossians is tied to his death, resurrection, and ascension; and his ascension, in particular, is understood as a sign of his cosmic eschatological victory. Höhne declares, "The Messiah's ascent to the Father's right hand spells defeat for all the enemies of God's reign in all the creation."[49] Though the cross appeared to spell certain defeat for believers and triumph for earthly rulers (Col 2:12), it instead resulted in life and freedom for believers and the defeat of every wicked ruler and authority (2:13–14; cf. 1:12–13). The language Paul uses in Colossians places particular emphasis on the satanic powers in this age having been

---

45 See Robert Letham, *The Holy Trinity: In Scripture, History, Theology, and Worship* (Phillipsburg, NJ: P&R, 2004), 386ff.
46 Michael Bird and Scott Harrower, *Trinity Without Hierarchy: Reclaiming Nicene Orthodoxy in Evangelical Theology* (Grand Rapids: Kregel, 2019), 63; Köstenberger and Swain, *Father, Son and Spirit*, 169.
47 F. F. Bruce, *The Epistles to the Colossians, to Philemon, and to the Ephesians*, NICNT (Grand Rapids: Eerdmans, 1984), 110.
48 Beale, *New Testament Biblical Theology*, 285.
49 Höhne, *Last Things*, 125.

"disgraced" or "stripped" (ἀπεκδυσάμενος) of their power, a violent action that has removed their standing and exposed them to open disgrace.[50] Whether the aspect of ἀπεκδυσάμενος primarily reflects military or political conquest, it gives the sense of a shameful defeat of satanic rulers and authorities. Satan's power (and the power of satanic rulers and authorities) over believers has been defeated and even put to open shame due to its lack of eschatological power.

Why would the satanic rulers and authorities be put to shame? In a significant way, they are put to shame because their longstanding ability to accuse the elect (see Job 1, Zech 3, Rev 12) has been curtailed by the atoning work of Christ:[51]

> The events of the eschatological consummation are not merely detached events lying in the future about which Paul speculates. They are rather redemptive events that have already begun to unfold within history. The blessings of the Age to Come no longer lie exclusively in the future; they have become objects of present experience. The death of Christ is an eschatological event.... Christ has already defeated the powers of evil that have brought chaos into the world.[52]

Paul follows this announcement of the declaration of satanic defeat (Col 2:15) by exhorting Christians that they should "therefore let no one pass judgment on you" (Col 2:16), and "let no one disqualify you" (Col 2:18). Satan's defeat accompanies the justification of those who are in Christ; therefore, Satan can no longer pass judgment on the elect nor disqualify them in their commissioned work. Through the work of Christ, *this age* has already begun to give way to *the age to come*, resulting in the inaugurated defeat of satanic rulers and authorities in the present age. Christ's triumph through the cross has disarmed and even disgraced Satan's forces, curtailing Satan's ability to accuse the elect.

---

50 This term possibly reflects either a political or military conquest (or both). See Melick, *Philippians, Colossians, Philemon*, 265.
51 Beale observes: "Until the death of Christ, it could appear that the devil had a good case." Beale, *New Testament Biblical Theology*, 217. See also John Calvin, *Commentaries on the Epistles of Paul the Apostle to the Philippians, Colossians, and Thessalonians*, ed. and trans. John Pringle (Bellingham, WA: Logos Bible Software, 2010), 190.
52 Vos, *Pauline Eschatology*, 51.

Ephesians 1:20–23, 3:10, 6:11–12

> For we do not wrestle against flesh and blood, but against the rulers, against the authorities, against the cosmic powers over this present darkness, against the spiritual forces of evil in the heavenly places. (Eph 6:12)

The satanic rulers and authorities (ἀρχὰς καὶ ἐξουσίας) mentioned in Colossians 2 are most likely the same evil spiritual entities that Paul addresses in Ephesians as "the rulers" (ἀρχὰς), "the authorities" (ἐξουσίας), and "the cosmic powers [κοσμοκράτορας] over this present darkness" (Eph 6:12).[53] Having reminded the Ephesian believers of their unity in Christ in this age, Paul relates the redemptive work of Christ to the consequential defeat of Satan (the ἄρχων)—and the resultant defeat of those satanic subordinates (ἀρχὰς) operative in this world. O'Brien observes:

> These authorities [in Ephesians] probably include the whole host of heavenly beings, good and bad alike, although the apostle's particular concern is obviously with hostile forces. The fact that evil powers are present in the heavenly realm indicates that heaven, like earth, must participate in Paul's two-age eschatological framework. It, too, is involved in this present evil age, and the powers which reside there have already been defeated through Christ's death and now await their final overthrow.[54]

These satanic forces are described as spiritual rulers and authorities in the heavenly places (τοῖς ἐπουρανίοις; Eph 6:12), yet Ephesians makes clear that the Father has now raised Christ above every spiritual authority in the heavenly places (τοῖς ἐπουρανίοις; Eph 1:20–21) so that Christ may employ the church to proclaim his glory above every ruler and authority in

---

53 Charles Hodge observes: "That these terms refer to angels is plain from the context, and from such passages as Rom. 8, 38. Col. 1, 16. Eph. 3, 10. 6, 12." Charles Hodge, *Commentary on the Epistle to the Ephesians* (Grand Rapids: Eerdmans Company, 1994), 83.

54 Peter T. O'Brien, *The Letter to the Ephesians*, PNTC (Grand Rapids: Eerdmans, 1999), 246–47. O'Brien maintains that this spiritual victory inhibits the powers and authorities from preventing the spread of the gospel. (This commentary has been recalled, but this eschatological observation remains unique in its clarity.) See also Sam Storms, *Biblical Studies: Ephesians* (Edmond, OK: Sam Storms, 2016), Eph 3:10–12; Stephen E. Fowl, *Ephesians: A Commentary*, New Testament Library (Louisville: Westminster John Knox, 2012), 112.

the heavenly places (τοῖς ἐπουρανίοις; Eph 3:10).⁵⁵ As in Colossians, the narrative of Ephesians reflects an eschatological shift in the dynamics of power and authority in the spiritual realm, with satanic forces being evicted following the work of Christ's first coming. There is a palpable spiritual victory that is being achieved over evil forces, a cosmic reclamation of territory and authority from the forces of this present darkness (τοῦ σκότους τούτου; 6:12). Just as his earthly ministry was characterized by the exorcism of satanic forces from this world, the ongoing New Testament testimony shows that Christ's work has brought true deliverance to the captives of this world from the power of Satan and his rulers (Acts 10:38; 26:18).⁵⁶

The defeat of satanic forces in Ephesians has a particularly eschatological tone, clearly drawing out the spiritual conflict that erupts in the New Testament between *this age* and *the age to come*.⁵⁷ The powers and authorities in this world are put under the feet of Christ, subjugated to a place of submission and defeat (Eph 1:22). The specific identity of these satanic powers is not made clear, though they are surely spiritual/angelic/demonic forces of this age that have been conquered by the work of Christ.⁵⁸ The earthly reality of this world reveals spiritual conflict existing behind the scenes. Scobie notes: "Beyond the historical adversaries encountered by Jesus and the early church lie powers of evil that belong to the created order. These are spoken of in three main ways: as Satan or the devil, as evil spirits or demons, and as 'powers' of evil."⁵⁹

The placement of the rulers (πάσης ἀρχῆς) "under [Christ's] feet" (ὑπὸ τοὺς πόδας αὐτοῦ; Eph 1:22) is a dominant posture that is evocative of Psalm 110:1: "The Lord [יהוה] says to my Lord [לַאדֹנִי]: 'Sit at my right

---

55 See discussion on "cosmic geography" in Heiser, *Unseen Realm*, 121–22.
56 Thielman, *Theology of the New Testament*, 126; Vlach, "The Trinity and Eschatology," 207.
57 Fung observes that Eph 1:21, in particular, is "the only instance in the Pauline corpus where the contrast is explicitly stated" between the Jewish scheme of this present evil age and the age to come of righteousness and regeneration. Fung, *Epistle to the Galatians*, 40. Hodge maintains that the Jewish conception of *this age / the age to come* is present, while the primary focus in Ephesians is "here and hereafter." Hodge, *Commentary on the Epistle to the Ephesians*, 84–85.
58 Fowl, *Ephesians: A Commentary*, 61; Ben Witherington III, *The Letters to Philemon, the Colossians, and the Ephesians: A Socio-Rhetorical Commentary on the Captivity Epistles* (Grand Rapids: Eerdmans, 2007), 243.
59 Scobie, *Ways of Our God*, 251.

hand, until I make your enemies your footstool [τῶν ποδῶν σου; LXX].'" The depiction of subjugated spiritual rulers cowed under the feet of the triumphant Christ reflects the eschatological victory over Satan that was achieved in Christ's first coming. Regardless of what cosmic powers exist in this age, they have been made subordinate to Christ in his victory (cf. Ps 110).[60] This mystery of the expansive authority of the gospel was a mystery hidden in ages past (τῶν αἰώνων), yet it has now been made known to all "rulers and authorities [ταῖς ἀρχαῖς καὶ ταῖς ἐξουσίαις] in the heavenly places" (Eph 3:10).[61] With the inbreaking of the age to come, Christ's defeat and expulsion of satanic rulers and authorities has been made clear in heaven as on earth.

Christ's victory over Satan gives believers the ability to "be strong in the Lord and in the strength of his might" in order to "stand against the schemes of the devil [τοῦ διαβόλου]" (Eph 6:10–11). Concomitant with standing against the schemes of ὁ διάβολος, Paul clarifies that the true spiritual conflict is not against "flesh and blood [αἷμα καὶ σάρκα]" but against "the rulers [τὰς ἀρχάς], against the authorities [τὰς ἐξουσίας], against the cosmic powers [τοὺς κοσμοκράτορας] over this present darkness [τοῦ σκότους τούτου], against the spiritual forces of evil [τὰ πνευματικὰ τῆς πονηρίας] in the heavenly places" (Eph 6:12). The devil (ὁ διάβολος) is depicted in Ephesians as a spiritual enemy who is opposed to both God and his people, a spiritual adversary that uses a variety of means to attack and oppose God's plans in this age (see Eph 4:27; 6:16).[62] Paul refers to these demonic entities using his preferred nomenclature of "rulers" (ἀρχάς) and "authorities" (ἐξουσίας) to denote evil spirits in this world (see Eph 1:21, 3:10), while also including the *hapax legomenon* of τοὺς κοσμοκράτορας—"world" or "cosmic" powers of evil (Eph 6:12).[63] Precise hierarchies of angelic pow-

---

60 O'Brien, *Letter to the Ephesians*, 142. See also Storms, *Biblical Studies: Ephesians*, Eph 1:20b–21; Daniel M. Gurtner, "Ephesians," in *The Bible Knowledge Background Commentary: Acts–Philemon*, eds. Craig A. Evans and Craig A. Bubeck, 1st ed. (Colorado Springs: Cook, 2004), 550.
61 Fowl, *Ephesians: A Commentary*, 61.
62 Arnold, *Ephesians*, 445.
63 Arnold observes: "The possessive genitive 'of this darkness' (τοῦ σκότους τούτου) casts these so-called 'world powers' as thoroughly evil, for they belong to the realm of darkness. 'Darkness' is the sphere in which these believers formerly belonged (5:8)—a realm that constituted a dominion of authority over their lives and from which they were rescued by the Lord (Col 1:13)." It should be noted that ἀρχάς and ἐξουσίας are the most common Pauline designations for demonic spirits, while the use of τοὺς

ers are not outlined within Paul's work,[64] though these rulers and authorities are clearly related to satanic power and influence. The spiritual powers and authorities that exist behind the scenes of this age have been exposed, addressed, and evicted in the work of Christ.[65] Both Colossians and Ephesians build similar pictures surrounding the current state of satanic rulers and authorities—their power is associated with the evil of *this age*, they have been exposed and defeated in the work of Christ, and their power is now bound in light of the inbreaking of *the age to come*.

Satan's Cosmic Destruction

Hebrews 2:14

> THAT THROUGH DEATH HE MIGHT DESTROY THE ONE WHO HAS THE POWER OF DEATH, THAT IS, THE DEVIL. (HEB 2:14)

The book of Hebrews begins on an eschatological note, observing that God has decisively spoken to us through Christ "in these last days [ἐσχάτου τῶν ἡμερῶν τούτων]" (Heb 1:2). The writer of Hebrews describes these as the "last days" in direct connection with Christ's victorious status since even now Christ reigns on high (Heb 1:3, 8, 13; 8:1; 10:12–13), even though the culmination of his victory is still yet to come (Heb 9:28; 10:37).[66] Victory was achieved in the satanic exorcism of the first coming, though the writer of Hebrews observes the paradox of the present inaugurated state: "At present, we do not yet see everything in subjection to him" (Heb 2:8). Christ has subjected the satanic rulers and authorities of this age as the victorious Son of Man (Heb 2:6), the one who has had all his enemies placed in subjection under his feet (Heb 2:8; cf. Ps 110:1). Christ has exorcised Satan from this world and subjected satanic rulers underfoot, thus accomplishing the redemption of the elect from the eternal consequences of sin and death (Heb 2:3, 6, 10–13). After describing this redemptive work in the opening chapters, the writer of Hebrews specifies that Christ has "left nothing outside his control" (Heb 2:8), since through his death he has destroyed (καταργήσῃ) the devil himself (τὸν διάβολον; 2:14). Though

---

κοσμοκράτορας is that word's only usage within the New Testament or LXX. See Arnold, *Ephesians*, 447.

64 Lutzer and Sproul, *God's Devil*.
65 Arnold, *Ephesians*, 448.
66 Horton, *Christian Faith*, 940.

this relatively short passage referring to Satan is often overlooked in favor of focusing on larger thematic developments within Hebrews, this passage carries significant eschatological weight as the defeat of Satan is placed in conjunction with the themes of Christ's redemption of the elect and cosmic spiritual rule.

The concept of the death of death is a biblical theme related to the eschatological power that Satan exercised in this age prior to the first coming. The salvation of the elect in Hebrews 2 likewise demonstrates that Satan and his forces have been subjected underfoot by Christ, even as Christ has destroyed Satan's power of death through his redemptive work. Paul observed that "death (ὁ θάνατος) reigned from Adam to Moses" (Rom 5:14), since death has reigned in this age since the sin in the Garden: "You shall not eat, for in the day that you eat of it you shall surely die" (θανάτῳ; Gen 2:17 LXX).[67] The hope of eschatological restoration involves an expectation and hope of the defeat of death—death signified this present evil age, while the age to come brought life. The hope of "those who sleep in the dust" was that they would "awake ... to everlasting life" (ζωὴν αἰώνιον; Dan 12:2 LXX), even though when reflecting on Adam's sin, it still had monumental ramifications in this age since "because of one man's trespass, death [ὁ θάνατος] reigned through that one man" (Rom 5:17). The believer's hope anticipated a day when death would be destroyed—when the coming age would be made manifest in eternal life. The hope of God's people was that "He will swallow up death [ὁ θάνατος, LXX] forever; and the Lord God [יְהֹוָה יֶהְגֶּה] will wipe away tears from all faces, and the reproach of his people he will take away from all the earth, for the Lord has spoken" (Isa 25:8).

The death of death is an indication of the inbreaking of the age to come—the fulfillment of all of God's promises in the person of Jesus Christ (see 2 Cor 1:20). The inaugurated blessings of the age to come are that although "in Adam all die [ἀποθνῄσκουσιν], so also in Christ shall all be made alive" (1 Cor 15:22), and further that Christ "died [ἀπέθανεν] for

---

67 Venema contends: "The first Word of the Lord, spoken to our first parents after the Fall into sin in Genesis 3, announces the future birth of a Redeemer who will crush the head of the serpent and vindicate God's gracious rule within his creation. In Genesis 3:15, we find this so-called 'mother promise' in the history of redemption, the protoevangelium, the 'first gospel' announcement: And I (the Lord God) will put enmity between you and the woman, and between your seed and her seed; he shall crush you on the head, and you shall bruise him on the heel.'" Venema, *Promise of the Future*, 14.

all, that those who live might no longer live for themselves but for him who for their sake died [ἀποθανόντι] and was raised" (2 Cor 5:15).⁶⁸

The devil (Satan) and death personified are closely related to one another in the text of Hebrews 2:14. The writer of Hebrews associates "Satan" and "death" so closely that "the power of death" serves as an all-encompassing designation of Satan's activity, while "devil" and "death" likewise represent conjoined terms for satanic resistance against God and his believers.⁶⁹ The author of Hebrews prefers the lexical use of "devil" (διάβολος) in referring to Satan, which possibly places a particular focus on his activities as a liar and deceiver.⁷⁰ The work of Christ's first coming is made manifest in Hebrews 2:14, wherein Christ's redemptive work through his death, burial, and resurrection also served to bring eschatological defeat to his enemies, namely death and the devil.⁷¹ Satan is portrayed as death personified, and the author of Hebrews describes him as having been "destroyed" by the first coming of Christ.

With the fulfillment of Old Testament promises in Christ, including the defeat of Satan and death itself, the inbreaking of the blessings of the age to come are apparent in new-creational fulfillment. Beale summarizes:

> In this manner, Christ has decisively defeated the power of the devil and death (2:14), a reality not expected to occur until the eschatological new creation. The writer to the Hebrews can even refer in 9:26 to Christ's mission "to put away sin by the sacrifice of himself" as happening at the "consummation of the ages" (cf. 10:10, 12,

---

68 See also Strachan, *Reenchanting Humanity*, 376–77.
69 Philip Gordon Ziegler argues, "The gospel tells of the saving advent of (1) God for the sake of (2) human beings and against those (3) supra-human powers which have ensnared and depleted them. These antithetical powers of 'Sin, Death, and the Devil'—sometimes named together, sometimes interchangeably, and sometimes deployed as synecdoches—are arrayed against both God and humanity, and actively so, being the recurrent subjects of transitive verbs. Common to them all is fundamental enmity against God and so also against God's good creatures." Philip Gordon Ziegler, "'Bound Over to Satan's Tyranny': Sin and Satan in Contemporary Reformed Hamartiology," *ThTo* 75.1 (2018): 93.
70 The term διάβολος as an adjective carries the sense of gossip or malicious talk. Satan's deception is related to preventing belief and preserving unbelief, as Harris observes: "He deceives because it is part of his personality to do so." Harris, "Satan's Work as a Deceiver," 190.
71 Mathison, *From Age to Age*, 146.

14). Consequently, as seen elsewhere in the Gospels, Acts, and Paul, Christ's first coming commences the beginning of the end times, which had been prophesied by the OT [Old Testament].[72]

Hebrews tells us that Christ is "crowned with glory and honor because of the suffering of death, so that by the grace of God he might taste death [θάνατος] for everyone" (2:9). Because Christ partook of death, it was through death that the paradoxical defeat of death was accomplished (Heb 2:14). In the context of his death on the cross, Christ has destroyed (καταργήση)[73] the power of death—and even the devil himself. The promise of death's defeat is associated with the last things, and the advent of the last things has begun with the work of Christ.

Just as Satan will "soon" be crushed underfoot (Rom 16:20, cf. Rev 20:10), Satan can accurately be described as having been destroyed *already* through the work of Christ (Heb 2:14).[74] The destruction of the devil's works (Heb 2:14) stopped his enslavement of Abraham's offspring (Heb 2:15; cf. 2:16), ended his claim of finality in death (Heb 2:14; cf. 2:10–11), and restricted his ability to tempt those who are in Christ (Heb 2:18). In addition to destroying the "one who has the power of death, that is, the devil" (Heb 2:14), through his own death, Christ has delivered those who were enslaved (δουλείας) under the power of death (Heb 2:15). Because the power of death (τὸν διάβολον) is destroyed, death itself is destroyed (cf. Hos 13:14; 1 Cor 15:26, 55; 2 Tim 1:10; Rev 20:14, 21:4).[75]

Death's defeat is accomplished in order to "help" (or "deliver"— ἐπιλαμβάνεται) God's children (Heb 2:16; cf. Jer 31:32; Heb 8:9)—because Christ experiences death on the believer's behalf (see Heb 2:10), believers are delivered from the final death of eternal destruction (cf. ὁ θάνατος ὁ

---

72 Beale, *New Testament Biblical Theology*, 142–43.
73 The term καταργέω conveys the meaning of "destroy, stop, bring to nothing"; similar usage occurs in Rom 6:6; cf. 1 Cor 6:13, 15:24, 15:26. See *DBL*, s.v. "καταργέω."
74 Mathison, *From Age to Age*, 585. Mathison thus counts Heb 2:14 (along with Rom 16:20 and Rev 12:1–17) as a New Testament allusion to the *protoevangelium* being eschatologically fulfilled; 26n40. See also Luke T. Johnson, *Hebrews: A Commentary*, ed. C. Clifton Black, M. Eugene Boring, and John T. Carroll, 1st ed., *The New Testament Library* (Louisville: John Knox Press, 2012), 100.
75 See καταργέω in both Hebrews 2:15 and 1 Corinthians 15:24–26. Johnson, *Hebrews*, 100.

δεύτερος, Rev 21:8).[76] Christ's death defeated the ruler of this age and the power of death itself (see John 12:31; 14:30; 16:11), accomplishing Satan's destruction as well as the liberation of all believers through his atonement for their sins (Heb 2:14–15; cf. Col 2:13–15).[77] The work of the cross has stripped Satan of his power (Heb 2:14; Col 2:15) just as it has stripped believers of the condemning effects of sin (Col 2:14; Heb 2:15).[78]

A similar passage that bears a striking resemblance to Hebrews 2:14 is found in Paul's first letter to the Corinthians. Paul has provided the Corinthians with a summation of the gospel in 1 Cor 15, followed by a reminder of the hope that believers possess in the coming resurrection due to Christ's inaugural resurrection.[79] In 1 Cor 15:24–27, Paul assures the Corinthians: "Then comes the end [τὸ τέλος], when he delivers the kingdom to God the Father after destroying every rule [ἀρχὴν] and every authority [ἐξουσίαν] and power. For he must reign until he has put all his enemies under his feet. The last [ἔσχατος] enemy to be destroyed is death [ὁ θάνατος]. For 'God has put all things in subjection under his feet.'" In the coming resurrection of the body, finality and judgment of death itself is defeated for the believer—Christ is thus the "firstfruits" (ἀπαρχὴ) of all who "belong to Christ" (1 Cor 15:23) because Christ has defeated all powers (15:24), enemies (15:25), and death itself (15:26). In 1 Corinthians 15 Paul contrasts Christ to Adam in his role as the eschatological second man who comes to redeem what the first man lost. Paul speaks of Christ destroying (καταργήσῃ) every rule (πᾶσαν ἀρχὴν), every authority (πᾶσαν ἐξουσίαν), and [every] power (δύναμιν). Paul likewise recognizes that this group of defeated foes will be made a footstool for Christ (1 Cor 15:25, 27; cf. Ps 8:6), a theme that the writer of Hebrews develops at length in the passages preceding Hebrews 2:14 (Heb 1:13; 2:8; cf. 10:13; Ps 110:1).

Finally, in 1 Corinthians 15:26 Paul observes that the last (ἔσχατος) enemy to be destroyed is death. Paul's depiction of the end of the age is that Christ conquers all opposition, triumphantly concluding with the defeat of death itself (ὁ θάνατος)—the "last [ἔσχατος] enemy." Hebrews echoes this eschatological triumph by using strikingly similar language to relate the

---

76 Johnson, *Hebrews*, 100, 102; BDAG, s.v. "ἐπιλαμβάνομαι."
77 Stott, *Cross of Christ*, 228ff.
78 Stott, 230.
79 The term παρουσία is used in 1 Cor 15:23; Matt 24:3, 37; 1 Thess 2:19; 3:13; 4:15; 5:23; 2 Thess 2:1, 8; Jas 5:8; 2 Pet 3:4, 12; 1 John 2:28.

destruction of death to the redemptive work of Christ accomplished in his death and resurrection.[80]

The work of Christ liberated the elect from the domination of death, a liberation that is writ large in the eschatological defeat of the one who holds the power of death, Satan.[81] The death of death is an eschatological reality that has both personal and cosmic ramifications, as it also incurs consequences that are both present and future. The condition of this age is one in which humanity dwells in "the region and shadow of death [σκιᾷ θανάτου]" (Matt 4:16), while Christ appears with the promise that those who abide in his word will neither see nor taste death (John 8:51–52).[82] Christ's work (in the first coming, generally—but specifically in his death, burial, and resurrection) gave light to those who sat in the "shadow of death [σκιᾷ θανάτου]" (Luke 1:79; cf. Isa 9:2, 42:7, 60:1–2; Matt 4:16), promising that "whoever hears my word and believes him who sent me ... has passed from death [θάνατος] to life" (John 5:24). Christ suffered physical death on the cross, yet through his death, he brought liberty from death to all God's children (Matt 20:18; 26:66; Mark 10:33; 14:64; Luke 24:20; Phil 2:8). The physical death of Christ, therefore, ironically brought true life (John 10:10)—reconciling enemies to God (Rom 5:10, 14; 8:2, 38; Heb 2:9; Col 1:22) because death could not exercise its hold on him (Acts 2:24; Rev 1:18).[83] Paul thus observed that "our Savior Christ Jesus ... abolished death and brought life and immortality to light through the gospel" (2 Tim 1:10). Recognizing the inaugurated aspects of the death of death is vital for

---

80 This passage in 1 Corinthians 15 and its relationship to Hebrews 2 (alongside 2 Corinthians 4:4) deserves a more careful exegetical inspection than the current work is able to provide. Storms, for example, believes that the entire amillennial/premillennial debate might be solved if the "end" of 1 Corinthians 15:24 is conclusively defined (Storms, *Kingdom Come*, 145ff.). 1 Corinthians also maintains that in Christ, the sting of sin (death) is removed (15:54–57; cf. Isaiah 25:8). See Mathison, *From Age to Age*, 549; Strachan, *Reenchanting Humanity*, 367ff.

81 On the correlation of cosmic/future and personal/present eschatology, see Hoekema, *Bible and the Future*, 1, 6; White, "Agony, Irony, and Victory in Inaugurated Eschatology," 108; Grudem, *Systematic Theology*, 1091; cf. also Vos, *Pauline Eschatology*, 5.

82 Ironically, though, Jesus was accused of being demon-possessed (John 8:52).

83 Christ's death on the cross accomplished the Christus Victor theme alongside, or, more precisely, *through* penal substitutionary atonement. See Stott, *Cross of Christ*, 227–53. The foundational tenet of Christ's work on the cross remains penal substitutionary atonement, the soteriological apex through which the various related redemptive accomplishments flow (cf. Matt 1:21; 1 Cor 15:3–4; Heb 9:22).

a robust eschatology of satanic exorcism—death is defeated both *now* and *not-yet*, and the believer has life both *now* and *not-yet*.

Christ's death brings new life to the believer now, accomplishing the defeat of death, sin, and Satan (Rom 5:17, 21; 6:4–5; 1 John 3:14). Furthermore, Christ's defeat of death through the cross makes believers a "new creation" in this age: "The old has passed away; behold, the new has come" (2 Cor 5:17).[84] The new life that believers presently enjoy (and the concomitant defeat of death) is eternal life that is experienced already in this age (Rom 6:9, 23), because death is defeated in Christ's atoning work and death's final defeat is certain (1 Cor 15:54–56; Rev 20:14). The curse of death has been reversed in the work of Christ, the "last [ἔσχατος] Adam":

> For as by a man came death, by a man has come also the resurrection of the dead. For as in Adam all die, so also in Christ shall all be made alive. But each in his own order: Christ the firstfruits, then at his coming those who belong to Christ. Then comes the end, when he delivers the kingdom to God the Father after destroying every rule and every authority and power. For he must reign until he has put all his enemies under his feet. The last enemy to be destroyed is death. (1 Cor 15:21–26)

The final defeat of death comes when every tear is wiped away from our eyes, as the resurrection of Christ has delivered the defeat of death as well as assuring its ultimate eschatological destruction (cf. Isa 25:8b LXX; see Rev 21:3–4).[85] Christ's atoning redemption and victorious triumph are both present as his reign is accomplished and his enemies are subjected under his feet (1 Cor 15:25; cf. Ps 8:6; Gen 1:28).[86]

The inbreaking of the age to come has occurred because Christ has begun the new-creational reign of the kingdom, commencing in his first coming. The kingdom of God and the advent of the new creation are inseparably interconnected. Though we live in *this age* where sin and death persist, believers experience *the age to come* as the secured victory that is presently realized through the power of Christ. Beale recognizes:

---

84 White observes, "Eschatology can instead provide perspective, as the *eschaton* is inherently personal—it is a vital source of the teaching life of the church." White, "Agony, Irony, and Victory in Inaugurated Eschatology," 108.

85 Verlyn D. Verbrugge, "1 Corinthians," rev. ed., in *EBC* 11, eds. Tremper Longman and David E. Garland, rev. ed. (Grand Rapids: Zondervan, 2008), 404.

86 Verbrugge, 397.

We have observed repeatedly that new creation and kingdom are two sides of one coin. Accordingly, it should not be surprising that Jesus's death itself is viewed as establishing his rule. And this is precisely what Heb. 2:14–15 indicates in direct connection to identifying Christ as an eschatological Adam (2:6–9). . . . Christ's power is likely linked in some way to the authority of his Adamic office. Thus, his death is a victory over Satan, perhaps understood as divesting the devil's kingdom of his captive subjects.[87]

In this way, the witness of the New Testament testifies that Christ has destroyed Satan, while Satan's final judgment is yet to come.

This expectation of future consummative judgment is why Paul could observe that "the last enemy to be destroyed [καταργήσῃ, same root καταργέω as in Heb 2:14][88] is death" (1 Cor 15:26), while simultaneously observing that "through the appearing of our Savior Christ Jesus, [he] abolished [καταργέομαι] death" (2 Tim 1:10). The mortal blow to both Satan and death itself has been dealt through Christ's first coming, and it will come to full fruition when he returns in the final judgment of the second coming (Rev 20:14).[89] Mathison observes, "The author of Hebrews says that through death, Jesus 'destroyed' the devil (Heb. 2:14). If such language is appropriate for what Christ accomplished on the cross in the first century, it is not inappropriate to speak of the binding of Satan as having already occurred. This binding is the penultimate judgment of God's ancient enemy (Gen. 3)."[90]

Death and Satan are defeated in an eschatological undoing of the Fall— just as in Adam all died, so in Christ "shall all [πάντες] be made alive" (1 Cor 15:22; cf. Rom 5:12–21; 6:1–14; 2 Cor 5:16–19).[91] The believer's experience of death in this time between the ages reveals that death has lost its spiritual finality, even though believers are not yet physically glorified. Therefore, death's physical effects still abide in this age, but they do not

---

87 Beale, *New Testament Biblical Theology*, 907–8. Beale subsequently links this fulfillment to Colossians 2, noting that this is the Christus Victor concept. Beale, *New Testament Biblical Theology*, 908n25, 285.
88 This use of καταργήσῃ / καταργέω is the only use of the term in Hebrews.
89 Mathison, *From Age to Age*, 610.
90 Mathison, 689.
91 These references are all related to the Pauline theme of resurrection and new creation. Verbrugge, "1 Corinthians," 397.

hold the last word for the believer.[92] In his commentary on 1 Corinthians 15:26, Luther fittingly summarizes: "In that way we might learn to know and regard our Lord as an enemy of death; his kingdom is intent on engaging death in combat, in putting him in subjection under his feet, until he has utterly destroyed him."[93] The recognition of Christ's comprehensive defeat of death subsequently leads Paul, later in 1 Corinthians, to observe the "mystery" that "we shall not all sleep, but we shall all be changed" (1 Cor 15:51)—death no longer holds the believer in the grip of fear (Heb 2:15) because Christ's victory has both liberated believers and defeated their satanic foe (1 Cor 15:57). Paul, therefore, concludes that when immortality and the imperishable body are realized in the consummation of Christ's final victory, these words will be fully realized: "Death is swallowed up in victory" (1 Cor 15:54; cf. 1 Cor 15:53–57; Isa 25:8). The death of death in Hebrews explains the New Testament outworking of the satanic exorcism witnessed in the Gospel accounts—namely, that Satan and death itself have experienced penultimate eschatological exorcism in this age.

1 John 3:8b

> THE DEVIL HAS BEEN SINNING FROM THE BEGINNING. THE REASON THE SON OF GOD APPEARED WAS TO DESTROY THE WORKS OF THE DEVIL. (1 JOHN 3:8)

Christ destroyed both death (θάνατος) and the devil (διάβολος)—the one who holds the power of death in this age (Heb 2:14)—through the work of his first coming. The one true God unmistakably rules over all the nations of the earth (Ps 22:28), and no created power or authority truly challenges or rivals God in all of his creation (Isa 44:6–8). Yet the New Testament also speaks of a tangible satanic rule over this age—John observes that "the whole world [ὁ κόσμος ὅλος] lies in the power of the evil one [τῷ πονηρῷ]" (1 John 5:19).[94] In the work of his public ministry, Christ identified Satan as

---

[92] John Calvin (Ioannis Calvini), *Opera quae supersunt omnia*, 59 vols., Corpus Reformatorum 29–88, cited in *1 Corinthians*, ed. Scott M. Manetsch, RCS, 9A (Downers Grove, IL: InterVarsity Press, 2017), 374.

[93] Martin Luther, *Luther's Works*, Amer. ed., 28:131–32, 133), cited in Manetsch, ed., RCS 9A, 374. Luther followed that conclusion with an admonition: "It would be proper to inscribe this verse with golden letters and to hold it before the eyes of Christians constantly."

[94] Alexander, *From Eden to the New Jerusalem*, 100, cf. 75. The clear distinction is still maintained between creature (Satan) and Creator (God).

the "ruler [ἄρχων] of this world [τοῦ κόσμου]," though he also made clear that "[Satan] has no claim on me" (John 14:30; see 12:31, 16:11). Satanic power prior to Christ possessed ἐξουσία in the world, while Christ's first coming laid claim to that power with the advance of the new-creational kingdom—the inauguration of the age to come. The New Testament portrays Satan as a usurping ruler in this world/age, one who uses deception to lead unbelievers to oppose Christ.[95]

In a cosmic reversal of that satanic program of deception and rebellion, John observed that a primary facet of Christ's earthly mission was to destroy the work (ἔργον; cf. 1 Cor 15:58, Rev 22:12) of the devil (ὁ διάβολος). Destroying the work of the devil includes destroying the demonic rulers and authorities (ἀρχὰς καὶ ἐξουσίας; Eph 1:20–23; 3:10; 6:11–12), destroying the power of death (θάνατος, Heb 2:14), and finally destroying the satanic ruler as well (ὁ ἄρχων; John 12:31; 14:30; 16:11). Following the satanic exorcism described in the Gospels and explicated in the New Testament epistles, Christ is revealed to be the true "ruler [ὁ ἄρχων] of kings of the earth [τῆς γῆς]" (Rev 1:5). The false ruler has been cast out, and the true ruler has destroyed all evil works and displaced all evil powers.[96] John reflects on this eschatological victory by observing that Satan, who "has been sinning from the beginning" (cf. Gen 3:14–15), has been destroyed along with his works. Satan, the one whose revolt against God precedes even man's rebellion, has been defying God from the beginning (ἀπ' ἀρχῆς).[97] Christ's first coming concludes with the Son of Man's ascension, which conclusively establishes his dominion over this world (cf. Dan 7:13–14), a dominion which brings conclusive defeat to the satanic powers that are operative in this age.

---

95 Bruce, *Gospel of John*, 266–67; Pink, *Exposition of the Gospel of John*, 272.

96 The "works of the devil" destroyed in 1 John reflect the results of kingdom advance and satanic exorcism throughout the New Testament. Chris Forbes observes, "In Colossians, Christ created all the ἀρχαί; he is their head, and the Christian's salvation consists in his stripping them of their power.... In Ephesians, the Church's continuing warfare is against these (still resisting) powers, and its task is to display the wisdom of God to them." Chris Forbes, "Paul's Principalities and Powers: Demythologizing Apocalyptic?" *JSNT* 23.82 (2001): 87.

97 Paul Barnett, *The Second Epistle to the Corinthians*, NICNT (Grand Rapids: Eerdmans, 1997), 82.

The "God of this World"

2 Corinthians 4:4

> The god of this world has blinded the minds of the unbelievers, to keep them from seeing the light of the gospel of the glory of Christ. (2 Cor 4:4)

One passage that must be examined is a particularly difficult passage presented in 2 Corinthians 4:4. After reflecting on the ministry of the gospel (4:1–2) that follows the "veil" of the "old covenant" being removed (3:7–18), as well as the persistent recalcitrance of the unbelieving world (αἰῶν) that does not see the gospel with clarity (4:3), Paul gives a brief word of explanation in 4:4 that has garnered interpretive controversy. Paul states that, regarding the unbelieving world (4:3–4), the "god of this world" (ὁ θεὸς τοῦ αἰῶνος τούτου) has "blinded" (τυφλόω) their minds to prevent them from seeing the light of the gospel. One of the foundational issues with this passage is identifying the "god of this world." Is this a reference to the one true God, or is it a reference to a false "god" such as Satan?[98]

The interpretive issue arises because Paul uses somewhat imprecise language concerning the referent of the phrase ὁ θεὸς τοῦ αἰῶνος τούτου—this phrase is found nowhere else in the New Testament, and it is atypical for a Pauline passage to utilize θεὸς to describe a satanic or demonic entity.[99] Though there is no direct lexical parallel available for the designation ὁ θεὸς τοῦ αἰῶνος τούτου, this title is certainly evocative of the satanic "ruler of this world" identified by John (ὁ ἄρχων τοῦ κόσμου τούτου; John 12:31). Paul's description in 2 Corinthians 4:4 of Satan having a modicum

---

98 Advocating the identity of God the Father in this passage is Ivor Poobalan, "Who Is the 'God of This Age' in 2 Corinthians 4:4?," *JAET* 24.1 (2020): 41–56. Pooblan maintains this was the majority view for 1500 years until the Reformation. Most commentators identify the referent as Satan. See Paul, *The Second Epistle to the Corinthians*; David E. Garland, *2 Corinthians*, NAC 29 (Nashville: Broadman & Holman, 1999), 210; Thomas R. Schreiner, *New Testament Theology: Magnifying God in Christ* (Grand Rapids: Baker Academic, 2008); Ralph P. Martin, *2 Corinthians*, WBC 40 (Waco, TX: Word, 1986); Ladd, *Presence of the Future*; R. V. G. Tasker, *The Second Epistle of Paul to the Corinthians*, TNTC 8 (Grand Rapids: Eerdmans, 1974); Riddlebarger, *Man of Sin*, 66; Beale, *New Testament Biblical Theology*, 304.

99 This usage is similar to Paul's use of τῶν ἀρχόντων τοῦ αἰῶνος τούτου in 1 Corinthians 2:8. See Susan R. Garrett, "Christ and the Present Evil Age," *Int* 57,.4 (2003): 371; Garland, *2 Corinthians*, 210.

of rule and authority in "this age" (τοῦ αἰῶνος τούτου) is comparable, and ὁ θεὸς τοῦ αἰῶνος τούτου seems to be the same Satan that Paul has previously referenced within 2 Corinthians (see 2:11; cf. later in his epistle, 11:14; 12:7).[100]

The theological objection to Satan being identified as a "god" carries weight and is worthy of reflection. Scripture unmistakably teaches that there are no "gods" but God (Isa 42:10–13; 43:6–8), and that all evil spiritual entities are essentially imposters and usurpers within the created order. As noted earlier, Paul himself has observed in his first letter to the Corinthians that "the earth is the Lord's, and the fullness thereof" (1 Cor 10:26; cf. Ps 24:1). Paul's writings often reflect a great depth of monotheistic vigilance and theological dismissal of false gods, including in his letters to the Corinthians: "For although there may be so-called gods [θεοὶ] in heaven or on earth [γῆς]—as indeed there are many 'gods' [θεοὶ] and many 'lords' [κύριοι]— yet for us there is one God [θεὸς], the Father, from whom are all things and for whom we exist, and one Lord [κύριος], Jesus Christ, through whom are all things and through whom we exist" (1 Cor 8:5–6).[101]

A concern of biblical interpreters with respect to 2 Corinthians 4:4, one that arose even among theologians in the early church, was that assigning the label "god" to any false deity might risk ontological dualism, Marcionite ditheism, or similar theological heresies.[102] Yet Paul qualifies his description of this "god" by noting that this false god is only the god of this age (αἰῶν). Garland astutely notes about Paul's designation: "If Paul were actually referring to God here, it is strange that he does not characterize him as the God of all ages rather than simply the God of this age… [Paul] classifies Satan as a 'god' because he has a dominion, however limited by the one true God, and has subjects whom Paul labels 'unbelievers.'"[103] Though unusual in any canonical use, Paul makes the compelling assertion that Satan's power in this age is strong enough to warrant the title ὁ θεὸς τοῦ αἰῶνος τούτου.

---

100 Barnett, *Second Epistle to the Corinthians*, 219n45.
101 Garland, *2 Corinthians*, 210. Garland notes the heretical case of Marcion, who used this text to argue for an inferior God and a supreme, saving God.
102 Such a state of affairs was certainly the case since the time of the Reformation. See Poobalan, "Who Is the 'God of This Age' in 2 Corinthians 4?," 42n2.
103 Garland, *2 Corinthians*, 210–11.

Though it is undoubtedly unusual to hear Satan referred to as a "god" in any sense,[104] it seems clear that Paul refers to Satan as ὁ θεὸς τοῦ αἰῶνος τούτου in 2 Corinthians 4:4 in a similar fashion to his reference to Satan as τὸν ἄρχοντα τῆς ἐξουσίας τοῦ ἀέρος (the prince/ruler of the authority of the air) in Ephesians 2:2. The satanic title "the god of this age" (ὁ θεὸς τοῦ αἰῶνος) is unique, though it is consistent with regular New Testament formulations for him that are situated within the theological context of this present evil age (John 12:31; 14:30; 16:11; 1 Cor 2:6; 2 Cor 4:4; Eph 2:2; 6:12; possibly Matt 9:34; 12:24; 13:19; 1 John 4:4; 5:19).[105] In Second Corinthians as in Ephesians, Satan exercises a modicum of authority in the area human beings occupy—both in this world/age (αἰῶν, 2 Cor 4:4) as a temporal reference, and in this area that operates "below the heavens" as a geographical reference (ἀήρ / ἔρος, Eph 2:2).[106] Paul warns against satanic influence that is still at work in this age, observing that "even Satan disguises himself as an angel of light" (2 Cor 11:13–15).[107]

Consistent with the overlap of *this age* and *the age to come*, it is possible to call Satan "the god [θεὸς] of this age [αἰῶν]" (2 Cor 4:4) while still recognizing that "the reason the Son of God appeared was to destroy the works of the devil [τοῦ διαβόλου]" (1 John 3:8).[108] The eschatological overlap of the ages is of vital importance since it is only in this age that Satan exerts control, and that control is curtailed by the decree of God.[109] Paul's eschatological conception is that *this age* is an evil age (Gal 1:4; cf. 1 Tim 6:17) that overlaps with *the age to come* (Eph 1:21), such that the end of the ages has definitively come in the person of Jesus Christ (1 Cor 10:11).[110] Second

---

104 Such language is unusual, but it is certainly not unprecedented. See John 10:34 (Ps 81:6); Exod 7:1; BDAG, s.v. "θεος."
105 Michaels, *Gospel of John*, 696n44. The phrase ὁ ἄρχων τοῦ κόσμου τούτου is used by John to refer to Satan, a phrase that is closely related to John's use of "the evil one" (John 17:15, "τοῦ πονηροῦ"). See also Tasker, *Gospel According to St. John*,153n31.
106 Cole, *Against the Darkness*, 101.
107 Martin, *2 Corinthians*, 78.
108 Geddert states, "Jesus taught that the Evil One was still in control of this present world, but that in some sense he was already defeated. Jesus taught that with his own coming, judgment on the world had come, but that nevertheless a future judgment was to be expected (Jn 12:31; 16:11)." Geddert, "Apocalyptic Teaching," 24.
109 Martin, *2 Corinthians*, 78.
110 Thomas Schreiner notes, "Just as Paul uses the language of the new creation, so also he adopts typical Jewish language of this age and the age to come (Eph. 1:21). This age is designated as 'the present evil age' (Gal. 1:4; cf. 1 Tim. 6:17), and believers are not to be

Corinthians 4:4 makes it clear that Satan's power is inherently limited—his authority applies only to this present evil age (Gal 1:4), an age that is surely passing away with the dawning of the age to come (1 Cor 2:6).[111]

The power that Satan exercises in this world entails that he "has blinded the minds of unbelievers, to keep them from seeing the light of the gospel of the glory of Christ" (2 Cor 4:4). The verb τυφλόω is only used three times in the New Testament: 2 Corinthians 4:4, John 12:40 (cf. Isa 42:19), and 1 John 2:11. All three uses of τυφλόω refer to the darkened state of the unbeliever in this age, with an implication of impending destruction imminently resulting from his blinded state. Satan's power is one of obfuscation, and thus, Satan's primary victims are those who lack faith and apart from God.[112] Though God is still the King of this age (1 Tim 1:17), Satan is permitted to hold the unbeliever in a continuing state of blindness resulting in their own destruction.[113] The nature of this blinding requires careful attention—the verb for "seeing" (αὐγάσαι) is a rare use of the verb, and the phrase "to keep them from seeing" is equally difficult to translate from a lexical standpoint.[114] The nature or effect of the blinding seems related to its objective referent in the "mind" (νόημα), denoting a method of attack that seems to be of particular danger to the Corinthians (2 Cor 2:11).[115] A blinded mind may relate to pride and arrogance, though it is certainly clear that it is inseparably connected to continuing unbelief and spiritual

---

conformed to this age (Rom. 12:2), as Demas was (2 Tim. 4:10), for the world dominates the lives of unbelievers (Eph. 2:2).... The present evil age is not the only reality, for the 'ends of the ages' have now dawned in Jesus Christ (1 Cor. 10:11 NRSV), and believers by virtue of the cross of Christ represent the intrusion of the new age, or as Paul says in Gal. 6:14–15, the new creation. The world in its present form is passing away (1 Cor. 7:31)." Schreiner, *New Testament Theology*, 32.

111 Garland, *2 Corinthians*, 211.
112 Martin, *2 Corinthians*, 78.
113 Ladd, *The Presence of the Future*, 118–19; Witherington, *Letters to Philemon, the Colossians, and the Ephesians*, 386. Though Tertullian argues (*Against Marcion 5.11*) that it was God that blinded the minds, it is undoubtedly Satan who blinds. See Garland, *2 Corinthians*, 210; Witherington, *Letters to Philemon, the Colossians, and the Ephesians*, 386.
114 Barnett makes the case that αὐγάσαι is transitive as opposed to intransitive. Barnett, *Second Epistle to the Corinthians*, 218n41. "To stop them from seeing" could imply shining, illuminating, or clearly viewing, though Martin prefers the latter. See Martin, *2 Corinthians*, 79.
115 Garland, *2 Corinthians*, 212. Garland maintains that attacking the mind is the "chief" ploy of Satan.

blindness.[116] Blind eyes accompany blind hearts (see Isa 6:9–10), and both lead to man's destruction.[117]

Satanic exorcism occurs in the context of *this age*—the eschatological age that is passing away even as *the age to come* is already shining (see Rom 13:12; Heb 9:26). Christ's first coming was a triumphant victory over the forces of darkness, one that brought defeat to demonic forces and the exorcism of Satan himself. Christ's victory brought deliverance for those who were previously held captive under satanic authority, removing the authority and power of satanic forces and destroying the power of Satan and death. Though Christ's victory over Satan is of great importance, satanic attack in this age continues while "this world" (see 2 Cor 4:4) experiences the final attacks of the defeated satanic foe.

---

116 On the effect of pride, see Barnett, *Second Epistle to the Corinthians*, 82. Tasker observes: "Unbelief and blindness of spiritual vision caused by this evil potentate are closely related, and it is impossible to state definitely which is cause and which is effect." Tasker, *Second Epistle of Paul to the Corinthians*, 70.

117 Poobalan remarks, "A careful reading shows that Isa 6:9–10 is alluded to in 2 Cor 2:14—4:6;" Poobalan, "Who Is the 'God of This Age' in 2 Corinthians 4?," 52.

Chapter 5

SATAN'S POWER AND AUTHORITY CURTAILED

Prior to the satanic exorcism that was accomplished in the first coming of Christ, Satan exercised a degree of power and authority in this world that was later curtailed. Though the references to Satan in the Old Testament account are rare, the few passages that reflect satanic activity show his possession of authority in this world, particularly concerning his interaction with humanity.[1] Satan's eschatological possession of power and authority does not suggest that satanic operation somehow exists outside the realm of God's control—on the contrary, God ever remains in sovereign control over creation and the powers that exist within it.[2] There is an ongoing tension in the New Testament between the victorious triumph of Christ's conquest and the ongoing persistence of evil in this world, yet there is a clear reclamation of power and authority accomplished in Christ's first coming.[3]

INABILITY TO ACCUSE

One of the most prominent descriptions of satanic activity in the Old Testament is Satan's work of accusation. Though there is a degree of narrative nuance to the activities of Satan within the pages of the Old Testament,[4] it is canonically consistent to recognize the figure of Satan as

---
1 See the analyses of passages involving satanic activity in Scripture in chapter 3.
2 On the divine decree and the presence of evil, see Letham, *Systematic Theology*, 168–70; John M. Frame, *The Doctrine of God* (Phillipsburg, NJ: P&R, 2002), 539–42; Van Til, *Introduction to Systematic Theology*, 389–94. See also Lutzer and Sproul, *God's Devil*, 129; cf. Pagels, "The Social history of Satan, the 'Intimate Enemy,'" 107.
3 Cf. Hoekema, *Bible and the Future*, 34–37, cf. 180.
4 For example, Stokes contends that שטן is primarily an "attacker" or "executioner" rather than an "accuser," which draws attention to the semantic range of שטן within the Old Testament. See Stokes, "Satan, Yhwh's Executioner," 252.

an accuser of believers and one who ultimately seeks their destruction. John further clarifies in Revelation: "The accuser [ὁ κατήγωρ] of our brothers has been thrown down, who accuses [ὁ κατηγορῶν] them day and night before our God" (Rev 12:10). The biblical depiction of Satan's activities reveals that he "accuses" (κατηγορέω) believers,[5] and John further highlights the extent of his accusatory schemes in his introduction of a personal title for Satan—"the "accuser" (ὁ κατήγωρ).[6]

This pattern of accusation holds true in the Old Testament accounts surveyed as well, since Satan is frequently depicted in a type of heavenly court setting, lobbying accusations against the people of God on the earth and requesting their destruction (Job 1–2; Zech 3). Satan's ability to accuse is greatly hindered with the satanic exorcism accomplished in Christ's first coming—a theme that the eschatological tension of the New Testament narrative brings to light. Satan's inability to accuse the elect particularly emerges into focus in passages of Revelation and Romans, to which the following section will now turn.

Revelation 12:7–12

> AND THE GREAT DRAGON WAS THROWN DOWN, THAT ANCIENT SERPENT, WHO IS CALLED THE DEVIL AND SATAN, THE DECEIVER OF THE WHOLE WORLD—HE WAS THROWN DOWN TO THE EARTH, AND HIS ANGELS WERE THROWN DOWN WITH HIM. (REV 12:9)

Revelation 12 begins a fresh vision in an ongoing series of apocalyptic visions, primarily presenting a picture of believers during the church age.[7] As with most of the visions in Revelation, John is primarily using the visionary palette of the Old Testament to fill in the colors of this current New Testament vision, so references to Old Testament imagery are frequently

---

[5] The New Testament authors' use of κατηγορέω almost always refers to bringing charges in a legal court setting. See BDAG, s.v. "κατηγορέω.". This term conveys the idea of "accuse," "bringing charges against," or "speaking against." See *DBL*, s.v. "κατηγορέω"; *LALGNT*, s.v. "κατηγορέω"; Souter, *Pocket Lexicon to the Greek New Testament*, s.v. "κατηγορέω."

[6] The sole New Testament occurrence of this word appears in Rev 12:10.; It is "an abbreviated vulgar form of κατήγορος" according to Souter, *Pocket Lexicon to the Greek New Testament*, s.v. "κατήγωρ." See also *LALGNT*, s.v. "κατήγωρ"; *DBL*, s.v. "κατήγωρ."

[7] Beale with Campbell, *Revelation*, 242; Leon Morris, *Revelation: An Introduction and Commentary*, TNTC 20 (Downers Grove, IL: InterVarsity Press, 1987), 151. Cf. Robert H. Mounce, *The Book of Revelation*, rev. ed. (Grand Rapids: Eerdmans, 1997), 231; Ladd, *Commentary on the Revelation of John*, 166.

woven into John's presentation of the events that unfold. Though the thematic background and discourse setting of Revelation 12 are unique in their presentation of a new visionary sequence, this new vision is nonetheless tied to visions previously presented in the book.

Revelation's unfolding series of parallel visions depict events that occur between the first and second comings of Christ from various perspectives, while Revelation 12 begins a new sequence in the parallel vision framework. While the first eleven chapters of Revelation primarily describe eschatological events from the perspective of an earthly struggle, the final eleven chapters shift into a description that describes these same events from the perspective of the heavenly realm (see Figure 5 below).[8]

SYNCHRONISTIC / PARALLELISTIC INTERPRETATION OF JOHN'S APOCALYPSE[9]

(Earthly Struggle)	First Coming	Seven Churches (1–3)	Second Coming
		Seven Seals (4–7)	
		Seven Trumpets (8–11)	
(Heavenly Conflict)		Woman and Dragon (12–14)	
		Seven Bowls (15–16)	
		Fall of Babylon (17–19)	
		Eternal State (20–22)	

FIGURE 5

This interpretive perspective is not intended to bifurcate the physical realm from that of the spiritual in an unnatural manner; in fact, it is quite

---

8 Beale with Campbell, *Revelation*, 241–42; William Hendriksen, *More Than Conquerors: An Interpretation of the Book of Revelation*, 75th anniv. ed. (Grand Rapids: Baker Books, 2015), 22–64; Hoekema, *Bible and the Future*, 223–25.

9 This chart is a visual depiction of the verbal argument made in Hendricksen, *More Than Conquerors*, 28.

the opposite—the earthly events through which the church perseveres are explained to be this-worldly manifestations of a heavenly, spiritual conflict that is occurring beyond humanity's natural scope of vision.

Of particular focus in this section of Revelation is the progressively-clearer depiction of the enemy—chapters 12–22 tell the same story as the first eleven chapters, though Satan is revealed to be the true evil entity that is operative behind the forces of darkness (see Rev 2:13; 6:8; and 9:11).[10] Satan, who previously has not received focal attention in the passages he occupies, now comes into direct focus in the context of heavenly warfare. John spotlights the identity of the enemy to whom he is referring by using the language of the Old Testament: "The great dragon was thrown down, that ancient serpent [ὁ ὄφις], who is called the devil [Διάβολος] and Satan [ὁ Σατανᾶς], the deceiver of the whole world" (Rev 12:9).

The passage in Rev 12:7–12 contains some familiar characters, yet much of the symbolism employed is unique within New Testament usage. The introductory verses of the chapter (12:1–6) describe the woman who gave birth to a son—a son who is described as "one who is to rule all the nations [πάντα τὰ ἔθνη] with a rod of iron" (12:5; cf. Ps 2:9, 66:7; Isa 7:14)—and was subsequently pursued into the wilderness by the dragon. Following this picturesque description of conflict with the dragon on earth (12:1–6), this current passage (12:7–12) proceeds to depict the spiritual conflict in heaven that corresponds to the earthly conflict below.[11]

On the heavenly side of the battle stands the angel Michael. Michael appears in various passages in both the Old Testament and New Testament (Dan 10:13, 21; 12:1; Jude 9), and is depicted as a warlike "archangel" (ὁ

---

10 Beale astutely observes, "Chs. 12–22 tell the same story as chs. 1–11, but explain in greater detail what the first chapters only introduce and imply. Ch. 12 now reveals that the devil himself is the deeper source of evil. Brief references to him have come already in 2:13; 6:8; and 9:11. The devil is the grand initiator of the trials and persecutions of the saints. He unleashes the beast and the false prophet. The harlot Babylon is also his servant. John pictures the four figures (the devil, the beast, the false prophet, and the harlot) rising in this order and then meeting their demise in the reverse order in chs. 12–20 in order to highlight the devil as the initiator, from first to last, of all resistance to God and His people." Beale with Campbell, *Revelation*, 241–42.

11 The two passages are connected by the phrase "another sign appeared in heaven." Beale maintains: "As will be seen, the three sections of the chapter, vv. 1–6, 7–12, and 13–17, are temporally and thematically parallel in order to tell the story over again from different perspectives." Beale with Campbell, *Revelation*, 252.

ἀρχάγγελος, a combination of ἀρχη + ἄγγελος; see Jude 9) who here commands the forces of heaven against Satan and his servants.[12] Just as in the previous section, there is a cosmic spiritual conflict occurring ("war ... in heaven") that is centered around the first coming of Christ. Michael stands against the dragon in the representation of Christ and the church, and just as Christ defeated Satan on earth through his redemptive work, Michael contends with Satan in the heavenly realm on behalf of Christ as his heavenly representative (cf. Dan 7:13–27; 10:13, 21; 12:1).[13]

Amid this conflict playing out in the heavenly arena, Satan appears so that he might make war on Christ and those who follow Him. Satan is referred to as "the great dragon" (ὁ δράκων ὁ μέγας; 12:9), a common term for Satan in Revelation—though John makes his identity abundantly clear with the additional descriptive terms used in this passage ("serpent," "devil," "Satan," "deceiver"). The background language of this passage (as with many others in Revelation) reflects similar language found in the apocalyptic passages of Daniel, specifically in Daniel 7 where the horn "makes war" with the saints—though the narrative reversal in Revelation is that the "horn" who overpowered the saints in Daniel is now instead overpowered by the victorious Christ.[14]

This eschatological reversal seems to be reflected in similar references in Revelation 11:7 and 13:7, wherein the enemy makes war upon the saints with ferocious and terrible power. Similar to Paul's discussion of ἀρχὰς καὶ ἐξουσίας in Ephesians, John's vision in Revelation 12 exposes the existence of a larger spiritual conflict that rages beyond earthly events—one that involves spiritual forces of angelic and demonic entities engaged in battle.[15] John's description of the dragon as "that ancient serpent" seems to be an overt allusion to the serpent in the Garden (Gen 3), the evil serpent who

---

12 Ladd, *Commentary on the Revelation of John*, 171; Morris, *Revelation*, 156.
13 Beale with Campbell, *Revelation*, 252–53. Fee offers this explanation: "This unusual moment wherein John actually names the archangel Michael belongs to a somewhat foggy history that developed in the intertestamental period, where the various angels were ranked and given names. In most of these cases Michael is understood to be the leading angel among the (usually) seven highest-ranking angels, called 'archangels.' The name itself apparently derived from three passages in Daniel (10:13, 21; 12:1) where a mysterious figure so-named is the keeper of the heavenly books." Gordon D. Fee, *Revelation*, NCC (Eugene, OR: Cascade, 2011), 168–69.
14 Beale with Campbell, *Revelation*, 253.
15 Morris, *Revelation*, 156.

is now clearly identified as both a "slanderer" (Διάβολος) and "adversary" (Σατανᾶς).[16] Satan accuses and slanders the elect and ultimately desires to lead the whole world astray (Rev 12:9).[17] The serpent that initially appeared to the first couple has now surfaced again to make war against the Lamb and those who follow Him—yet the serpent has now met decisive defeat (cf. Gen 3:15).

The outcome of the heavenly spiritual conflict is that Satan and "his angels" are defeated (οὐκ ἴσχυσεν) by Michael and "his angels." Though Satan had made war against the eschatological inbreaking of Christ's advent—Christ's first coming to earth, as pictured in the previous passage (Rev 12:1–6)—Satan has now been defeated, and his defeat is expressed with a heavenly depiction of the spiritual conflict that takes place. Michael victoriously emerges in this passage for the same reason the saints in the Revelation are victorious over the dragon: it is because of "the blood of the Lamb" and, subsequently, through "the word of their testimony" (12:11). Christ has achieved victory over Satan and exorcised him in this age, and the redemptive work of the cross is brought into particular focus in this passage. It is "by" (διὰ) or "because of" (so NASB) Christ's blood that Satan is defeated. The particular focus in this passage is the triumphant victory of the Lamb, corresponding with the crushing defeat of the serpent.[18]

---

16   Ladd, *Commentary on the Revelation of John*, 171; Beale with Campbell, *Revelation* 254. Morris clarifies: "In this significant moment he is described very fully. He is the *great dragon*, and *that ancient serpent*, which is probably meant to awaken recollections of Genesis 3. He is both *the devil* (the word means 'slanderer') and *Satan*. This latter is the older name. It transliterates a Hebrew word which means 'adversary;'" Morris, *Revelation*, 156. Emphasis in original.

17   Morris observes, "This name for the evil one would have made a specially strong impact in the first century, for there was a well-known and well-hated figure called the *delator*, the paid informer. He made his living by accusing people before the authorities. It is not a large step from 'accuser' to 'slanderer' and thus 'the satan' is not infrequently called 'the devil'. In addition to accusing and slandering, the evil one deceives and John brings out the scope of this activity by saying that he *leads the whole world astray*." Morris, *Revelation*, 157. Emphasis in original.

18   Ladd contends: "In redemptive history the victory over Satan was won by Christ through the shedding of his blood on the cross. John, however, is not here concerned with the way the victory is won but merely with the fact that Satan is defeated." Ladd's focal attention is appreciated, though it should be qualified that the *way* of Christ's victory is vital to the redemptive *ends*. See Ladd, *Commentary on the Revelation of John*, 170–71.

As a result of Satan's defeat, the great dragon "was thrown down" (ἐβλήθη; *lemma* βάλλω). The language that John uses in Revelation to describe Satan's exorcism is used elsewhere to denote spiritual conflict—particularly spiritual conflict involving the violent expulsion of evil.

Satan's expulsion from heaven—what can accurately be described as a cosmic exorcism in this age—was a violent expulsion (βάλλω) of judgment inflicted upon an evil ruler (ἄρχων). John conveys that Satan and "his angels" had lost access to their previous place in heaven: "There was no longer any place for them in heaven [ἐν τῷ οὐρανῷ]" (Rev 12:8). Morris notes, "The result of the battle is the defeat of the dragon, so that he and his angels lost their place in heaven. He had been the accuser of God's people (Job 1:6–9; 2:1–6; Zech. 3:1ff.), but now he has no place in heaven."[19] Though Satan had frequently occupied the heavenly places in times past, his defeat in the first coming of Christ eliminated his access to that place of power and authority.

As noted previously, Satan's "casting down" from heaven in Revelation 12 continues the narrative method of drawing on the tapestry of Daniel to illustrate this fresh revelatory vision. Daniel's prophecy in Daniel 2 describes a mighty image made of strong materials (iron, clay, bronze, silver, and gold), which is subsequently destroyed by a stone. The stone was revealed to represent the inbreaking of God's kingdom (Dan 2:44), while the statue (and its composite materials) represented the sinful, earthly kingdoms that ultimately stood against the one true God (Dan 2:38–43).[20] After the stone has rolled into the statue and crushed the elements representing the earthly kingdoms, Daniel's wording closely resembles what is found later in Revelation—"not a trace of them could be found" (Dan 2:35; cf. Rev 12:8 "there was no longer any place for them in heaven").[21]

The satanic opposition to Christ, an opposition which manifests in both the earthly and heavenly arenas (cf. the earthly viewpoint of Revelation 1–11 and the corresponding heavenly viewpoint of Revelation 12–22),

---

19 Morris, *Revelation*, 156.
20 See Beale with Campbell, *Revelation*, 254.
21 Beale with Campbell, 254. Beale notes that many commentators identify the Son of Man in Daniel 7 with the rock of Daniel 2, reflecting the work of Christ that He identified in his own ministry (Luke 20:17–18). Beale concludes, "The point of Dan. 2:35 and the allusion to it in Rev. 12:8b is that opposition to God's kingdom and his people is decisively thwarted."

is crushed by the victorious work of Christ and the establishment of his kingdom—realities established in his first coming that await their final consummation in his second coming. John draws the reader's attention to the victorious nature of Christ's exorcism of Satan (12:10–11) while recognizing that satanic attack and persecution will nonetheless persist for those who live in this age (12:12).[22] Satan and his demonic forces fell at the outset of the initial creation (Gen 3), and, similarly, he has fallen at the outset of the new creation in Christ (see 2 Cor 5:14–17; Gal 6:15).[23] There is great spiritual power exerted in Satan's exorcism—three times in one verse (Rev 12:9) John repeats his observation that Satan was "thrown down" (ἐβλήθη; ἐβλήθη; ἐβλήθησαν) along with his angels. John portrays this cosmic battle using the biblical language of satanic defeat (Dan 2; cf. Luke 10:18; John 12:31), showing the triumph of Christ over the forces of evil and this age.[24]

As is portrayed in Revelation, Satan's exorcism is not meant primarily to describe Satan's physical place of residence—as if some sort of corporal relocation had occurred.[25] Similar to the observation that Christ made in the Gospels ("I saw Satan fall like lightning from heaven"; Luke 10:18), Satan's "casting out" in Revelation 12 draws attention to an eschatological reorientation of power—a dynamic change in the spiritual power and authority in this age. Using apocalyptic language to describe the heavenly realm, Satan's expulsion from heaven primarily conveys a curtailment of his activities:

> Satan's realm is often pictured as being the atmosphere above the

---

22 Fee divides this passage (Rev 12:10–12) into three parts, arranged as a song: the death and resurrection (10), the victory and witness (11), and the coming wrath (12). Fee, *Revelation*, 170.

23 Beale concludes, "Christ's death and resurrection have resulted in Satan's excommunication from heaven. Just as Satan and his hosts fell at the beginning of the first creation (Isa. 14:11–16; Ezek. 28:12–19 [possibly]; 2 Pet. 2:4; Jude 6), so he had to fall at the start of what Scripture tells us is the second, new creation (see 1:5 and 3:14; cf. 2 Cor. 5:14–17; Gal. 6:15). Satan's job had always been to accuse the saints (Job 1:6–11; 2:1–6; Zech. 3:1–2), and from these texts it can be concluded that the devil was permitted by God to accuse His people of sin. Implicit also in the accusations was the charge that God's own character was corrupt." Beale with Campbell, *Revelation*, 256. The use of "excommunicated" is interesting here—denoting many of the same themes as exorcism (cast away from previous place; spiritual warfare; expulsion due to sin; etc.). Beale also infers that Isaiah 14 is prophetically reflecting a satanic fall behind its contextually immediate referent.

24 Beale with Campbell, 256.

25 Ladd, *Commentary on the Revelation of John*, 172.

earth. He is called "the prince of the power of the air" (Eph. 2:2); his angels are "spiritual hosts of wickedness in heavenly places" (Eph. 6:12). However, in Job, he is pictured as having access to the very presence of God. The present passage [in Rev 12] describes a victory over Satan by virtue of which his accusations against God's people lose their force (vs. 10).[26]

Satan has lost his previous ability to accuse God's people. Though he may attack and even tempt believers until his final defeat, Satan may no longer be found in heaven impugning and making accusations against the elect.

John describes this eschatological expulsion as something that has already taken place—there is not only the expectation of a futurely awaited victory but this casting out is a reality presently experienced by the church in this age.[27] As opposed to a solely futurist or proleptic statement, John describes this vision in Revelation 12 in the context of Christ's first coming.[28] Characterized in its consummated state in Revelation 11:15,[29] John describes the inaugurated reclamation of power and authority that Christ has achieved in the exorcism of Satan: "Now [Ἄρτι] the salvation and the power [ἡ δύναμις] and the kingdom of our God and the authority [ἡ ἐξουσία] of

---

26 Ladd, 171–72.
27 Contra the premillennial interpretation of Ladd: "This announcement [in Rev 12], like that in 11:15, is proleptic and looks forward to the consummation which has not yet occurred; but it has occurred in principle, for Satan is already a defeated foe. Even though John has described the heavenly warfare and the downfall of Satan in mythological terms, this defeat leads to the establishment of *the authority* of the Messiah in the world. The result is that Satan's accusations against God's people are frustrated." Ladd, *Commentary on the Revelation of John*, 172. Emphasis in original.
28 Beale notes, "The similar ascriptions of power to God and the Lamb in [Rev] 4:11 and 5:11–12 confirm that here, as in those chapters, the focus is on Christ's resurrection, which has launched the initial stage of the kingdom. The introductory word now emphasizes the beginning aspect of fulfillment. Therefore, v. 10 is not a mere anticipation of the future kingdom, but celebrates the fact that the kingdom has begun immediately following Christ's death and resurrection. This is the direct fulfillment of the prophecy of the beginning of the Messiah's rule in Ps. 2:7–9 (alluded to in v. 5); the combination of God or "Lord" and his Christ, as in this verse, occurs in the Old Testament only in Ps. 2:2. The resurrection is the turning point of all human history. It represents the moment at which the power of the enemy in heaven was crushed and his kingdom came crashing down to earth." Beale with Campbell, *Revelation*, 255.
29 Beale with Campbell, 255.

his Christ have come, for the accuser [ὁ κατήγωρ] of our brothers has been thrown down, who accuses [ὁ κατηγορῶν] them day and night before our God" (Rev 12:10). With the completed work of Christ's first coming, the δύναμις and ἐξουσία of this age have been stripped from Satan, along with the removal of his ability to make accusation against the people of God from a heavenly vantage point.

Satan's relatively few appearances in the Old Testament highlight his exercise of immense power and authority, centrally seen in his accusation of the elect. Satan is depicted before the very throne of God making accusations against believers, sometimes seeming to occupy an official capacity (Zech 3:1–5) and, at other times, carrying out violence on earth by divine permission (Job 1–2). It is from this place of power that Satan has been "thrown down"—he is no longer able to successfully impugn the saints before the throne of God. With the advent of the age to come in the completed work of Christ, Satan's appeals against the elect are overthrown, and his access to the heavenly realms is curtailed.[30]

Romans 8:33, 38

A passage in Romans 8 may bring further clarity to the twin themes of satanic defeat and Christological victory that John describes in Revelation 12. Romans 8 comprises one of the most doctrinally packed chapters in one of the most theologically dense books in the New Testament corpus. In it, Paul conveys two key themes that are in keeping with the overall eschatological development of Revelation 12:7–12. Specifically, Paul recognizes that no one can bring a charge against God's elect because of the completed work of Christ (Rom 8:33), and he likewise notes that neither angels, rulers, nor powers can separate believers from the love of God which is in Christ (Rom 8:38–39).[31]

---

30 Morris notes, "The picture is one of implacable hostility on the part of Satan as well as of the complete triumph of God. Satan urged the sins of the brothers in the highest court. But now he has been overthrown and is completely powerless against them." Morris, *Revelation*, 157.

31 The presence of satanic or demonic powers behind these and similar passages is often underdeveloped, either due to academic skepticism or popular-level overemphasis. See Scobie, *Ways of Our God*, 265; Forbes, "Paul's Principalities and Powers," 87. Discussion of the post-Enlightenment skeptical influence of such scholars as Friedrich Schleiermacher and Rudolf Bultmann is helpful in Cole, *Against the Darkness*, 161.

Romans 8:33

WHO SHALL BRING ANY CHARGE AGAINST GOD'S ELECT?
IT IS GOD WHO JUSTIFIES. (ROM 8:33)

The heavenly battle scene in Revelation 12 describes Satan as a defeated foe, one who has been exorcised from heaven and thereby prevented from making accusations before God against the elect. Satan cannot accuse because the victorious work of Christ—"the blood of the Lamb" (Rev 12:11)—has restrained Satan's ability to impugn those who are covered by Christ's propitiatory blood. Paul explicates this theme of protection against satanic charges in Romans 8:33, a passage beset with interpretive challenges.[32] The opening question of this narrative section is direct: "Who shall bring a charge?" The verb form translated as "bring a charge" (ἐγκαλέσει) is typically a forensic term that is rendered in the future tense—it is very likely referring the question forward in time, directed toward the coming eschatological judgment that will emerge with Christ's second coming.[33]

Who is it who will ostensibly "bring a charge" of accusation against believers? Satan, the ancient accuser of believers throughout the Old Testament and New Testament alike, is undoubtedly in view in the narrative background of this question. Moo observes,

> "Bring a charge" is the first of the explicitly judicial terms in this context. The future tense of the verb focuses attention on the last judgment. Who will stand and accuse us at that time? To be sure, Satan, the "accuser," may seek to do so; so may our enemies and, perhaps most persuasively of all, our own sins. But no accusation will be effective because it is against God's "elect" that the accusation is being made; and, as Paul has shown in vv. 28–30, those who are God's "elect ones" by virtue of his calling and purpose are assured of glory.[34]

---

32 Moo finds at least six possible ways to interpret this verse, while Schreiner observes that even the punctuation is disputed. See Douglas J. Moo, *The Epistle to the Romans*, NICNT (Grand Rapids: Eerdmans, 1996), 541; Thomas R. Schreiner, *Romans*, BECNT (Grand Rapids: Baker Books, 1998), 461.
33 The verb ἐγκαλέω occurs six times in Acts (19:38, 40; 23:29, 38; 26:2, 7) and is also found in the LXX (cf. Prov. 19:5; Zech. 1:4; Wis. 12:12; Sir. 46:19). See Moo, *The Epistle to the Romans*, 541–42; Schreiner, *Romans*, 462, 467.
34 Moo, *Epistle to the Romans*, 541–42.

Precisely because God is counted as being "for us" (8:31), Paul assures believers of the coming eschatological blessings that are still yet to come (8:32), and he concludes with the promise that no satanic force can bring accusation successfully against the elect (8:33).[35] For the believer, Satan no longer holds any power of spiritual indictment due to the work of Christ. Beale, therefore, observes: "It is not coincidental that Rev. 20:11–15 is a picture of the judgment at the final resurrection, in which not only is Satan conspicuously absent but also those raised whose names are 'written in the book of life' will be exempted from the judgment narrated there."[36] Satan's capacity of successfully accusing the elect has ended in his exorcism, though his attacks and influence continue as this age is yet passing away.

The strong denial of Satan's power in Romans 8:33 is due to the victory of Christ. In this relatively brief verse, Paul employs forms of θεός twice for additional emphasis—underscoring that God is the key actor at work in the defeat of Satan.[37] Possibly lingering in the background of Paul's words in Romans 8:33 is a passage from Isaiah 50:8–9a: "He who vindicates me is near. Who will contend [ὁ κρινόμενός, LXX] with me? Let us stand up together. Who is my adversary [ὁ κρινόμενός, LXX]?[38] Let him come near to me. Behold, the Lord God helps me; who will declare me guilty?"[39] If Paul is indeed alluding to Isaiah 50:8–9, then Romans 8:33 uses the same forensic language (ἐγκαλέσει) as the Servant Song in Isaiah, appealing to God to vindicate his elect from Satan's eschatological calls for judgment.[40]

---

35 Beale ties this section to a resurrection theme. Beale, *New Testament Biblical Theology*, 503.
36 Beale, 504.
37 Robert H. Mounce, *Romans*, NAC 27 (Nashville: Broadman & Holman, 1995), 190n205.
38 "Adversary" is a gloss of the Hebrew term בַּעַל מִשְׁפָּטִי (ba-'al miš-pā-ṭî) and of the Greek term ὁ κρινόμενός (LXX).
39 Moo, *Epistle to the Romans*, 541–42.
40 Contra Fitzmeyer, who denies that Satan is intended as the inferred accuser in Romans 8:33. Joseph A. Fitzmyer, *Romans: A New Translation with Introduction and Commentary*, AB 33 (New Haven: Yale University Press, 2008), 532–33.

Romans 8:38–39

> FOR I AM SURE THAT NEITHER DEATH NOR LIFE, NOR ANGELS
> NOR RULERS, NOR THINGS PRESENT NOR THINGS TO COME,
> NOR POWERS, NOR HEIGHT NOR DEPTH, NOR ANYTHING ELSE IN
> ALL CREATION, WILL BE ABLE TO SEPARATE US FROM THE LOVE OF
> GOD IN CHRIST JESUS OUR LORD. (ROM 8:38–39)

Further in the discourse of Romans 8, Paul includes a list of entities that are unable "to separate us from the love of God in Christ Jesus," including some familiar forces that are defeated in the spiritual victory of Christ's first coming (death, angels, rulers, powers, etc.). Paul's outline of the myriad forces that are rendered impotent in the face of Christ's victory (and Satan's defeat) includes nearly every category of power that could attack the believer. Mounce notes: "[Paul's] list of ten terms moves from physical danger through the hierarchy of superhuman powers, those that now exist or ever will, powers from on high or from below, and culminates in the inclusive phrase 'anything else in God's whole world.'"[41] Paul lists several pairs of concepts that are readily identifiable such as "death" and "life," though the abrupt inclusion of "powers" (δυνάμεις) seems to interrupt the consistent progression in the passage.[42]

The identity of these "powers" seems to be in keeping with the forces of spiritual conflict present elsewhere within the narrative progression: death (θάνατος), angels (ἄγγελοι), and rulers (ἀρχαί) are all concepts that Paul regularly uses to describe the cosmic spiritual conflict that accompanied the earthly ministry of Christ.[43] The "powers" are almost certainly evil (they seek to separate believers from Christ), representing spiritual forces

---

41 Mounce, *Romans*, 192.
42 Moo, *Epistle to the Romans*, 544. Mounce further observes, "The list is composed of four pairs interrupted by a single term after the third pair and a catch-all at the close. Commentaries discuss at length the various possibilities for each item. Some take the various designations in a general way to depict the extremes of life as we experience it, the supernatural world, time, and space." Mounce, *Romans*, 192n213.
43 Schreiner argues, "In the Byzantine text the word δυνάμεις is inserted before οὔτε ἐνεστῶτα. This is an obvious attempt to repair the order so that all angelic powers are kept together, and the very disjunction speaks of the originality of the text in NA[27]. In a few manuscripts scribes have added ἐξουσία in various places, presumably because the word is associated with ἀρχαί elsewhere in Paul (Eph. 3:10; 6:12; Col. 1:16; 2:10, 15)." Schreiner, *Romans*, 468.

at work who oppose the outworking of Christ's victory in creation.[44] These evil spiritual forces would include "powers" in the same category of angelic created beings whose authority over believers has been curtailed by Christ's work.[45] Paul makes clear that no spiritual forces, including the ruling evil spirits of this age, can spiritually threaten the elect.[46] The evil powers of this age have been defeated along with their satanic ruler.

The things above (ὕψωμα) and below (βάθος) no longer separate the believer from God due to the work of Christ. Included in these defeated powers is "death" itself (θάνατος), presented along with the contrasting category of "life" (ζωή).[47] The fundamental inability of death to destroy the believer is consistent with the death of death in Hebrews 2:14, as death itself has lost its power in this age—even while physical death persists. Augustine similarly hinted at this element of the inaugurated defeat of death when reflecting on this eschatological tension: "For sin first loseth its reign, and so perisheth. In this life then, as far as the Saints are concerned, it loseth its reign, in the other it perisheth. For here it loseth its reign, when we *go not after our lusts*; but there it perisheth, when it shall be said, *O death, where is thy contention?*"[48] Satan is still active, and death is still a reality in

---

44 Schreiner, *Romans*, 465.

45 Schreiner observes, "The second pair, ἄγγελοι οὔτε ἀρχαί, refers to angelic powers, as does the term δυνάμεις which is inserted later. One could possibly see a reference to governmental authorities in the term ἀρχαί (cf. Titus 3:1), but in Paul this word usually refers to angelic rulers (1 Cor. 15:24; Eph. 1:21; 3:10; 6:12; Col. 1:16; 2:10, 15) as does the term δυνάμεις when personal beings are intended (1 Cor. 15:24; cf. 2 Thess. 1:7)." Schreiner, *Romans*, 465. Douglas Moo observes that although the rulers are most likely evil, this cannot be stated with certainty from the text—though he further allows that "the occurrence of 'powers' with 'rulers' to denote spiritual beings suggests rather that some kind of spiritual forces are denoted here." Moo, *Epistle to the Romans*, 545–46.

46 Again, this does not negate persecution. Fitzmyer contends, "Spirits probably of different kind, order, or rank, such as both Jews and Gentiles of Paul's day often considered to be cosmic powers or supramundane rulers of this world. Because they are lined up like 'death' and 'life' or 'height' and 'depth,' which express extremes, it may be that these too are supposed to express extreme kinds or ranks of spirits. The pair *pasa archē kai pasa exousia* occurs also in 1 Cor 15:24, but they are here separated and used in the plural." Fitzmyer, *Romans*, 535. Cf. Col 1:16; Eph 1:21; 3:10; 6:1.

47 Moo believes θάνατος is likely referring to martyrdom, though he allows that "we must avoid introducing more precision in Paul's choice of terms than his evident rhetorical purpose would justify." Moo, *Epistle to the Romans*, 545.

48 Augustine of Hippo, *Sermons on Selected Lessons of the New Testament*, Vol. 2, Library of Fathers of the Holy Catholic Church (Oxford: J. H. Parker, 1845), 748. Emphasis in original.

this age—though the dawning of *the age to come* is evident in the defeat of death for the believer who is in Christ.[49]

The descriptions of death (θάνατος), angels (ἄγγελοι), and rulers (ἀρχαὶ) in Romans 8:38 illustrate the spiritual forces who are unable to bring accusation against the elect (Rom 8:33).[50] Though Satan is not specifically named in this passage, these evil forces are consistent with the spiritual manifestations of Satan at work in this age. Johnson observes the consistency of Paul's description of "powers" and "authorities" with the progression of satanic description throughout the New Testament:

> At the personal level, Paul speaks of Satan as a constant threat, one lying outside the community yet capable of causing damage within. More cosmically he envisages "powers and principalities" which, though conquered by the death and exaltation of Christ, remain capable of opposing believers, who must continue to do battle "against the cosmic powers of this present darkness, against the spiritual forces of evil in the heavenly places" (Eph 6:12).... John declares that "the whole world lies under the power of the evil one." Finally, the Book of Revelation imagines the world caught in a cosmic battle between Christ and Satan, the great beast waging ceaseless war against the saints in unholy alliance with the corrupt power of an empire that buys and sells human lives and brands them with its mark.[51]

Despite the threats of satanic assault present in the New Testament, Satan's power has been irrevocably curtailed in the work of Christ's first coming. Paul clarifies that Satan can no longer successfully bring accusation

---

49 Beale notes, "Believers have begun to be 'saved' from bondage to Satan and from final judgment through Christ's death and resurrection. Christ has come and suffered the end-time penalty of that sin, so the price has finally been paid. Nevertheless, it is clear that Satan is still active in blinding unbelievers (Acts 26:18, 2 Cor. 4:3–4) and attempting to influence God's people to sin or trying to harm them (2 Cor. 11:14; 23:7; Rev. 2:9–10)." Beale, *New Testament Biblical Theology*, 902.

50 This does not necessarily suggest delineating classes or levels of angelic beings, as Forbes observes: "Apocalyptic Judaism was fascinated by the differing duties and ranks of angels, and the organization and 'specialities' of demons, and, more particularly, with knowing the names and types of both angels and demons. These are subjects in which Paul displays no interest whatsoever." Forbes, "Paul's Principalities and Powers," 86.

51 Luke T. Johnson, "Powers & Principalities: The Devil Is No Joke," *Commonweal* 138.17 (2011): 14.

against the believer and that this prohibition extends to all satanic powers and authorities operative in this age.[52]

Loss of Satanic Authority over the Nations

The territory of the "nations" of this world is the battlefield on which the cosmic exorcism of Satan takes place. The spiritual space of the "nations" is a theme that runs across the canon, particularly coming into focus within passages dealing with God's covenantal commissioning of his people. The Edenic commission given to Adam and Eve (Gen 1:28) included the entire scope of the "earth" (הָאָרֶץ; τῆς γῆς LXX), an expansive terrain similar to what is found in later Great Commission language that included the "nations" (τῆς γῆς; Matt 28:18; cf. πάντα τὰ ἔθνη; Matt 28:19).[53]

Adam and Eve were first commissioned to expand God's glory among all creation, yet they sinned and failed in their task—subsequently being expelled from the Garden in the process.[54] Adam and Eve's expulsion was followed by the rebellious ingathering of the nations in Genesis 10–11, nations that were subsequently scattered by divine action. These nations shared a common lineage (Acts 17:26), yet they were spiritually foreign to the people of Israel: "When the Most High gave to the nations [גּוֹיִם; ἔθνη LXX] their inheritance, when he divided mankind, he fixed the borders of the peoples according to the number of the sons of God. But the Lord's portion is his people, Jacob his allotted heritage" (Deut 32:8–9).[55] Early on in the storyline of Scripture, the nations gather together in a show of self-reliance and idolatry at Shinar (and are divided,

---

52 Beale summarizes that Romans 8:38–39 "indicates that Satan and his angelic hosts are among those who had maliciously treated and wrongly accused Christians and whose slander will be nullified at the vindication of the final resurrection. No one, including Satan, can 'bring a charge against God's elect' now (Rom. 8:33 [see also Rev. 12:7–10]) or on the last day." Beale, *New Testament Biblical Theology*, 503–4.

53 On Matthew 28:18–20 as a recommissioning of Genesis 1:26–28 (cf. Daniel 7:14), see Beale, *Temple and the Church's Mission*, 175.

54 On the theme of vice-regency and divine commission, see Mathison, *From Age to Age*, 22ff; Alexander, *From Eden to the New Jerusalem*, 89ff; Dumbrell, *Search for Order*, 19; Dempster and Carson, *Dominion and Dynasty*, 59; Beale, *Temple and the Church's Mission*, 392.

55 Heiser, *Supernatural*, 81–82. Heiser's larger argument concerning "sons of God" is not in view in this present work.

called "Babel"), nations that are subsequently given over to darkness and deception (see Rom 1:18–25).[56]

Following Babel, God's exercise of authority over the nations is re-established through Abraham's family, with God promising Abraham a "great nation [לְגוֹי]" as an inheritance (Gen 12:2; 17:4). God's covenantal promises to Abraham that his seed would be a blessing to the nations is preserved in the New Testament (Rom 4:17–18; cf. Gen 17:5; Gal 3:6–9), where the promise of the seed ultimately finds fulfilment in Christ (Matt 2:13–15; cf. Hos 11:1). This theme of cosmic promise and fulfillment among the nations is recurrent throughout the biblical witness, where the nations are understood to be both under God's providential jurisdiction as well as constituting a group that is separate from God's people. God's people in the Old Testament retain a task of being set apart among the nations, though this mission receives far greater clarity with the advent of Christ and the commissioning of the New Testament church. The mission of God's people to the nations is directly tied to his authority over the nations—authority that Christ victoriously reclaimed in the work of his first coming. This theme that will now be briefly outlined in its New Testament context.

It is necessary to acknowledge that there is a sense in which authority is the eternal possession of Christ since God ultimately and perpetually holds authority over all things: "To the only God, our Savior, through Jesus Christ our Lord, be glory, majesty, dominion [κράτος], and authority [ἐξουσία], before all time [παντὸς τοῦ αἰῶνος] and now and forever [πάντας τοὺς αἰῶνας]" (Jude 25). God holds the authority (ἐξουσία) in "all the ages" (πάντας τοὺς αἰῶνας), both in *this age* and in *the age to come*. Yet there is a clear redemptive-historical theme of authority (ἐξουσία) in this age that lies in the power of Satan, an authority which infected the creation following the Garden and is inaugurally revoked in the first coming of Christ. This is the progressive testimony of the New Testament witness—Christ has reclaimed eschatological power and authority from the satanic

---

56 Heiser, *Unseen Realm*, 112–13. This current project is not arguing for "territorial spirits" in the theological vein of C. Peter Wagner, who postulates extra-biblical demonic hierarchies and demonic geographic assignments against which believers are to do battle. See C. Peter Wagner, *Territorial Spirits: Practical Strategies for How to Crush the Enemy Through Spiritual Warfare* (Shippensburg: Destiny Image, 2012); C. Peter Wagner, *Confronting the Powers: How the New Testament Church Experienced the Power of Strategic-Level Spiritual Warfare*, The Prayer Warrior Series (Ventura: Regal, 1996).

forces of this world and is bringing about the full consummation of that eschatological reclamation.

An eschatological transfer of power and authority in this world seems to have occurred in the first coming of Christ. Various passages have been examined that describe this transfer of authority, many of which use the language of a cosmic satanic exorcism that has occurred in this age. Along with the context of cosmic satanic exorcism, there is a corresponding transfer of authority over the nations. There is an eschatological expectation within the Old Testament that the Lord would bring judgment to the nations and spread the knowledge of the Lord (Isa 49), giving the nations to the Son (Ps 2:4–9) and bringing all the nations from the "ends of the earth" under the rule of Yahweh (Ps 22:27–28). The pages of the New Testament reveal that due to the victorious triumph of Christ, the Father has now given Christ authority over the nations—for both judgment and salvation, conquest and deliverance (Matt 25:31–33; John 5:25–29).[57] With the in-breaking advent of the age to come, Christ has been given authority over "all things [τὰ πάντα]" (Heb 1:2–3), authority over "all flesh" (John 17:2), and authority over an elect people chosen from among the nations (John 17:6, 16).[58] This is why John subsequently describes Christ as "Jesus Christ the faithful witness, the firstborn of the dead, and the ruler [ὁ ἄρχων] of kings of the earth [τῆς γῆς]" (Rev 1:5).

Christ's power and authority over the nations do not imply that all the nations will follow Him in fealty and repentance during *this age*—that is an expectation that is more appropriately associated with the full consummation of *the age to come* and the second coming (Isa 2:1–4; 65:17–25). Instead, Christ warns his followers that the nations will hate them, even as those same nations hated Christ (Matt 24:9, Rev 11:18). This consistent refrain of victory-through-suffering must be recognized properly, even amid Christ's epochal triumph over Satan in the work of his first coming. The nations continue to stand in opposition to God, prophetically reflecting the spiritual heritage of the ancient nations that rebelled against both God's commands and his commission (see Gen 10–11). The church in the New Testament continues to triumph through victorious suffering, following the Christological pattern through which its Head (Col 1:18) likewise

---

57 Köstenberger and Swain, *Father, Son and Spirit*, 35, 166.
58 Köstenberger and Swain, 169.

triumphed through the suffering of Calvary (Heb 12:2). Authority over the nations has been won by Christ, though these nations are still held in judgment for their ongoing sin and wickedness (see Lev 18:28–30; 20:23; Deut 29:24). An examination of two key passages regarding power and authority over the nations will serve to clarify the eschatological situation of Christ's authority.

Matthew 28:18–20

> AND JESUS CAME AND SAID TO THEM, "ALL AUTHORITY IN HEAVEN AND ON EARTH HAS BEEN GIVEN TO ME. GO THEREFORE AND MAKE DISCIPLES OF ALL NATIONS." (MATT 28:18)

The Great Commission text of Matthew 28:18–20 helps to illuminate the overlapping dynamics of satanic exorcism, kingdom advance, and authority in this age.[59] This commission begins with the victorious words of the risen Christ stating that He possesses "all authority" (ἐξουσία) both "in heaven [οὐρανῷ] and on earth [γῆς]" (Matt 28:18). The following command that he delivers likewise reflects this comprehensive authority, and the comprehensive nature of Christ's authority unites the successive sections of the commission together. O'Brien correctly observes that "the three sections [of the Great Commission] are tied together by the word 'all' (Greek *pas*): 'all authority', v. 18; 'all the nations', v. 19; 'all things', v. 20; 'always', v. 20. The three statements are bound together. They are all-embracing and all-inclusive."[60]

The "nations" of this age again form the backdrop of the commission given in Matthew 28. As opposed to referring to the Gentiles and pagan nations using the more generalized phrase τὰ ἔθνη, the commission addresses the broader area of πάντα τὰ ἔθνη, emphasizing that the totality of Jews and Gentiles are in view in the sweep of the commission's authority.[61] Based on the authority that Christ claims in his post-resurrection

---

59 Similar "commissional" passages are also found in Mark (16:14–18)*, Luke (24:44–49), and John (20:19–23), though these passages contain different thematic emphases reflective of the diverse human authorship and theological intention of the Gospels. See Edwin Luther Copeland, "Great Commission and Missions," *SwJT* 9.2 (1967): 79–80.

60 Peter T. O'Brien, "Great Commission of Matthew 28:18–20: A Missionary Mandate or Not?," *RTR* 35.3 (1976): 71.

61 Benjamin L. White, "The Eschatological Conversion of 'All the Nations' in Matthew 28.19-20: (Mis)Reading Matthew through Paul," *JSNT* 36.4 (2014): 355.

address, Christ calls his followers to make disciples of "all nations" (πάντα τὰ ἔθνη). Christ instructs his disciples to baptize and to teach his followers to observe all the things that he commanded, with the evident antecedent of "them" (αὐτοὺς) being "all the nations" (πάντα τὰ ἔθνη) that were referenced previously.[62] The nations that occupied the spiritual space outside the boundaries of Israel are now specifically included in the disciple-making task because a change of authority has transpired. An eschatological victory has been achieved. In the final post-resurrection address given to believers just prior to his ascension, Christ assured his disciples that all authority (πᾶσα ἐξουσία) in both the realm above and the realm below (οὐρανῷ καὶ τῆς γῆς) had been given to him (Ἐδόθη μοι).[63] All authority is in the power of Christ, and it is from that authority that he commissions his disciples to go into the world (John 20:21).

The commission given to the followers of Christ was to make disciples, thus both proclaiming the glory of God and fulfilling the canonical call to the nations (see Gen 1:26–28),[64] clarified by the instruction to make disciples of "all nations" (πάντα τὰ ἔθνη; Luke 24:44–47). The Great Commission breathed expansive scope and life into the commission given in Eden (Gen. 1:28), bringing creation into obedient worship of the sovereign Christ and reflecting his image amid the created order. Christ's work on the cross fulfilled the eschatological promises of the Old Testament (2 Cor 1:20) and ushered in a culminating period of redemptive history, "the

---

Krentz concludes here that the entire Gospel of Matthew is, therefore "a missionary text," though that is likely an overgeneralization. See Edgar Krentz, "'Make Disciples': Matthew on Evangelism," *CurTM* 33.1 (2006): 25.

62 Krentz, "Make Disciples," 6; Robert L. Thomas, "The Great Commission: What to Teach," *TMSJ* 21.1 (2010): 6.

63 The operative verb δίδωμι, here rendered in the aorist passive indicative (Ἐδόθη), reflects a past action with ongoing consequences.

64 Beale observes: "The resurrection of Jesus is a further development of the new creation (e.g., Matt. 27:57–28:15). Resurrection is a full-blown new creation notion, since the way the righteous were to enter in and become a part of the new heavens and earth is through God recreating their bodies. Jesus's claim that 'all authority has been given to Me in heaven and on earth' (Matt. 28:18) alludes to Daniel 7:13–14, which prophesied that the 'son of man' would be 'given authority, glory and sovereignty' forever. Then, as we noted at the introduction of this chapter, he immediately gives the disciples the so-called 'Great Commission.'... This edict not only continues the allusion to the Daniel 7 prophecy (v. 14, 'that all the peoples, nations, and men of every language might serve him'), but is itself a renewal of the Genesis 1:26–28 commission to Adam." Beale, *Temple and the Church's Mission*, 175.

end of the ages" (1 Cor 10:11). The Great Commission was fundamental for the immediate task of the disciples (cf. "made known to all nations," Rom 16:26; "proclaimed among the nations," 1 Tim 3:16), and it carried eschatological expectation in the scope of its command: "the gospel must first be proclaimed to all nations [*panta ta ethnē*]" (Mark 13:10; cf. Matt 24:14). The mission to the nations employed all-encompassing language: Christ possesses "all" authority over "all" nations and called his disciples to teach "all" things with the promise that his Spirit would be with them "always" (Matt 28:19–20).[65] Christ established both the means by which his followers' mission was to be carried out (He holds authority over the nations), as well as the manner in which the nations would be reached (the presence of "God-with-us" to the end of the age).[66]

Christ commissioned his disciples in his power during his earthly ministry (Luke 10:18–19), and he proclaimed that the works that the Spirit would accomplish through his disciples would exceed even their highest expectations (John 14:12). The New Testament commission entailed the territory of the world that lay in spiritual darkness, a territory that languished under the rule of the satanic rulers and authorities that were defeated in the conquering work of Christ. Satan's authority and power have been curtailed, and therefore (οὖν) the expansive call to the nations was issued. The nations are now invited through gospel preaching to partake in unity with the covenant community of believers.[67] The language used in the commissioning of Christ's followers is reflective of divine warrior language—God himself would fight for his people among the nations into which they were called to go.[68] The elect of the nations would be given as disciples of Christ, as the Lord gathers "all peoples" to himself (Isa 56:6–7; cf. Matt 21:13; 28:18–20).[69]

Christ's statement of divine authority in Matthew 28:18 is the enabling power that drives the Great Commission: "All authority in heaven and on

---

65 Krentz, "Make Disciples," 6.
66 O'Brien, "Great Commission of Matthew 28," 77.
67 White, "The Eschatological Conversion of 'all the Nations' in Matthew 28.19–20," 354.
68 Hertig, "Great Commission Revisited," 349–50.
69 White, "Eschatological Conversion of 'all the Nations' in Matthew 28.19-20," 354; Thomas, "Great Commission," 6.

earth has been given to me."⁷⁰ Christ proclaimed his authority (ἐξουσία) in a dramatic fashion, having been questioned by various earthly figures throughout the Gospel accounts before effectively establishing the basis by which the Great Commission should be carried out.⁷¹ Christ's statement of authority not only promised the power by which the commission is made possible, but it also assured Christ's presence with his followers throughout the course of their earthly task. The ongoing presence of Christ is, therefore, a monumental development in the eschatological narrative of Scripture. Christ did not leave his disciples to struggle alone—rather, he completed the Matthean theme of "God-with-us" in the climactic fulfillment of his promise.⁷²

Christ gave the commission as a redemptive-historical capstone of the inaugurated eschatological fulfillment that his death and resurrection brought to this world. The stated intent and scope of the commission is enabled by the authority of the resurrected Christ (Matt 28:18), which both ensures the success of the commission and confirms Christ's presence with his disciples who are engaged in this task. Christ, therefore, appears as the reigning and sovereign King, commissioning his followers to carry out the work of an earthly commission through which the Spirit reaps eternal spiritual victory. Hertig thus observes, "The climactic great commission text is an enthronement speech."⁷³ Christ's victorious claim of authority in this age includes the eschatological expectation of divinely orchestrated victory, alongside the persistent expectation of worldly opposition and persecution. The Great Commission is made possible by Christ's defeat of Satan, his curtailment of sin, and his inauguration of progressive renewal of the created order.

---

70 The term ἐξουσία in this passage reflects BDAG's third definitional grouping, carrying the sense of "the right to control or command, authority, absolute power, warrant." See BDAG, s.v. "ἐξουσία."

71 So also Hertig, "Great Commission Revisited," 345–46.

72 O'Brien, "Great Commission of Matthew 28," 77. Hertig likewise observes, "The worldwide mission task requires the assurance of God's presence because of the magnitude of the task. The Immanuel promise ('God with us') was first announced in Isaiah 7:14 during a time of desperation when the hearts of the people were shaken by the fear of ruthless enemy aggression. The God-with-us theme is utilized in the context of enemy threat (cf. Isaiah 8:8; Exodus 3:14). Divine presence in the Old Testament carries with it the import, 'I will fight for you.' In the same way, the mission of the disciples requires the presence of the risen Christ." Hertig, "The Great Commission Revisited," 349–50.

73 Hertig, "Great Commission Revisited," 343.

Luke 10:1–20

> BEHOLD, I HAVE GIVEN YOU AUTHORITY TO TREAD ON SERPENTS
> AND SCORPIONS, AND OVER ALL THE POWER OF THE ENEMY,
> AND NOTHING SHALL HURT YOU. (LUKE 10:19)

Returning to the key passage in Luke 10, there is a dynamic of spiritual authority in Satan's fall that warrants further examination. Satan's fall from heaven portrayed his eviction from a level of spiritual access that he no longer enjoys. Satan previously exercised a measure of access to the heavenly places (τοῦ οὐρανοῦ), yet he has now been expelled from that place of power and authority, in keeping with the advance of the kingdom (Luke 10:9, 11).[74] The former spiritual territory and authority wielded by Satan have been cut off and restricted from his control, even though curtailment of control is not synonymous with complete cessation of activity. Christ uses the imagery of witnessing Satan "falling" to explain his disciples' missional triumph over demonic forces (Luke 10:9,17).

This scene in Luke bears a striking resemblance to the scene later described in Revelation 12:7–12. In that later apocalyptic passage, the great dragon (Satan) is defeated and cast down from heaven, having his powers against the elect restricted and curtailed in direct consequence to Christ's victory.[75] In Luke's passage, Christ explained that his disciples had been able to perform demonic exorcisms as a direct consequence of the cosmic overthrow of Satan due to the victory being achieved in his earthly work.[76]

In Luke's narrative, the theme of authority emerges early on during the wilderness conflict between Christ and Satan, in which Satan offers to give Christ authority over the nations (Luke 4:5–8 // Matt 4:8–10 // Mark 1:12–13). Luke's record of the wilderness temptation includes the eschatological concept of the transference of authority in this age: "And [Satan] said to [Christ], 'To you I will give all this authority [ἐξουσίαν] and their glory, for it has been delivered [παραδέδοται / παραδίδωμι] to me, and I give [δίδωμι] it to whom I will. If you, then, will worship me, it will all [πᾶσα] be yours'" (Luke 4:6–7). Satan claimed to exercise a measure of authority in the world—a continuing degree of power in this age that continued into

---

74 Job 1:6 is an example of a relevant Old Testament text regarding Satan's activity before the throne of God in the heavenly realms.
75 See Canoy, "Time and Space, Satan," 254ff.
76 See Ladd, *Presence of the Future*, 156.

the advent of Christ's first coming. Christ did not dispute Satan's claim of possessing authority over the kingdoms of this age,[77] though his response to this temptation rejected every satanic offer of authority by referring to God's greater authority in Scripture (Luke 4:4, 8, 12; cf. Deut 6:13).

As proof of this inaugurated victory, Christ demonstrated a significant eschatological reversal, one that emerges throughout the public ministry of his first coming. While Satan offered to "give" (δώσω / δίδωμι) Christ the authority in this world (Luke 4:6), the victory of Christ's first coming was made evident when he victoriously "gave" (δέδωκα / δίδωμι) his disciples authority over "the enemy" (i.e., Satan himself; Luke 10:19). Christ subsequently sent the disciples on an eschatological mission of acting as God's representatives throughout the world: "Behold, I have given you authority [ἐξουσίαν] to tread on serpents [ὄφις, cf. Gen 3:14 LXX] and scorpions and over all the power [δύναμιν] of the enemy, and nothing shall hurt you" (Luke 10:19).[78] The power that Christ gave to the disciples was previously brandished by Satan in the wilderness, while Satan's defeat and the work of Christ's first coming achieved his exorcism in this age. As Christ victoriously emerged in the accomplishment of his earthly work, he embodied the Old Testament theme of the divine warrior by accomplishing victory over Satan and his forces.

The consequences of Christ's authority in this age are clarified in the surrounding context of this event's position in redemptive history. Christ's first coming resulted in the cosmic exorcism of the demonic ruler of this world, attendant with Christ receiving divine authority over the nations and kingdoms of this world. Christ observed that comprehensive authority "has been given to me" (Ἐδόθη μοι; Matt 28:18), in effect a reversal of the previous reality that similar authority had been given to Satan (ἐμοὶ παραδέδοται; Luke 4:6). Christ's declared purpose in the first coming was to "give" (δοῦναι / δίδωμι) his life for the redemption of many (Mark 10:45), giving himself to redeem lost sinners (ἔδωκεν / δίδωμι; Titus 2:14) and deliver the redeemed from the present evil age (δόντος / δίδωμι; Gal 1:3–4). Just as Christ gave himself for the redemption of a people, so the

---

77 Joel B. Green, *Gospel of Luke*, NICNT (Grand Rapids: Eerdmans, 1997), 194; Stein, *Luke*, 147. Contra William Hendriksen, *Luke: New Testament Commentary* (Grand Rapids: Baker Books, 1978), 236.

78 Bruce A. Ware, *Father, Son, and Holy Spirit: Relationships, Roles, and Relevance* (Wheaton, IL: Crossway, 2005), 132–33; Hoekema, *Created in God's Image*.

authority of this world was accordingly given to him to rule in this age. This language is reflective of the Danielic Son of Man, who "was given (ἐδόθη / δίδωμι; LXX) dominion and glory and a kingdom, that all peoples, nations, and languages should serve him" (Dan 7:13–14).[79] It is no surprise that Christ self-identifies as the Son of Man in the Gospels—the eschatological fulfillment to whom all nations and authority are achieved in his victory-through-suffering.[80]

In response to the eschatological development of authority given to Christ, Christ then proclaims the preservation of his people (Matt 16:18) and the ingathering of disciples from all nations (πάντα τὰ ἔθνη; Matt 28:18–20). The commission of Matthew 28 is preceded by the mission of the disciples in Luke 10, though the theological emphases are similar— Christ's followers are given the authority in this age that he has likewise been given and are subsequently guaranteed dominion over the satanic forces in this world. Because Christ now has authority, the nations are prevented from prematurely rising in satanic rebellion against Christ and his church (Rev 12:9–10; 2 Thess 2:6–7) until the appointed time of the final judgment and second coming (Rev 20:7–10). It is in the context of this divine providence that Christ issues the Great Commission to his disciples, reflecting his authority over the nations (Matt 28:18–19) and assuring them of his ongoing presence with them in their task (Matt 28:20).[81] Christ has been given (δέδωκέν; John 10:29) a particular people, and has subsequently given to that particular people (δέδωκα; Luke 10:19) authority to exercise over the nations and evil forces of this age (Luke 10:1ff.; cf. Acts 4:23–31).

What then has changed in the satanic exercise of authority in this age? Christ's victorious first coming was a spiritual conquest over the forces of evil, aptly described using the militaristic terms of "disarming" and "triumphing" (ἀπεκδυσάμενος; θριαμβεύσας)[82] over the forces of Satan in this

---

79 Again, see discussion of the messianic context of this passage in Miller, *Daniel*, 210; Carl Friedrich Keil and Franz Delitzsch, *Commentary on the Old Testament*, vol. 9 (Peabody, MA: Hendrickson, 1996), 645.
80 Beale, *Redemptive Reversals*, 99–100. "Son of Man" is Jesus's favorite self-designation, occurring thirty times in Matthew, fifteen times in Mark, twenty-five times in Luke, twelve times in John; James Stalker, "Son of Man, The (ὁ υἱὸς τοῦ ἀνθρώπου, *ho huiós toú anthrōpou*)," in *ISBE* 5:2829; *ODCC*, s.v. "Son of Man."
81 Hoekema, *Bible and the Future*, 228; Riddlebarger, *Case for Amillennialism*, 211.
82 BDAG, s.v. "ἀπεκδύομαι" and "θριαμβεύω."

world (Col 2:15). Christ's authority over the nations means that the advance of the kingdom cannot be thwarted, and final eschatological rebellion is restrained—Satanic power over the nations is curtailed in this respect. Christ has triumphed over the satanic rulers and powers of the nations in this age, and he now divinely reigns over the church (Eph 1:20–23). The satanic ruler of this world has been cast out (John 12:31; Matt 12:22–32), and all authority over this world has been given to Christ (Matt 28:18).

A number of discourses in the Gospels are filled with earthly rulers who question Christ's authority (e.g., Luke 20:2), yet soon after such encounters, Christ is given all authority over the nations, establishing the fulfillment of Old Testament covenantal promises (πάντα τὰ ἔθνη, cf. Gen 18:18 and 22:18 LXX).[83] Christ has achieved authority and final victory (yet eschatologically penultimate; cf. Isa 65:17–25; Rev 11:15), and he now gathers a people to himself from among the nations while satanic evil is restrained from preventing this ingathering (Ps 2:8; cf. Rev 5:9; 7:9). Christ's authority over the nations (Rev 1:7; 2:26) is manifest to exercise his iron rod of judgment: "From his mouth comes a sharp sword with which to strike down the nations [τὰ ἔθνη]" (Rev 19:15). Christ thus triumphantly and eternally establishes his church amid the nations (Matt 16:18),[84] even while this world still hates Christ's followers as it likewise hated Christ (Matt 24:9; Rev 11:18).

Christ's eschatological authority over the nations results in the spread of the glory of God in this age (cf. Ps 96:1–3), as the nations will be gathered together in response to the light of Christ (Dan 7:13–14; cf. Ps 82).[85] God's house is described as a place of prayer for the nations (Mark 11:17), and the consummated New Jerusalem will convey God's healing provision for the nations (Rev 22:2). Christ's exorcism of Satan has provided an inaugurated taste of the eschatological freedom of the nations, as all power in this age has been established in Christ (Matt 28:18–20), and it is in that divine eschatological power that Christ commissions his followers into the world (Luke 10:1–20).

---

83 O'Brien, "Great Commission of Matthew 28," 74–77.
84 Heiser describes this as a reclamation of sacred space. See Heiser, *Supernatural*, 113.
85 See Wright's discussion of Psalm 82 in N. T. Wright, *The New Testament and the People of God*, 1st North Am. ed. (Minneapolis: Fortress, 1992), 56–57, 90.

Satanic Deception as Revolt

Satanic deception is essentially a revolt against God. When successful, satanic deception incurs the ultimate destruction of those who are deceived, because satanic deception is a revolt against the one true God who has revealed himself to man. When satanic deception is left unrestrained by divine permission (see Rev 20:3, 8), the inevitable result is a level of creaturely revolt that incurs the uncompromising wrath of God.[86] Therefore, the divine prevention of satanic deception is a key component of the New Testament paradigm of satanic exorcism. Christ conquered and exorcised Satan in the victory of his first coming, and the restraint of satanic deception in this age is a key component for understanding the effects of satanic exorcism. Deception is a quality that is inseparable from Satan, whom John calls "the deceiving one"—a spiritually seducing figure who habitually seeks the destruction of others.[87] Following a definitional examination of the concept of deception, the present work will observe the restraint of satanic deception in two closely related New Testament passages (2 Thess 2:6–7; Rev 20:1–3).

Deception is a lie that is proffered in place of the truth. The concept of deception is typically rendered in the Greek by either πλανάω (see Rev 20:3, 8; Matt 24:4–5) or ἀπατάω—though πλανάω is used far more frequently, especially in eschatological passages.[88] One sense of πλανάω refers to "leading astray" or "deceiving," which seems to be its primary sense in context in the key passage in Revelation 20.[89] The common Hebrew equivalent for πλανάω is העת (tāʿâh), a term that in its LXX translation often refers to "being led astray" and "deceived" (see Deut 27:18) and is tied closely to the concept of human rebellion against God (cf. πλανῆσαί, Deut 13:5 LXX).[90] The New Testament conception of deception (πλανάω/ἀπατάω)

---

[86] The idea of "revolt" in connection with deception appears in Ladd, *Commentary on the Revelation of John*, 262.

[87] Harris notes about Revelation 12:9: "The word 'deceives' renders a present active participle (ὁ πλανῶν), which speaks of deception that is 'a continuous action which has become ... habitual.' Satan is involved in much more than random occurrences; he deceives because it is part of his personality to do so." Harris, "Satan's Work as a Deceiver," 190.

[88] Harris, "Satan's Work as a Deceiver," 193–95. The term ἀπατάω occurs in Ephesians 5:6, 1 Timothy 2:14, and James 1:26.

[89] BDAG, s.v. "πλανάω."

[90] *LALGNT*, s.v. "πλανάω"; Jones, "Apostasy." In the LXX, העת occurs sixteen times, while הגש occurs another five times.

involves a destructive lie, one that stands in opposition to God's revealed truth, and one that inexorably leads to the destruction of those who are deceived.[91]

Matthew's Gospel warns of false "Christs" and false prophets who "lead astray" (πλανήσῃ; Matt 24:4–5, 11, 24) those who are being deceived. Believers are warned against satanic deception that leads to destruction (ἐξαπατήσῃ; 2 Thess 2:3), just as the serpent deceived Eve in the garden to their mutual destruction (ἐξηπάτησεν 2 Cor 11:3, ἠπατήθη / ἐξαπατηθεῖσα in 1 Tim 2:14). The satanic quality of deception is also exercised in the New Testament by demonic spirits (see 1 Tim 4:1–2; 1 John 4:1),[92] as certain elements within early Judaism anticipated that such activity would bring about immense conflict within the covenant community in the last days (Dan 11:30–45, cf. 2 Thess 2:3).[93] Paul, therefore, warns believers to beware of those who "deceive [ἐξαπατῶσι] the hearts of the naive" (Rom 16:18), as satanic deception is recognized as "one of the primary means" Satan utilizes to attack humanity.[94]

Particularly in John's writings, the unbelieving crowds accused Christ of deceiving the people (πλανᾷ; John 7:12), and the Pharisees accused those sympathetic to Christ of likewise being deceived (πεπλάνησθε; John 7:47). John warned believers against deceiving themselves (πλανῶμεν; 1 John 1:8) and warned believers to beware of those who actively seek to deceive others (πλανώντων, 1 John 2:26; πλανάτω, 1 John 3:7). Deception is a key dynamic throughout Revelation—Jezebel deceived Christ's servants (πλανᾷ; Rev 2:20), Babylon was judged for deceiving the nations of this world (ἐπλανήθησαν; Rev 18:23), and the dragon is consistently described as a great deceiver of the world (ὁ πλανῶν, Rev 12:9) along with those he gives power to, such as the second beast (πλανᾷ; Rev 13:14) and the false prophet (ἐπλάνησεν; Rev 19:20). Satan is restricted from deceiving the nations

---

91 Gregory H. Harris, "Does God Deceive?: The 'Deluding Influence' of Second Thessalonians 2:11," *TMSJ* 16.1 (2005): 74.

92 Harris, "Satan's Work as a Deceiver," 74. See also "Falsch, Falschheit," in *Calwer Biblical Lexicon*, ed. Zeller, 175.

93 Beale, *New Testament Biblical Theology*, 156, 190, 202. See also Vos, *Pauline Eschatology*, 111.

94 On Rom 16, see Beale, *New Testament Biblical Theology*, 219, 221–22. On deception as a satanic method, see Erickson, *Christian Theology*, 448. Erickson references 2 Cor 4:4 and 1 Thess 2:18 as deception (alongside 2 Cor 11:14–15), while Rev 12:9 and 20:8, 10 are also referenced.

(πλανήσῃ; Rev 20:3) during the thousand years, but his eventual release results in the abrupt deception of all the nations of the earth (πλανῆσαι, Rev 20:8; ὁ πλανῶν, Rev 20:10).

2 Thessalonians 2

> AND YOU KNOW WHAT IS RESTRAINING HIM NOW SO THAT HE MAY BE REVEALED IN HIS TIME. FOR THE MYSTERY OF LAWLESSNESS IS ALREADY AT WORK. ONLY HE WHO NOW RESTRAINS IT WILL DO SO UNTIL HE IS OUT OF THE WAY. (2 THESS 2:6–7)

Paul's second letter to the Thessalonian church begins with words of comfort and encouragement offered to believers during a time of reflection on final things.[95] Paul gives thanks for the faith of the Thessalonians (2 Thess 1:3) and assures them that those who persecute them will not escape the Lord's judgment (1:6–9). Beyond the letter's opening remarks and encouragements in the first chapter, the following eschatological content of the letter is notoriously difficult.[96] In 2 Thessalonians 2, Paul refers to a spiritual force that he describes as "the mystery of lawlessness" (2:6–7), an entity that operates alongside (or in conjunction with) an ominous figure he refers to as "the man of lawlessness" (2:3, 8–9). This coming "lawlessness" (τῆς ἀνομίας; 2:7) is associated in this discourse with the eschatological last days, and it stands in direct opposition to the covenantal God (i.e., the God of lawgiving). Paul warns the Thessalonian church that this "man of lawlessness" will come in the last days in opposition to God (2:3–4), yet he also asserts that the "mystery of lawlessness" is "already at work" in this age (2:7). This "lawlessness" (τῆς ἀνομίας) is most palpably revealed in the form of a satanic figure who opposes the true worship of God, even while attempting to claim God's glory for himself (2:3–4).[97]

---

95 Michael D. Martin, *1, 2 Thessalonians*, NAC (Nashville: Broadman & Holman, 1995); Kevin J. Vanhoozer, Daniel Treier, and N. T. Wright, eds., *Theological Interpretation of the New Testament: A Book-by-Book Survey* (Grand Rapids: Baker Academic, 2008), 155ff.

96 Mathison observes, "The second chapter of Paul's second epistle to the Thessalonians contains one of the most difficult eschatological texts in all of Scripture. There are as many different interpretations, it seems, as there are interpreters, and even those who are in agreement concerning certain basic elements of the text disagree on secondary details." Mathison, *From Age to Age*, 519..

97 Compare the use of the term "lawlessness" (τὴν ἀνομίαν) in Matthew 24:12. See Beale, *New Testament Biblical Theology*, 203.

There are many distinct similarities between the "man of lawlessness" in 2 Thessalonians 2 and the "antichrist" figure of 1 John (ἀντίχριστος; 1 John 2:18). Just as John expected his readers to be alert for the coming of the antichrist (1 John 2:18; cf. 2:22, 4:3; 2 John 7), so too Paul reminds his Thessalonian readers that they previously received instruction and warning about the coming of the man of lawlessness (2:5). Many scholars identify this mysterious figure as a personified antichrist in John's epistles,[98] if not further identifying him with the Dragon of John's Apocalypse as well.[99] Although Paul does not specifically use the term ἀντίχριστος in the letter to the Thessalonians, the cryptic "man of lawlessness" occupies a similar eschatological role as the final and ultimate figure of opposition to Christ in the last days, one who directly precedes the final judgment and the consummated eternal state. Similar to the Johannine ἀντίχριστος, the Pauline "man of lawlessness" will speak words against the one true God and will seek to oppress and destroy the people of God in this age (cf. Dan 7:25; 11:36).[100]

Noting the eschatological similarities mentioned above, Beale identifies the Pauline "man of lawlessness" as the Johannine ἀντίχριστος and identifies the "mystery" in the passage as the mysterious presence of the spirit of antichrist, which is already at work in the world, even while the ultimate personification of antichrist is yet to come.[101] Therefore, the "mystery" is that the antichrist can be active in spirit while not yet (or possibly at all)

---

98 See Eugene E. Carpenter and Philip W. Comfort, *Holman Treasury of Key Bible Words: 200 Greek and 200 Hebrew Words Defined and Explained* (Nashville: Broadman & Holman, 2000), 226.

99 See Beale, *New Testament Biblical Theology*, 527. Hobert Farrell and Donald Lake draw attention to the parallel between the man of lawlessness and the antichrist because of their similar eschatological roles: "Both the apostle Paul and John saw present events as leading up to the events of the future. Instructing the church at Thessalonica about the second coming of Christ (2 Thess 2:1–12), Paul stressed that the appearance and rebellion of the man of lawlessness must occur beforehand. That man would oppose the worship of any gods or God and even proclaim himself to be God (2 Thess 2:4). He would subsequently be destroyed by Christ at his return (2 Thess 2:8)—an indication that those events are set in the final days of history." Hobert K. Farrell and Donald M. Lake, "Antichrist," in *Baker Encyclopedia of the Bible*, eds. Walter A. Elwell and Barry J. Beitzel (Grand Rapids: Baker Books, 1988), 1:119.

100 Hoekema, *Bible and the Future*, 154.

101 Beale, *New Testament Biblical Theology*, 943–44, 953. Sam Storms notes that he would not be convinced of a personified eschatological antichrist were it not for this passage in 2 Thessalonians chapter 2. Storms, *Kingdom Come*, 521.

present in the flesh. Within this context, Paul describes this satanic force of lawless opposition to Christ as being "restrained" (κατέχων). The nature of this restraint is ambiguous at first glance, yet Paul again qualifies this restraint as the result of the work of Christ that is curtailing the eschatological powers previously held by Satan.[102] It is also a current and ongoing restraint—this lawlessness is "now" (νῦν/ἄρτι; 2:6, 7) restrained.[103] Beale observes: "The death and resurrection of Christ have banished the devil from this privileged place and prosecutorial role formerly granted him by God. This is because Christ's death was the penalty that God exacted for the sins of all those who were saved by faith."[104] The atoning work of Christ in the salvation of the elect has likewise brought an eviction of the satanic enemy in this age.

Satan's restraint that is resultant from the work of Christ in no way negates his responsibility and culpability for the vicious attacks that he makes upon the people of God.[105] Satan previously enjoyed the ability to levy charges of sin and unfaithfulness against the people of God, even attempting to impugn God's character (especially his justice and holiness) in the process. Particularly in Second Thessalonians, Paul describes Satan's work as "lawlessness" that will yet be revealed fully—Satan opposes the law and rule of God through devious subterfuge, yet his deceptions and lawlessness are restrained and will soon be laid bare. Satan's lawlessness is restrained from prematurely hastening the final eschatological conflict that precedes

---

102 Note that Paul previously used the term "restrain" or "hold fast" (κατέχετε, lemma κατέχω) in 1 Thessalonians 5:21: "Hold fast what is good."

103 The KJV incorrectly applies this temporal ἄρτι to the Thessalonians' knowledge, yet its referent is certainly the restraint itself. See Storms, *Kingdom Come*, 536–37; Gordon D. Fee, *The First and Second Letters to the Thessalonians*, NICNT (Grand Rapids: Eerdmans, 2009), 287.

104 The position temporarily enjoyed by Satan is by divine permission and is reclaimed in God's right timing. Beale, *New Testament Biblical Theology*, 217. Mathison stipulates that it is the Holy Spirit who restrains, contra Beale. Mathison, *From Age to Age*, 528n105. Storms helpfully concludes: "Whatever view one finally embraces, it seems reasonable to conclude that the ultimate origin of this restraining influence is God." Storms, *Kingdom Come*, 535.

105 Beale observes the parallel pictures of Satan's restraint in both 2 Thessalonians 2 and Revelation 12:"Satan's wrath is directed toward the believing community on earth during the interadvent [church] period more than in previous ages. [...] The 'place' that the devil lost (Rev. 12:8: 'there was no longer a place found for them in heaven') was his hitherto privileged place of accusation, formerly granted him by God. His accusations throughout pre-Christian times were ceaseless." Beale, *New Testament Biblical Theology*, 216–17.

the *parousia*—a concept alluded to here through the "man of lawlessness" that is clarified later in the New Testament. Even though Satan's hostility is fierce, his powers have been curtailed by the work of Christ. Satan's ongoing activity explains the prevailing theme of deception in 2 Thessalonians 2, as Paul warns believers not to be deceived (ἐξαπατήσῃ / ἐξαπατάω; 2 Thess 2:3) while the "coming of the lawless one" (2:9) is characterized by deception (ἀπάτη; 2:10).[106] Following the warnings against evil deception, Paul describes a final delusion that would be sent by God (πλάνης / πλάνη; 2:11) against those who did not believe the truth and had pleasure in unrighteousness, again coinciding with the theme of culminating judgment.[107]

Satan remains active in *this age*, yet his powers of lawlessness are restrained due to the inauguration of the *age to come*.[108] Paul, therefore, warns the Thessalonians to beware of the workings of satanic lawlessness, even when there is a satanic subterfuge (μυστήριον; 2 Thess 2:7). Paul similarly warned the Corinthian church that lawless men would disguise themselves even as followers of Christ (2 Cor 11:13, 15), just as Satan disguises himself as an angel of light (2 Cor 11:14).[109] Paul is building on a theme developed in First and Second Thessalonians of eschatological comfort and hope amid suffering. In 1 Thessalonians 4, Paul reassures the Thessalonian church regarding the state of their loved ones who had passed away before them. In 1 Thessalonians 5, Paul introduces the hope and expectation of the "day of the Lord," a day which is yet coming and for which the elect are to wait in watchful expectation. When the age to come arrives in full on the "day of the Lord," believers' hope is that they will bear witness to the presence of the Lord's second advent. Paul has described this as the Lord's coming (παρουσία—1 Thess 4:15; 2 Thess 2:1), which is commonly described as

---

106 Harris contends: "It is fitting that Scripture presents Satan at both the first and last efforts to deceive mankind, because ultimately all religious deception is traceable to Satan, 'the serpent of old .... who deceives the whole world' (Rev 12:9)." Harris, "Does God Deceive?," 73. Compare also John 8:44; 2 Cor 11:3; 1 Tim 2:14.

107 Harris notes: "Second Thess 2:11 is of special interest in discussions of deception during that future time, because God is the agent who sends the 'deluding influence' (*energeian planēs*) among unbelievers. Two Old Testament passages which present God as in some way deceiving are analogous to God's future activity of this kind, 1 Kgs 22:22 and Ezek 14:9." Harris, "Does God Deceive?," 73.

108 Vos, *Pauline Eschatology*, 12.

109 See Beale, *New Testament Biblical Theology*, 201–2.

the *parousia*.¹¹⁰ After Satan's restraint is lifted, the events portrayed which precede (and coincide with) the *parousia* take place.

In effect, Satan's restraint coincides with the postponement of the consummation of this age—that is to say, Satan is restrained from prematurely hastening the final eschatological conflict before its appointed time. Satan is now hampered in his scope of activity, yet he is so with the qualification "that he may be revealed in his time" (2 Thess 2:6). Satan's subterfuge is limited, and his time is short—but he will be unleashed for one last attack toward the end of human history.

Revelation 20

> Then I saw an angel coming down from heaven, holding in his hand the key to the bottomless pit and a great chain. And he seized the dragon, that ancient serpent, who is the devil and Satan, and bound him for a thousand years, and threw him into the pit, and shut it and sealed it over him, so that he might not deceive the nations any longer, until the thousand years were ended. After that he must be released for a little while. (Rev 20:1–3)

One final critical passage to consider that describes Satan's inability to deceive the nations occurs in Revelation 20. Revelation serves as a capstone that secures and holds together many eschatological stones, as it serves as a theological locus where various redemptive threads coalesce.¹¹¹ Despite the difficulties in navigating the divergent interpretations of this book (and this chapter in particular), Storms observes that "the book of Revelation is believed by most to be the key to biblical eschatology."¹¹²

Several interpretive issues arise in Revelation 20, so a brief note is in order concerning the particular methodology utilized here to interpret this passage. The interpretive method followed in this study of Revelation follows what is commonly designated progressive parallelism or a recapitulation

---

110 See detailed discussion on this topic in Storms, *Kingdom Come*, 523ff.
111 Mathison views the book of Revelation as the capstone of Scripture, where all its redemptive threads come together. Mathison, *From Age to Age*, 641. The Apocalypse of John (Ἀποκαλυψις Ιωαννου), introduced as the Apocalypse of Jesus Christ (Ἀποκάλυψις Ἰησοῦ Χριστοῦ) in 1:1, is typically titled "[the] Revelation" in the Christian canon.
112 Its interpretation, however, should be consistent and congruous with the eschatological content that precedes it. Storms, *Kingdom Come*, 387.

reading of the text—an approach that recognizes that there are seven progressive, parallel sections operating within the book of Revelation that describe the church age from various perspectives. This methodology typically observes parallel depictions in the general sections of Revelation chapters 1–3 (the seven churches), chapters 4–7 (the seven seals), chapters 8–11 (the seven trumpets), chapters 12–14 (the woman and the dragon), chapters 15–16 (the seven bowls), chapters 17–19 (the fall of Babylon), and chapters 20–22 (the eternal state).[113] (See Figure 6.)

PROGRESSIVE PARALLELISM/RECAPITULATION IN JOHN'S APOCALYPSE[114]

1st Coming of Christ							2nd Coming of Christ
Seals	1	2	3	4	5	6	7
Trumpets	1	2	3	4	5	6	7
Bowls	1	2	3	4	5	6	7

FIGURE 6

Interpreted through the recapitulation perspective, Revelation 20 describes Satan's binding at the first coming of Christ (20:1–3) as well as his final release, defeat, and eternal exorcism to the lake of fire (20:7–10). Using rather broad strokes, the chain of symbolic apocalyptic depictions is most important in this passage's interpretation, while a wooden chronological sense of time persistently fails to explain the text adequately.[115] Revelation 20 is thus closely tied to development from the previous three chapters, encapsulating the narrative of Satan's inaugurated and

---

113 Hoekema, *Bible and the Future*, 223–25; Hendriksen, *More Than Conquerors*, 22–64. Storms maintains that Hendriksen represents "strict parallelism" while Storms (cf. Beale) advocates for more "progressive parallelism," though the differences for our purposes are insignificant (primarily concerning the relationship between the trumpets and the bowls). See Storms, *Kingdom Come*, 396–402; Beale, *Book of Revelation*, 48.

114 This chart is presented in Storms, *Kingdom Come*, 402.

115 The visionary and symbolic levels must not be confused with the historical level, as more wooden literal interpretations often insist on doing. Beale with Campbell, *Revelation*, 421. Poythress observes four levels of interpretation here: linguistic, visionary, referential, and symbolic. Vern S Poythress, "Genre and Hermeneutics in Rev 20:1–6," *JETS* 36.1 (1993): 41–54; Storms, *Kingdom Come*, 408.

consummated defeats in a manner that further clarifies the narratives in chapters 16 and chapters 17–19.[116] A close and consistent reading of the text leads to understanding Revelation 20:1–6 as a description of the entire New Testament church age, describing the events that transpire between Christ's first and second coming.[117]

The concept of the "millennium," or the "thousand years" (χίλια ἔτη), is mentioned in each of six successive verses in Revelation 20 (vv. 2–7) in referring to the duration of Satan's binding.[118] As it impacts the theme of eschatological satanic defeat, the "millennium" referenced in Revelation 20 is best regarded as the period that "stands for the whole time between the life of Jesus on earth and his second coming."[119] The χίλια ἔτη that John refers to is a lengthy period of time, following Christ's first coming and preceding his second coming, during which Satan is bound as a result of the satanic exorcism accomplished in Christ's earthly ministry.

Much scholarly debate surrounds the interpretation of Revelation 20, though it bears noting that a recognition of the symbolism at work in this

---

116 Beale observes: "This chapter [20], though we have treated it as a separate section, is closely related literarily to the previous major segment extending from 17:1 to 19:21. That section dealt with the announcement of the fall of Babylon at the end of time (ch. 17), the elaboration of Babylon's fall, especially the responses drawn forth both from unredeemed and redeemed multitudes (18:1–19:10), and Christ's judgment of the ungodly world forces at the end of history (19:11–21). Our comments will argue that 20:1–6 refers to the course of the church age, which temporally *precedes* the narration of final judgment in chs. 17–19, while, on the other hand, 20:7–15 recapitulates the description of final judgment in 19:11–21 (as well as 16:14–21)." Beale with Campbell, *Revelation*, 420.
117 At the same time, further discussions of chiliasm are beyond the scope of this current work. Chiliasm, or millennialism (from the Gk χίλια), is extremely nuanced. For example, Lorraine Boettner and B. B. Warfield (both postmillennial) understand this passage in a manner traditionally held to be "amillennial." See Hoekema, *Bible and the Future*, 179. For a thorough presentation of the historic premillennial position on this passage, see Ladd, *Commentary on the Revelation of John*, 259ff. Ladd's presentation is an accepted "eclectic" approach to Revelation. See also Mathison, *From Age to Age*, 648–49.
118 The phrase χίλια ἔτη is also found in a symbolic reference in 2 Peter 3:8: "But do not overlook this one fact, beloved, that with the Lord one day is as a thousand years [χίλια ἔτη], and a thousand years [χίλια ἔτη] as one day."
119 Morris, *Revelation*, 222–23; Beale with Campbell, *Revelation*, 421; cf. Fee, *Revelation*, 281–282; contra Ladd, who states, "This suggests that this binding [Rev 20:3] is different from the binding of Satan accomplished by our Lord in his earthly ministry; the latter had special reference to demon exorcision [*sic*] by which individuals were delivered from satanic bondage (Matt. 12:28–29)." Ladd, *Commentary on the Revelation of John*, 262.

passage does not diminish the veracity of the text. Sam Storms aptly notes, "We must also be careful to remember that simply because something is portrayed in figurative or non-literal terms does not mean it is less truthful or less real. In other words, *literal* is not synonymous with *true* nor is *symbolic* synonymous with *false* or *mythological*."[120] The thousand-year period denotes an extensive period of time, in this case encompassing the entirety of the church age: "One thousand is the cube of ten, the number of completeness. We have seen it used over and over again in this book to denote completeness of some sort and John is surely saying here that Satan is bound for the complete time that God has determined."[121] Recognizing Satan's binding during the church age is associated with the perspective of inaugurated eschatology—there are aspects of last things (such as satanic defeat) that have been inaugurated in Christ's first coming, yet these things remain to be consummated ultimately in his second coming.[122]

The passage contained in the opening verses of Revelation 20 depicts (in apocalyptic vocabulary) Satan being restrained or bound (ἔδησεν)[123] by an angel of the Lord. As Gordon Fee notes, John clearly identifies Satan as the restrained party, using eschatological language to depict him:

> So the angel then seized the dragon, who is now also given his other biblical designations, beginning with that in Eden, and thus the reason for the imagery of a dragon, who first appeared in John's narrative in chapters 12 and 13, beginning with 12:3. The dragon, of course, as noted earlier, is none other than that ancient serpent who makes his first appearance in the biblical narrative in Genesis 3:1, as the malevolent opponent of God and therefore of all that is good. But for the sake of his Gentile readers, who may miss the imagery,

---

120 Storms, *Kingdom Come*, 410. Emphasis in original.
121 Morris, *Revelation*, 224. Fee agrees with Morris's appraisal of Revelation 20:1–6: "John's major concern here is not with time as such, but with the special place God has reserved for those who have been killed by the state simply because they were followers of the once slain, now risen Lamb. In any case, John's obvious concern lies with the second paragraph (vv. 4–6), and thus not with the time period as such." Fee, *Revelation*, 282.
122 This perspective is held by both those with amillennial and postmillennial perspectives, although the variances within both views are extensive. Common to all amillennial views is the foundational paradox of *already/not-yet*. See Beale, *Revelation*, 420; Morris, *Revelation*, 223; Augustine, *City of God*, 20.486; 20.3–29.
123 This verb conveys the sense of "binding" or "imprisoning". See BDAG, s.v. "δέω" (cf. Matt 12:29).

John at this point makes sure that no reader will mistake the dragon's identity. Thus recalling the identifiers in 12:9, the great enemy of humankind is further designated by his descriptive title, the devil, and then by his name, Satan.[124]

Having thus seized Satan (identified using all four of Revelation's descriptive titles for him), the angel restrains him for "a thousand years" (χίλια ἔτη). Having traced this concept of satanic defeat across the New Testament witness, a correct interpretation of the binding of Satan in Revelation 20 should bear an eschatological resemblance to what has been penned before it. Christ's triumphant victory in his first coming accomplished a true and lasting defeat of Satan—a satanic exorcism that bears cosmic, ongoing results.[125] Revelation 20 describes Satan as having been seized by "an angel" (ἄγγελον; Rev 20:1) describing the same satanic exorcism accomplished by the angel Michael in the corresponding description in Revelation 12 (ὁ Μιχαὴλ καὶ οἱ ἄγγελοι αὐτοῦ; Rev 12:7). Satan has been seized by a righteous angelic force on behalf of Christ, he has been bound and sealed, and he has been kept restrained for the entirety of the church age.[126]

The extent and nature of Satan's binding warrants further clarification. Satan is said to have been restrained or bound (ἔδησεν) in the bottomless pit by a great chain so that (ἵνα) he can no longer deceive the nations (20:4). The ἵνα clause describes causality in the function of Satan's binding,

---

124 Fee, *Revelation*, 281.
125 Mathison observes, "There is, however, evidence in the Gospels that the binding of Satan had begun already during the earthly ministry of Christ (Matt. 12:26-29; Mark 3:26-27; Luke 10:18). . . . Since the binding of Satan is associated with the first advent of Christ, the thousand years represents a period of time that began then. And since the events associated with the end of the thousand years (i.e., the resurrection of the dead and the final judgment) have not occurred yet, then it would appear that the thousand years is intended to be understood as a symbolic number representing a long but indefinite period of time." Mathison, *From Age to Age*, 689. Mathison writes from a postmillennial, not amillennial, viewpoint.
126 See Scobie, *Ways of Our God*, 262–63; Fee, *Revelation*, 284. Ladd allows a consistent theme of binding, though he questions its application to Rev 20: "It is clear that the gospels do represent Jesus as having bound Satan (Matt. 12:29) and toppled him from his place of power (Luke 10:18); and this victory over Satan is reflected in Revelation (see note on 12:9); it is an open question as to whether the binding of Satan in Rev. 20 is the same as that in Matt. 12 or is an eschatological event." Ladd, *Commentary on the Revelation of John*, 260.

which, as stated, is specifically to curtail his powers of deception.¹²⁷ Satan's restraint resultant from his exorcism is neither absolute nor comprehensive—it is not a binding of every imaginable activity, but a binding with a specific purpose in mind. Satan is not constrained from all forms of evil and nefarious activity as this age is still passing away. Satan's restraint is specific, and the passage under examination reveals that he is held back so that (ἵνα) he might not deceive (πλανήσῃ) the nations (τὰ ἔθνη) any longer—nations that are triumphantly declared to be under the authority of Christ and those whom he commissions in his name (Matt 28:18–19).

John describes Satan as being bound in a pit (Rev 20:3), a descriptive setting that further sheds light on the nature of his defeat and binding. The "pit" (τὴν ἄβυσσον) into which Satan is committed is a functional spiritual holding pen, a space in which demonic spirits are kept awaiting the final judgment of Christ's second coming. In a vernacular understanding of the first century, some listeners would have considered the pit to be "a vast subterranean cavern which served as a place of confinement for disobedient spirits awaiting judgment."¹²⁸ The ἄβυσσον is mentioned in nine New Testament passages, seven of which occur in Revelation (9:1, 2, 11; 11:7; 17:8; 20:1, 3).¹²⁹ The other two New Testament uses of ἄβυσσον emerge as the place of judgment for the demonic "legion" in the Gadarene/Gerasene demoniac passage (Luke 8:31) and in Paul's conception of the place of the dead (Rom 10:7). The pit was where the demons begged not

---

127   See Morris, *Revelation*, 224. Morris observes, "Again and again [John] uses the expression 'is given' when he speaks of the authority to do any evil act. Here he says specifically that Satan was restrained, not from all evil, but *from deceiving the nations* during *the thousand years*. From verse 8 we see that this means that Satan cannot gather the nations for the final cataclysm. The End is in God's control, not Satan's. John may also mean that, though Satan is busy, he is restrained from doing his worst. He cannot destroy the church. He cannot even destroy the martyrs, for they reign with Christ. The period of restraint will end, for Satan *must* (*dei*) be loosed, though only *for a short time*." Morris, *Revelation*, 224–25. Emphasis in original.

128   Mounce, *Book of Revelation*, 352. Sam Storms observes: "The word translated 'abyss' [ἄβυσσον] occurs nine times in the New Testament, eight of which refer to the abode of demons (the exception being Romans 10:7 where it refers to the abode of the dead in general)." Storms, *Kingdom Come*, 429n7.

129   There are fifty-one occurrences of ἄβυσσον in forty-nine verses in the LXX (including deuterocanonical books), often with the English gloss "the deep" (cf. Gen 1:2, 7:11, 8:2). Henry B. Swete, *The Old Testament in Greek: According to the Septuagint* (Cambridge: Cambridge University Press, 1909); *LALGNT*, s.v. "ἄβυσσον."

to be imprisoned (Luke 8:31), and it is the spiritual prison that portrays Satan's restraint following his exorcism by Christ. Satan is thus identified in Revelation as "the angel of the bottomless pit" (Rev 9:11), a pit from which demonic forces emanate (9:1–3; 11:7; 17:8) during Satan's eschatological incarceration that extends throughout the interadvental period.[130]

Satan is described in Revelation 20:1–3 as an incarcerated, outcast, and defeated foe. Though he exerts influence in this age over those who persist in unbelief (i.e., the "god of this world"; 2 Cor 4:4), Satan has been exorcised from his place of authority in this world. As a result of his exorcism, Satan has been prevented from deceiving the nations toward their own destruction (Rev 12:9), and the spiritual authority in this world has been given to Christ in eschatological fulfillment (with the subsequent commission to advance the gospel among the nations—Matt 28:18–20). Satan is not rendered wholly impotent, but he is restrained and bound so that he cannot prevent Christ's commission and the work of the church.[131] Revelation 20:1–3 describes a cosmic spiritual victory, one that has achieved a curtailment of Satan's powers of deception and destruction, resulting in his inability to prevent the divinely ordained spread of the gospel message.[132] The effects of Satan's binding become apparent as the following passage in Revelation 20 is taken into account, in which Satan is permitted to resume his deceptive efforts (20:8, 10) and his violent opposition against the people of God (20:8–9).[133] This theme will be explored further in the following section.

Revelation 20:7–10

> AND WHEN THE THOUSAND YEARS ARE ENDED, SATAN WILL BE RELEASED FROM HIS PRISON AND WILL COME OUT TO DECEIVE THE NATIONS THAT ARE AT THE FOUR CORNERS OF THE EARTH, GOG AND MAGOG, TO GATHER THEM FOR BATTLE; THEIR NUMBER IS LIKE THE

---

130 See Storms, *Kingdom Come*, 429n7.
131 Hoekema rightly qualifies: "This does not imply that Satan can do no harm whatever while he is bound. It means only what John says here: while Satan is bound he cannot deceive the nations in such a way as to keep them from learning about the truth of God. . . . We conclude, then, that the binding of Satan during the gospel age means that, first, he cannot prevent the spread of the gospel, and second, he cannot gather all the enemies of Christ together to attack the church." Hoekema, *Bible and the Future*, 228.
132 Hoekema, 238.
133 See also Fee, *Revelation*, 285.

> SAND OF THE SEA. AND THEY MARCHED UP OVER THE BROAD PLAIN OF THE EARTH AND SURROUNDED THE CAMP OF THE SAINTS AND THE BELOVED CITY, BUT FIRE CAME DOWN FROM HEAVEN AND CONSUMED THEM, AND THE DEVIL WHO HAD DECEIVED THEM WAS THROWN INTO THE LAKE OF FIRE AND SULFUR WHERE THE BEAST AND THE FALSE PROPHET WERE, AND THEY WILL BE TORMENTED DAY AND NIGHT FOREVER AND EVER. (REV 20:7–10)

The overall testimony of the New Testament concerning the satanic defeat of Christ's first coming conveys that Satan is bound and restrained during the duration of the interadvental church age. His binding began with Christ's incarnational work in *this age*, and it will conclude with Christ's return in the final consummation of *the age to come*. Satan's binding is inaugurated—it has begun due to the present dawning of *the age to come*, and yet it remains to be consummated once *this age* has been eclipsed. Scobie observes: "For the New Testament these [supernatural/spiritual] powers are real. They have been defeated by Christ in the decisive battle of the war between good and evil, though they will be totally eliminated only at the final consummation."[134] It is to this final, yet-future satanic defeat that the present work now turns.

Following the sweeping vision of Satan's restraint during the church age (Rev 20:1–6), John describes the conclusion of Satan's incarcerated epoch with his final release (v. 7). This passage depicts Satan's eschatological emancipation in relatively succinct form, though John's indefinite use of "when" (ὅταν, "whenever") looks to indicate the indefinite duration of the "millennium" itself.[135] When the period of Satan's restraint (τὰ χίλια ἔτη) has ended, Satan is released from his prison (φυλακῆς; v. 7).[136] Immediately upon his release, Satan prepares the nations of the earth (τὰ ἔθνη ... τῆς γῆς; v. 7) for war, and his deception of the nations and assault on the elect are now permitted to reach global proportions.[137]

---

134 Scobie, *Ways of Our God*, 265.
135 Morris, *Revelation*, 227. BDAG notes that ὅταν is a temporal particle that in Revelation 20:7 seems to reflect "marker of a point of time that coincides with another point of time." See BDAG, s.v. "ὅταν."
136 BDAG here notes, "The fallen city of Babylon becomes a φυλακή [*haunt*] for all kinds of unclean spirits and birds [in Rev] 18:2ab." BDAG, s.v. "φυλακή."
137 "Gog and Magog" is a designation that is representative of all nations, previously appearing in genealogies (Gen 10:2; 1 Chr 1:5, 5:4) and in the prophecy of Ezekiel 38–39. See Fee, *Revelation*, 285ff; Morris, *Revelation*, 227ff. "Armageddon" [Ἁρμαγεδών; Rev

The end result of unrestrained satanic deception now becomes clear: those who are deceived are plunged headlong into destruction (cf. Matt 8:32 // Mark 5:13 // Luke 8:33). John's depiction of a final battle in Revelation 20:8–10 contains the same imagery seen earlier in 19:17–21 and 16:12–16, denoted by the repeated phrase "gather them together for war."[138] The nations of the earth are gathered against "the camp of the saints and the beloved city" who are representative of the people of God throughout the earth (cf. Ezek 38), though instead of a war that the elect must win, fire from heaven (ἐκ τοῦ οὐρανοῦ) consumes the forces of evil (Rev 20:9).[139] The number of the rebellious nations "is like the sand of the sea" (ἡ ἄμμος τῆς θαλάσσης; v. 8), language that is reminiscent of the past times that the nations had gathered around in overwhelming force to threaten the people of God in the Old Testament (see Josh 11:4; Judg 7:12; and 1 Sam 13:5).[140]

Satan's gathering of the nations for war immediately upon his release sheds light on the nature of his interadventual binding, explicitly showing that he is bound in order to restrict his powers of deception (Rev 20:3) and to curtail his premature gathering of the nations for eschatological conflict against Christ and his church (v. 8).[141] Satan will only deceive the nations to make war against Christ when he is given divine permission, following his release from eschatological incarceration. Satan's response to his eventual release further clarifies that the purpose of Satan's original binding is

---

16:16] is symbolic of the earthly scene of spiritual battle. Storms, *Kingdom Come*, 433ff; Hendriksen, *More Than Conquerors*, 163. The description of enemy nations as coming from the four corners is a familiar Hebrew idiom for the whole earth (cf. Isa 11:12; "four winds" in Ezek 37:9; Dan 7:2); Beale with Campbell, *Revelation*, 452.
138 Beale with Campbell, *Revelation*, 423. Beale also sees strong allusions to Ezek 38–39 in Rev 19:17–21 and 20:8–10, as well as Zech 12–14 (and possibly Zeph 3:8 LXX).
139 Beale with Campbell, 453.
140 Beale with Campbell, 454.
141 Storms observes, "Note well what John does and does not say. He does *not* say that Satan was bound so that he should no longer persecute Christians, or so that he should no longer prowl about 'like a roaring lion' (1 Pet. 5:8) devouring believing men and women. He does *not* say that Satan was bound so that he should no longer concoct schemes to disrupt church unity (2 Cor. 2:11), or so that he should no longer disguise himself as an angel of light (2 Cor. 11:14). He does *not* say that Satan was bound so that he should no longer hurl his flaming missiles at Christians (Eph. 6:16), or so that he should be kept from thwarting the plans of the Apostle Paul (1 Thess. 2:18) or other church planters." Storms, *Kingdom Come*, 439. Emphasis in original.

to restrict him from his powers to incite eschatological rebellion prematurely through deception.[142]

Once the nations are gathered and the final satanic assault has commenced, Satan's methods of attack are exposed, and the nature of his previous restraint is clarified. All three of John's depictions of this final battle (Rev 16:12–16; 19:19–20; 20:8) depict Satan's assaults occurring through his power of deception (πλανῆσαι)[143]—the nations that are gathered together for war have been satanically deceived into openly rebelling against Christ.[144] The binding of Satan and the restraint of his deceptive activities illuminate that Revelation 20 clarifies the "casting down" of Satan pictured in 12:9—Satan (the serpent—12:9; 20:2) is the great deceiver (of the world, 12:9; of the nations, 20:3) who has been cast down in the work of Christ (12:8–9; 20:1–3).[145]

Following this final battle, Satan is revealed to be the one who has deceived (20:8), though his armies are now laid waste (20:9), and he is committed to final and permanent restraint and eternal torment (20:10). Satan's exorcism is now completed—he is "thrown down" (ἐβλήθη / βάλλω) into the lake of fire forever (εἰς τοὺς αἰῶνας τῶν αἰώνων; 20:10). Satan's final defeat/restraint indicates the advent of the *parousia* and the end of this age. The finality of this defeat is palpable: "There is no intermission and no end."[146] Satan's powers of deceiving the nations and uniting them in war against the Lamb have been removed through his decisive defeat by Christ.

---

142 Storms, *Kingdom Come*, 439.
143 The verb πλανάω is also used by the apostle John in John 7:47; 1 John 1:8; 2:26; 3:7; Rev 12:9; 13:14; 18:23; 19:20; 20:3; 20:8; 20:10.
144 Beale with Campbell, *Revelation*, 425–26.
145 Beale with Campbell, 426. The beast/false prophet is likely related to the New Testament theme of antichrist—the unspecified, primarily impersonal opposition to the work of Christ. See Storms, *Kingdom Come*, 488.
146 Morris, *Revelation*, 228.

Chapter 6

SATANIC ASSAULT PERSISTS IN THIS AGE

Satan is a defeated foe. Though Satan has demonstrated a degree of authority and power at times in the biblical narrative, his exorcism that was accomplished in Christ's first coming has curtailed his power and authority in this age. Although Satan is a defeated foe, satanic assaults persist in this age, even while he is restrained from deceiving the nations and from prematurely bringing about eschatological rebellion. The following sections will briefly survey relevant New Testament passages that reflect on the ongoing attacks of Satan in *this age*, concluding with a consideration of Satan's final defeat in the consummation of *the age to come*.

MATTHEW 6:13

> AND LEAD US NOT INTO TEMPTATION,
> BUT DELIVER US FROM EVIL. (MATT 6:13)

In Jesus's teaching about prayer in the Sermon on the Mount (often called the "Lord's Prayer"; Matt 6:9–13), Christ's words convey the depth of the believer's hope in this age—a hope grounded in the work of God that properly recognizes the current habitation of believers in this world ("Your kingdom come, your will be done, on earth as it is in heaven"). This prayer contains several words of petition to the Lord from his people, though the prayer notably begins with the theological grounding that God and his purposes are of primary interpretive importance ("Our Father in heaven, hallowed be your name").[1] Believers are later told at the end of the third petition to pray that the Father would "lead us not into temptation, but

---

1 Sam Storms, *Biblical Studies: The Sermon on the Mount* (Edmond, OK: Sam Storms, 2016), Matt 6:5–15.

deliver us from evil" (6:13). Believers are instructed to pray for deliverance from "evil," though there is good reason to favor the translation of τοῦ πονηροῦ as "the evil *one*," thus constituting an inferred reference to Satan rather than a generalized notion of evil.[2] The πονηρός referred to in this context fits with the canonical descriptions of Satan, the figure who is the personification of evil itself.[3]

Believers are thus instructed to pray for the Father's deliverance from the evil of Satan in this age—so that the "Father of lights" (Jas 1:17) would defeat the "father of lies" (John 8:44).[4] This mention of deliverance from Satan would then continue the Matthean theme of victory over Satan's temptations (Matt 4:1–11), though in the Lord's Prayer it is the believer who petitions the Father for deliverance "from" (ἀπὸ) evil.[5] The admonition for the believer is thus to pray earnestly that he would not be led into temptation, which is contrasted with the corresponding peril of "the evil one" (τοῦ πονηροῦ).[6] The recognition of Satan in this passage serves to place God's deliverance in opposition to Satan's destructive temptations, while it also properly places both the danger and blame for temptation on Satan in this context (cf. Jas 1:13–14; Matt 4:1, 3; 1 Cor 7:5; 1 Thess 3:5; Rev 2:10).[7]

Though Christ has exorcised Satan in this age, Satan remains active in this world in certain capacities, and believers are therefore warned to beware of Satan's evil temptations—temptations that ultimately lead to mutual destruction for both tempter and tempted (cf. Mark 14:38; Gal 6:1).[8] Therefore, Satan's current defeated state is eschatologically veiled. His defeat is certain and accomplished, yet his ongoing activity evokes the superficial

---

2 This lexical argument centers on whether πονηροῦ may be rendered masculine or neuter. There is great attestation among the Greek fathers (including Tertullian, Cyprian, Origen, and Chrysostom) and Reformers to favor a masculine interpretation. See Ulrich Luz, *Matthew 1–7*, ed. Helmut Koester, rev. ed., Hermeneia (Minneapolis: Fortress, 2007), 323, esp. 323n132; BDAG, s.v. "πονηρός."

3 It should be noted that the Greek noun πονηρός is masculine in gender as opposed to neuter. See BDAG, s.v. "πονηρός." Contra Leon Morris, *The Gospel According to Matthew*, PNTC (Grand Rapids: Eerdmans, 1992), 148–49.

4 The present author is indebted to Owen Strachan for this poignant observation made in a personal conversation.

5 Cf. Matt 13:19, 38; Eph 6:16; 1 John 2:13–14; 3:12; 5:19; Carson, "Matthew," 174; Chamblin, *Matthew*, 1:415–16.

6 Storms, *Biblical Studies: The Sermon on the Mount*, Matt 6:5–15.

7 Carson, "Matthew," 173.

8 Carson, 173; cf. J. V. Dahms, "Lead Us Not into Temptation," *JETS* 17 (1974): 229.

appearance of a ubiquitous and formidable foe.⁹ Believers accordingly live by faith in Christ's accomplished victory and authority and not according to the narrow viewpoint of this age that is passing away (2 Cor 5:7).

Matthew 12:43-45 // Luke 11:24-26
When the unclean spirit has gone out of a person, it passes through waterless places seeking rest, but finds none. (Matt 12:43)

In a didactic passage recorded by both Matthew and Luke, Christ makes use of a parabolic story concerning demonic actions and the eventual return of a demon to its host. The narrative focus of this passage is not the delineation of a detailed understanding of demonic activity, but instead, it is a condemnation of the "evil generation" that refused to listen to Christ's words (Matt 12:45; cf. Luke 11:29).[10] In order to explain the dangerous unbelief of the crowds, Christ employs the language of demonic exorcism by way of illustration. In both Gospel accounts, this parable of demonic activity follows the "strong man" passages (Matt 12:22–30 // Luke 11:14–23)—passages in which Christ responds to the objections against his healing on the grounds that he was in league with Beelzebul ("Beelzebul Controversy"). The narrative focus of Matthew 12:43 occurs in a setting of demonic exorcism and subsequent accusations made by religious leaders against Christ, a setting in which Christ clarifies the unbelief of both the religious leaders and the gathered crowds through the language and illustration of demonic exorcism.[11]

This parabolic mention of the wandering unclean spirit is instructive for the present study because it contains several overarching connections with the focal theme of satanic exorcism in this age. The current passage conveys the situation that "when" (ὅταν) an evil spirit leaves a person (τοῦ ἀνθρώπου),[12] it wanders through "arid" or "waterless" places in search of rest. There is a negative connotation commonly associated with the desert

---
9 Compare the advance of the kingdom in Matt 13:11–13. The experiences of the apostles and early church are instructive in recognizing true victory amid opposition and suffering.
10 See Chamblin, *Matthew*, 1:676.
11 See Doriani, *Matthew*, 1:525.
12 Carson, "Matthew," 298.

and "restless" places in Scripture (see Isa 13:20–21, 34:14; Rev 18:2), though the focus in this current passage is on the evil spirit's pressing desire to inhabit a host.[13] The demonic desire toward men (ἄνθρωπος) and the satanic desire for the world (κόσμος) are similar in this regard—their mutual evil desire is to retain a hold on their respective host, and ultimately bring about their host's destruction.[14] Christ preceded his words in this parable with the powerful expulsion of a demon from the demonized man (Matt 12:22, 43). In the parable, he proceeds to explain that the evicted evil spirit wanders about restlessly after being forced to depart from its previous host. Similar to the satanic exorcism that would soon follow in Christ's work (John 12:31), the evil spirit remains dangerous and has destructive intent, though it has been defeated and cast out from its previous residence by the work of Christ.

The warning that follows the parabolic teaching is that if the evil spirit in question were to return to its former place, the "house" ought not only be put in order but also properly occupied in order to prevent the evil spirit from again demonizing its host.[15] Were the evil spirit to find a vacant host upon its return, the resultant state would be "worse than the first"—a warning that Christ subsequently applies to the current "evil generation" (Matt 12:45).[16] Vacating the demonizing influence is insufficient—the territory that was previously demonized must be newly inhabited by Christ.

The application in Matthew 12:45 indicates that this is not merely a warning concerning individual demonization, but that it also speaks to the larger spiritual space of the world—evil must be replaced with good (cf. Rom 12:21), lest the evil return in an escalated assault that is worse than the first.[17] The former state that precedes the exorcism entails the presence of evil and the exercise of demonic/satanic authority, while the freed/exorcised state must be properly inhabited by the governing authority of Christ (cf. Rom 6:15–18).[18] This theme of Christological reclamation of territory (i.e., territory previously occupied by the demonic and satanic) is an

---

13 Carson, 298; Morris, *Gospel According to Matthew*, 328.
14 Cf. Luke 8:26–33; Doriani, *Matthew*, 1:532n1.
15 Morris finds ἐλθὸν to be a conditional use of the verb in Matthew 12:43. Morris, *Gospel According to Matthew*, 329. Cf. also Carson, "Matthew," 298.
16 The application to "this wicked generation" is not included in Luke's account. See a possible inclusio in Matthew 12:39 and 12:45. Carson, "Matthew," 298.
17 Chamblin, *Matthew*, 1:677.
18 See Blomberg, *Matthew*, 22:207; Doriani, *Matthew*, 1:532.

eschatological theme that holds true both for demonized individuals as well as the world/age whose "god" is identified as Satan (ὁ θεὸς τοῦ αἰῶνος; 2 Cor 4:4). Christ has come to free those in bondage to the demonic, to exorcise the evil spiritual forces of this world, and to proclaim his rightful eschatological authority in this age.

Satan's Persistent Influence

Christ is presently victorious in the overlap of *this age* and *the age to come*, and yet there is a persistent theme that has been recognized in the preceding analysis: Satan is still active in *this age*, and his attacks against those who follow Christ have not stopped—they will only finally cease in *the age to come*. Satan is bound through cosmic exorcism regarding deception of the nations and prohibition of gospel advance, yet his attacks against the church are both palpable and ongoing. While the crucifixion of Christ and the ongoing persecution of believers seems to indicate the triumph of evil in this world, Christ has achieved decisive eschatological defeat of Satan that awaits its final consummation. In light of this eschatological tension of satanic exorcism *now* and *not-yet*, the New Testament gives frequent warnings about the nature and extent of Satan's current, ongoing assaults against believers in this age.

John 8:44

> HE WAS A MURDERER FROM THE BEGINNING, AND DOES NOT STAND IN THE TRUTH, BECAUSE THERE IS NO TRUTH IN HIM. (JOHN 8:44)

John 8:44 follows a narrative section in this Gospel that is rich with a variety of Christ's recorded teachings—teachings that were given during Jewish religious celebrations and were directed particularly at the Jewish leaders who continued to oppose him and his ministry.[19] Christ had begun openly clarifying the nature of his ministry and mission in relationship to the Father (John 8:28; cf. 5:19; 6:38; 7:16), as well as foretelling his impending death on the cross (7:8, 30, 34; 8:14, 21).[20] Christ confronted the religious leaders with the depth of their unbelief, and in doing so he called into question the legitimacy of their belief that they were sons of Abraham

---

19 Borchert refers to these Jewish religious celebrations as the "Festival Cycle." Gerald L. Borchert, *John 1–11*, NAC 25A (Nashville: Broadman & Holman, 1996), 301.
20 Borchert, *John 1–11*, 301.

due to ethnicity or birth. Although the Jews claimed Abraham (and even God) to be their father (8:39–43; cf. Gen 18:1–19), Christ confronted them with the recognition that they were not children of God—further clarifying that while Christ heard from *his* Father, his Jewish opponents instead heard from *their* "father," the devil (John 8:44–47).[21] The spirit of Satan is evident in the sinful desires of Christ's opponents—whose will is to do their "father's desires" (v. 44b).[22]

Amid Christ's condemnation of the Jewish opponents as offspring of Satan, some insights into the character and activity of Satan emerge. Satan is at work through "his children." While Satan ultimately brings destruction to those who are "his" (v. 47b), Satan's intentions are also carried out in this age through the evil actions of those who belong to him (v. 44a). Satan is described in two primary ways in this passage, both as a "murderer" and a "liar" (v. 44).[23] Satan's followers (or "children") are murderers, just as their father, Satan, is a murderer—his lies and murderous intentions are evident in all those who oppose Christ.[24] Christ came to give eternal life to his children (John 14:6)—those who are set in contradistinction from others who reside in death (see Rom 5:12–14).[25] Standing in opposition to Christ, who is "the truth" (John 14:6) and "the life" (10:10), is Satan—the one who brings lies and death.

Satan is described as a murderer "from the beginning [ἀπ' ἀρχῆς]," bringing to mind his role of deception through the serpent's whisper: "you shall not surely die" (Gen 3:4).[26] The work of Christ exposes Satan's intentions and methods—Satan seeks to destroy (see John 10:10), and he does so through the proliferation of lies and deceit. Both Satan's intentions and

---

21 Jey J. Kanagaraj, *John*. NCC (Eugene, OR: Cascade, 2013), 95.
22 On the enslaved will of fallen man, see R. C. Sproul, *John*. St. Andrew's Expositional Commentary (Lake Mary: Reformation Trust, 2009), 166. Phillips observes: "This is the unbeliever's bondage under Satan: he is not only *unwilling*, but also *unable* to receive the gospel of Christ." Richard D. Phillips, *John*, 1st ed., REC 1 (Phillipsburg, NJ: P&R Publishing, 2014), 563–64. Emphasis added.
23 Craig S. Farmer, ed., *John 1–12*, RCS 4 (Downers Grove: InterVarsity Press, 2014), 323.
24 Gary M. Burge, "Gospel of John," in the *The Bible Knowledge Background Commentary*, eds. Craig A. Evans and Craig A. Bubeck (Colorado Springs: Cook, 2005), 89; Phillips, *John*, 560.
25 Burge, *Gospel of John*, 89.
26 So Phillips, *John*, 560; Borchert, *John 1–11*, 305–6. Note Burge's suggestion that either the Edenic temptation or the influence on Cain's murder of Abel may be in focus. Burge, *Gospel of John*, 89; cf. Kanagaraj, *John*, 96.

methods are therefore reflected in the deeds of his children (including the immediate context of those who opposed Christ directly), and his work of destruction and lies remains active in this age. Spreading destructive lies is more than merely something Satan *does*, but it is indeed a necessary reflection of who he *is*: "[Satan] does not stand in the truth, because there is no truth in him. When he lies, he speaks out of his own character, for he is a liar and the father of lies" (8:44b).[27] Satan is unable to stand in the truth of the revelation of Jesus Christ—thus, Satan's consistent desire is to destroy and to oppose the proclamation of the truth of Christ where he is permitted.[28]

1 John 4:1–6

> THIS IS THE SPIRIT OF THE ANTICHRIST, WHICH YOU HEARD WAS COMING AND NOW IS IN THE WORLD ALREADY. (1 JOHN 4:3)

Satan remains active in this age through an ongoing rebellion against God that John describes in his letters as the "spirit of antichrist" (τὸ τοῦ ἀντιχρίστου; 1 John 4:3).[29] John's depiction of the "spirit of antichrist" describes rejection of the person and work of Christ in this age, specifically in the manifestation of a spirit of rebellion and revolt against the Creator.[30] The spirit of ἀντίχριστος is more than an evil substitution for the things of God (though it entails that as well)—the spirit of ἀντίχριστος at work in this world is also evident in the enemies who directly oppose and attack Christ and his followers.[31]

---

27 Phillips, *John*, 561.
28 Calvin inferred that since Satan "did not remain in the truth," this passage further implies the post-creational fall of Satan. See John Calvin, *Commentary on the Gospel according to John*, ed. and trans. William Pringle (Bellingham, WA: Logos Bible Software, 2015), 1:351.
29 The term ἀντίχριστος (or its conjugation) in the Johannine corpus is found in 1 John 2:18, 2:22, 4:3, and 2 John 7; though there are distinct similarities to the "man of lawlessness" in 2 Thessalonians 2. See Edward Hayes Plumptre, "Antichrist," in *A Dictionary of Christian Biography, Literature, Sects and Doctrines*, eds. William Smith and Henry Wace, (London: Murray, 1977), 120; Beale, *A New Testament Biblical Theology*, 149, 527; Hobert K. Farrell and Donald M. Lake, "Antichrist," in *Baker Encyclopedia of the Bible*, eds. Walter A. Elwell and Barry J. Beitzel (Grand Rapids: Baker Books, 1988), 1:119.
30 I. Howard Marshall, *The Epistles of John*, NICNT (Grand Rapids: Eerdmans, 1978), 208.
31 See Stott's discussion of the preposition ἀντί" in John R. W. Stott, *The Epistles of John*, TNTC (Grand Rapids: Eerdmans, 1964), 104–5; see also Souter, *Pocket Lexicon to the Greek New Testament*, s.v. "ἀντί".

In the current passage in 1 John 4:1–6, John depicts the contrasting spiritual realities of the "Spirit of truth" versus the "spirit of falsehood" (4:6), entities who are presently at work in the "children of God" and the "children of Satan," respectively (2:29–3:12).[32] John identifies the spirit of ἀντίχριστος as the driving mechanism of false prophets (ψευδοπροφῆται) and as the spirit of error (τὸ πνεῦμα τῆς πλάνης). Though Satan's continuing work is discernable in various ways, the work of destructive human teachers is particularly in view in this context.[33] John's warning is that all teachings must be examined because the influence of Satan is manifest in this world—manifest in the time of John's writing, in the present day, and continuing until the end of this age (4:1–6).[34]

The manifestation of the spirit of ἀντίχριστος is greatly clarified through the lens of John's Christological focus (vv. 2–3).[35] The ongoing presence of satanic influence illuminates the dynamic of satanic ownership—those who are "not of God" are revealed to be "of Satan" (3:10; 4:3).[36] As the satanic spirit is manifested in fallen humanity's virulent opposition to the person and work of Christ, Satan's influence can likewise be discerned in every false teacher throughout the time between Christ's first and second comings.[37] The New Testament is replete with warnings for believers to be on guard against false teachers, as false teaching represents a principal means through which Satan's influence is active in this age (e.g., Matt 7:15; Acts 20:30; 2 Tim 4:3–4; 2 Pet 2:1; 3:16; 1 John 4:1). False teaching is destructive, following the satanic pattern of deception that leads to ruin—believers are therefore warned to "test the spirits" since "many false prophets have gone out into the world" (1 John 4:1). False teaching is satanic, and its outcome follows the satanic pattern of the destruction of its host. Not only does John mention false spirits and false teachers, but he also further clarifies that the power behind these evil forces is Satan himself—the evil one whom John describes as "he who is in the world" (ὁ ἐν τῷ κόσμῳ; 5:4).

---

32 Daniel L. Akin, *1, 2, 3 John*, NAC 38 (Nashville: Broadman & Holman, 2001), 169–70. There are also many notable lexical parallels between 1 John 4:1–6 and 2:18–28.
33 Douglas Sean O'Donnell, *1–3 John*, REC (Phillipsburg, NJ: P&R Publishing, 2015), 118.
34 Akin, *1, 2, 3 John*, 173; Sam Storms, *Biblical Studies: First John* (Edmond, OK: Sam Storms, 2016), 1 John 4:1–6. Logos Bible Software.
35 O'Donnell, *1–3 John*, 119.
36 Storms, *Biblical Studies: First John*, 1 John 4:1–6.
37 O'Donnell, *1–3 John*, 119.

John juxtaposes "he who is in the world" with Christ's victorious rule, observing that "he who is in you is greater than he who is in the world" (4:4). The juxtaposition is therefore also between the "children" of God (τεκνία—2:1, 12, 28; 3:7, 18; 4:4; 5:21) who are "from" God (3:9; 4:7; 5:1, 4, 18), and the satanic ruler whom Christ has defeated (see John 12:31; 14:30; 16:11).[38] Believers are therefore victorious because Christ is victorious, even amid persecution, as Christ assured his followers: "I have said these things to you, that in me you may have peace. In the world you will have tribulation. But take heart; I have overcome the world" (John 16:33).

Ephesians 2:1–3

> FOLLOWING THE COURSE OF THIS WORLD, FOLLOWING THE PRINCE OF THE POWER OF THE AIR, THE SPIRIT THAT IS NOW AT WORK IN THE SONS OF DISOBEDIENCE. (EPH 2:3)

Satan's persistent influence may be observed in the ongoing work of his spiritual children (ἐν υἱοῖς; "in [his] sons"), as Paul describes in the letter to the Ephesians. In Ephesians 2:3, Satan is referred to as the "prince [ἄρχων] of the power [ἐξουσία] of the air," using language that is similarly used elsewhere to evoke the power that Satan continues to exert in this age (see John 12:31; 14:30; 16:11; 2 Cor 4:4).[39] The title of ἄρχων is clearly recognized in the context of spiritual realities, while the ascription to Satan ruling the "air" [ἀέρος] is less evident. Satanic rule in the ἀέρος seems primarily to indicate the spiritual quality of this designation—Satan exercises his power (however limited and restrained) in the "air of this world," indicating the spiritual inbreaking of cosmic warfare into the earthly things of this age (see Rev 9:2; 16:17).[40] Satanic assault is not relegated solely to the spiritual realm but spills over into the "air of this world," indicating tangible consequences of spiritual warfare in this age.

---

38 O'Donnell, 122–23.
39 George G. Findlay, *The Epistle to the Ephesians*, in *The Expositor's Bible, Vol. 6: Ephesians to Revelation*, ed. W. Robertson Nicoll (Hartford: Scranton, 1903), 29; Bryan Chapell, *Ephesians*, REC (Phillipsburg, NJ: P&R Publishing, 2009), 80n3.
40 See the contention in BDAG that this usage signifies "political domain of transcendent beings or powers." BDAG, s.v. "ἀέρος." Findlay renders this Greek term as "spirit" or "breath," while Fowl believes this usage is not indicative of spiritual warfare. See Findlay, Epistle to the Ephesians, 29; Fowl, Ephesians, 66.

Paul's focus in this passage is to describe the darkness from which believers have been saved by God's grace: salvation from the power of "transgressions and sins" and from the death [νεκρός] that those sins incurred. Death epitomizes the depth of humanity's spiritual alienation from God and the physical death that accompanies the fallen spiritual state in this age (cf. 1 Cor 15:24–27; Rom 6:1–11).[41] The power of death is a defining characteristic of *this age*, one that is contrasted with the theme of "new life" that comes through Christ Jesus with the advent of *the age to come* (see John 3:3–7; Gal 6:15; 2 Cor 5:17). While Christ has come to bring abundant life (John 10:10), the former state of believers was described as one that followed "the course [αἰών] of this world [κόσμος]" (2:2). The "αἰών of this world" brings to mind the eschatological sense of the "age of this world"—pointing to the age or time in which the evil things of this κόσμος are still palpable (cf. Eph 1:21; 2:7; 3:9; Gal 1:4).[42] Paul combines the evil of this age with the concept of the "world"—denoting the area that stands in opposition to Christ and whose leaders oppose Christ and all those who follow Him (1 Cor 2:12; 11:32; Gal 4:3; Col 2:8, 20; 1 John 2:15–17).[43] Satan is the ruler (ἄρχων) who operates in the air (or age; αἰών) of this world (κόσμος), and in that regard he exercises a degree of "power" or "authority" (ἐξουσία). The realm of Satan's power lies in the areas of cosmic spiritual warfare in this age (Eph 6:12; cf. Col. 1:13), yet that space is likewise described as the area in which all people once walked and whose course all people once followed.[44]

Not only is Satan's influence wide-ranging, but it is also ongoing. Christ's work is the focal point of Ephesians 2:4, as He has saved believers by bringing them from death to life. Yet Satan is described as being "at work" (ἐνεργέω; present tense) in the "sons of disobedience"—language that is similar to the depiction of God being at work in this age (Eph 1:11,

---

41 Fowl, *Ephesians*, 68.
42 Αἰών may reflect a personal quality in this particular use. See BDAG, s.v. "αἰών"; Fowl, Ephesians, 69n6; Storms, Biblical Studies: Ephesians, Eph 2:2a.
43 Chapell, *Ephesians*, 79–80. Early attestation of this identity can be found in Clement of Alexandria and Jerome. See Fowl, *Ephesians*, 69n7.
44 Storms, *Biblical Studies: Ephesians*, Eph 2:2b. Calvin observes, "A more severe condemnation of mankind could not have been pronounced." John Calvin, *Commentaries on the Epistles of Paul to the Galatians and Ephesians*, ed. and trans. William Pringle (Bellingham, WA: Logos Bible Software, 2010), 220.

20; 5:8).⁴⁵ Believers are made a new creation and rescued from the bondage of sin and death in this age, while unbelievers continue in bondage as they follow the course of this world and its satanic prince (Rom 8:4; 2 Cor 10:2).⁴⁶

Satan's Ongoing Attacks

Though Satan has been exorcised from this world in the work of Christ's first coming, satanic assaults persist in the current overlap of the ages. Satan is restrained, but he is not completely inert. The biblical narrative gives insight into the nature of Satan's ongoing activity, especially with regard to the ongoing satanic devices of persecution and attack against believers in this age.

2 Corinthians 11:3, 14–15

> But I am afraid that as the serpent deceived Eve by his cunning, your thoughts will be led astray from a sincere and pure devotion to Christ. (2 Cor 11:3)

Satan's attacks are ongoing and persistent in this age as he awaits his final, consummative defeat that approaches with Christ's second coming. In 2 Corinthians 11:3, Paul warns the Corinthians against satanic attacks by calling to mind the oldest satanic attack recorded in Scripture: Paul warned that just as "the serpent" (ὁ ὄφις) had "deceived" (ἐξαπατάω) Eve by his cunning, he would likewise "lead astray" (φθείρω) the Corinthians. The background context of Paul's warning is the serpent's deception of Eve in the Garden (Gen 3:13; cf. 1 Tim 2:14), carrying the connotation that the serpent's deception, both in the Garden and now, is a deception that leads to corruption, destruction, and ultimately ruin (1 Cor 15:33; cf. Gen 6:11 LXX; Hos 9:9 LXX).⁴⁷ The serpent deceived Eve by casting doubt on God's commands, lying to her, and ultimately bringing about the destruction of both Adam and Eve as a result of their sin. In like manner, false teachers in this age mimic the ancient ploys of Satan through their "disgraceful, underhanded ways" of twisting God's words (2 Cor 4:2) and

---

45 Storms, *Biblical Studies: Ephesians*, Eph 2:2b.
46 Storms, Eph 2:2b.
47 Garland, *2 Corinthians*, 462.

causing the spiritual ruin of those whom they deceive.⁴⁸ Following the satanic method of mimicking the things of God (2 Cor 11:14), false teachers disguise destructive false teaching under the semblance of biblical doctrine.

Satan not only brings persecution in this age, but he also works through deceptive means to accomplish his goals. Rather than openly declaring themselves to be enemies of Christ, satanic false teachers "creep in" in a fashion similar to the serpent "creeping in" to the Garden, as they sought to "instill their poison by fawning artifices."⁴⁹ Paul warned, similar to what transpired in the Garden, that the Corinthian church might be "deceived" (ἐξαπατάω—cf. Rom 7:11; 2 Thess 2:3, Rom 16:18).⁵⁰ It is no surprise that Satan's servants would use similar means as he had previously employed with Eve. Satan disguises evil intentions under the guise of good things, though the reference to Eve reminds Paul's recipients that they are not unaware of the serpent's ploys (see 2 Cor 2:11).⁵¹ Paul observes that just as the false teachers disguise themselves as apostles, it is no surprise to his readers: "And no wonder, for even Satan disguises himself as an angel of light. So it is no surprise if his servants, also, disguise themselves as servants of righteousness" (11:14–15a). Though Satan's deceptive methods have not deviated from Eden, his defeat (and that of his servants) is secured: "Their end will correspond to their deeds" (11:15b).

1 John 5:18–19

> THE WHOLE WORLD LIES IN THE
> POWER OF THE EVIL ONE. (1 JOHN 5:19)

In keeping with similar New Testament warnings about the ongoing work of Satan in this age, John provides further caution of the power that Satan continues to exercise in this world—even after his exorcism by Christ. Building on the warnings concerning the "spirit of antichrist" that is already at work in this world (1 John 4:1–6), John gives a word of warning and comfort in 1 John 5. John assures his readers that "everyone who has been born [πᾶς ὁ γεγεννημένος] of God" (2:29; 4:9; 4:7; 5:1; 5:4) is protected from the "touch" of the "evil one" (4:18). The language John uses to

---

48 Garland, 462.
49 John Calvin, *Commentaries on the Epistles of Paul to the Corinthians*, ed. and trans. John Pringle (Bellingham, WA: Logos Bible Software, 2010), 2:342.
50 BDAG, s.v. "ἐξαπατάω."
51 Garland, *2 Corinthians*, 462–63; Harris, "2 Corinthians," 520.

describe the one who protects believers is less clear—the believers are protected by "he who was born of God" (ὁ γεννηθεὶς ἐκ τοῦ θεοῦ). Though the language is imprecise, this "protector" is surely referring to Jesus Christ, in keeping with the consistent New Testament witness of Christ's protection over those who are his children (see John 17:12; 1 Pet 1:5; Jude 24; Rev 3:10).[52] Though John admonishes the believers to stand against sin, Christ is clearly the victor in the fight against the evil one, as Calvin observed: "And we know that we fight with no other weapons but those of God. Hence the faithful keep themselves from sin, as far as they are kept by God (John 17:11)."[53] Christ, the μονογενής Son (1 John 4:9), is the protector who has defeated the evil one.[54]

The "evil one" (5:18, 19) in this passage is directly connected to the "world" that he has corrupted—the world (κόσμος) represents the place of hostility to God and perversion through sin.[55] John continues a clear line of delineation between those who are "in" Christ and those who are "in" the world (and, by extension, "in" the power of the evil one).[56] John describes the spiritual reality that "everyone" (πᾶς) who is "of God" (ἐκ τοῦ θεοῦ) and "born of God" (ὁ γεγεννημένος) is protected from the evil one—such that the believer has nothing to fear. On the other hand, the "whole world" (ὁ κόσμος ὅλος) lies in the power of the evil one (ὁ πονηρός) and is unable to withstand his assaults. Martin Luther observed: "The world is a realm of wrongdoing, and the devil is lord over it."[57] The apostle John portrays all human beings as residents in one of two spiritual positions—there is no "neutral ground" in this arena of spiritual

---

52 Note also the change from a perfect passive participle referring to believers (ὁ γεγεννημένος) to the aorist passive participle for Christ (ὁ γεννηθεὶς). Akin, *1, 2, 3 John*, 212. See also Storms, *Biblical Studies: First John*, 1 John 5:1–21; O'Donnell, *1–3 John*, 164.
53 John Calvin, *Commentaries on the Catholic Epistles*, ed. and trans. John Owen (Bellingham, WA: Logos Bible Software, 2010), 271.
54 For further discussion of the terms μονογενής and γεννάω, see Letham, *Holy Trinity*, 386; Keith E. Johnson, "Trinitarian Agency and the Eternal Subordination of the Son: An Augustinian Perspective," *Themelios* 36.1 (2011): 11, 14n31; cf. Ware, *Father, Son, and Holy Spirit*, 132–33; Köstenberger and Swain, *Father, Son and Spirit*, 77.
55 Cf. John 7:7; 8:23; 12:25, 31; 13:1; 14:30; 15:18; 16:11; 17:9, 25; 18:36; 1 John 4:4–5; 4:17. BDAG, s.v. "κόσμος."
56 Storms, *Biblical Studies: First John*, 1 John 5:1–21.
57 Martin Luther, "Lectures on the First Epistle of St. John," 326, cited in O'Donnell, *1–3 John*, 165.

conflict.⁵⁸ The believer physically resides in the world in this age (John 17:6, 9, 15–16, 18) but is kept from the power of the evil one (whose assaults and deceptions persist in limited measure).⁵⁹

If Satan, the ancient "evil one," still exercises such a degree of power in this world, how does John assure the believers that they are protected from Satan's touch? John assures his recipients that the evil one cannot "touch" or "harm" (οὐχ ἅπτεται) the one who has been born of God.⁶⁰ Some interpreters of this passage have thereby concluded that John is speaking of Satan's inability to harm the believer—that the reference to ἅπτεται indicates that Satan cannot touch a believer to the point of harm, even drawing on the saga of Job as a referential point of context (Job 1–2).⁶¹ Yet the context of this passage indicates something beyond physical persecution since the clear New Testament witness is that believers will experience persecution, including physical harm for some, in this present age (John 16:33; 17:18; Rev 2:10).⁶²

John's contention seems to be that, regarding the spiritual state of the believer—the state in which believers are "kept" from sinning and found to be "born of God"—Satan is unable to lay hold of those who are in Christ. Satan is restrained from advancing spiritual attacks that would separate the believer from Christ in this age, even though persecution is otherwise present and even normative (see Rom 8:31–39). The perseverance of the believer is, therefore, a testimony to the work of Christ's exorcism of Satan in this age, as Christ is the one "who was born of God [who] protects him" (1 John 5:18; cf. Heb 13:20–21; Phil 2:12–13).⁶³

---

58 Akin, *1, 2, 3 John*, 213.
59 A connotation of "power" (so ESV, NASB) or "control" (NIV) is implied in the phrase "the whole world lies in the evil one" (author's translation): ἐν τῷ πονηρῷ κεῖται.
60 The term ἅπτεται may be rendered as "touch" (ESV, NASB, KJV) or "harm" (NIV), with the semantic range being "making contact to cause harm." BDAG, s.v. "ἅπτω."
61 Akin contends, "That is, the evil one is not permitted to touch the believer to the point of doing harm to him." See Akin, *1, 2, 3 John*, 212.
62 Storms contends, "We can't press the term 'touch', for according to 1 Pt. 5:8 it is possible to be 'devoured' by the Devil! See also Rev. 2:10. Thus, whatever 'touch' means, it does not suggest that all Christians are automatically insulated against demonic attack." Storms, *Biblical Studies: First John*, 1 John 5:1–21.
63 Storms, *Biblical Studies: First John*, 1 John 5:1–21.

Ephesians 6:10–12

> For we do not wrestle against flesh and blood, but against the rulers, against the authorities, against the cosmic powers over this present darkness, against the spiritual forces of evil in the heavenly places. (Eph 6:12)

In the sixth chapter of Paul's letter to the Ephesians, Paul warns the believers in Ephesus to persevere against an array of diabolical spiritual enemies, employing the familiar Pauline language of "standing firm" (v. 14; see 1 Thess 3:8; 2 Thess 2:15; 1 Cor 10:12; 15:1; 16:13; Phil 1:27).[64] Paul encourages the church to "be strong" and to "put on the whole armor of God," urging the believers to prepare themselves for spiritual battle. The language Paul employs evokes the picture of the might and power of well-equipped soldiers, while the context is that of spiritual warfare. Believers are to gird themselves in the armor that is necessary to stand firm, while the primary function of this armor is defensive in nature. The defensive capacity of the armor is indicative of spiritual warfare that occurs in the overlap of the ages—the believer is not called to charge into an offensive assault, but instead is to stand his ground against the attacks (at times subtle, at other times ferocious) of Satan (see 1 Pet 5:8; Rev 12:17).[65] The military equipment described reflects the common armament of a foot soldier—so just as Paul has called on believers to "put on the new self" (Eph 4:24), he now calls the church to "put on" armor to stand firm against Satan's attacks.[66] Well-equipped soldiers are more likely to survive in battle, and the same holds true regarding the spiritual equipping of the church amid Satan's persistent assaults in this age (cf. Matt 28:18).[67]

The "spiritual forces of evil" that are aligned against the church are described using a range of terms: believers engage "against the rulers [ἀρχάς], against the authorities [ἐξουσίας], against the cosmic powers [κοσμοκράτορας] over this present darkness, against the spiritual forces of evil [τὰ πνευματικὰ τῆς πονηρίας] in the heavenly places" (v. 12). Paul's intention is not to present a systematized or hierarchical understanding of

---

64 Fowl, *Ephesians*, 200n2.
65 Fowl, 203–4.
66 Fowl, *Ephesians*, 203.
67 R. C. Sproul, *The Purpose of God: Ephesians* (Fearn, Scotland: Christian Focus, 1994), 147.

satanic forces, but this description is meant instead to give an overarching view of the vast array of spiritual forces that are aligned against the church in this age—often drawing from the themes developed elsewhere in the letter (Eph 1:21; 2:2; 3:10; 4:27; 5:8; 5:16; cf. Rom 8:38; 1 Cor 15:24; Col 1:13, 16; 2:10, 15; 1 Pet 3:22).[68] Paul's description of these evil entities exemplifies the darkened state of this world, even while he assures his readers of the inaugurated state of Christ's victory over those forces.

Paul's depiction of the manner of the attack against the church takes the form of a subtle, deceptive approach instead of a more obvious frontal assault. Paul warns the Ephesians against the "schemes" (μεθοδεία) of the devil—a word that carries the sense of something deceptive, crafty, and secretive (Eph 4:14).[69] The satanic "schemes" that Paul warns the Ephesians against likely represent a variety of satanic assaults, with false teaching (4:5) and challenges to believers' faith (6:16) among those that are in immediate view.[70] In response to this wide array of deceptive attacks from forces of evil, Paul exhorts his readers to "take up the whole armor of God, that you may be able to withstand in the evil day" (6:13). Paul's reference to "the evil day" (τῇ ἡμέρᾳ τῇ πονηρᾷ) is similar to his previous observation that "the days are evil" (5:16), though his inclusion of the definite article seems to point to something specific that is beyond the general recognition that this age constitutes "evil days." The reference to "the evil day" is likely meant to frame the context of the church's conflict with the "evil one" in the grand context of cosmic spiritual warfare—believers are to gird themselves for spiritual battle in order to be prepared for the final day of judgment that approaches (1 Thess 5:2–4).[71] Paul, therefore, warns believers to be aware of satanic persecution and deceit, noting that satanic attacks will intensify as the day of judgment approaches.

---

68 Fowl, *Ephesians*, 204; Chapell, *Ephesians*, 334–35.
69 BDAG, s.v. "μεθοδεία"; Fowl, *Ephesians*, 203n4; Storms, *Biblical Studies: Ephesians*, Eph 6:21–24.
70 Arnold notes, "What Paul does not say in this passage is how these schemes, which he will later refer to as 'flaming arrows' (6:16), are discerned and felt. Given the broader context of Paul's thought, it would seem prudent to see an expansive variety of ways that the devil hatches his attacks." Arnold, *Ephesians*, 445.
71 Chapell, *Ephesians*, 335; Fowl, *Ephesians*, 205.

1 Peter 5:8–9

YOUR ADVERSARY THE DEVIL PROWLS AROUND LIKE A ROARING LION,
SEEKING SOMEONE TO DEVOUR. (1 PETER 5:8)

Using the poignant visual imagery of a prowling, ravenous lion, Peter urges believers to remain vigilant against the attacks of Satan. Peter describes Satan as the "adversary" (ὁ ἀντίδικος) and "the devil" (διάβολος), two terms that are canonically familiar references to Satan and that bring to mind Satan's continued (yet unsuccessful) attempts to levy accusations against the people of God (cf. Rev 12:9).[72] Satan's hostility to believers is compared to the behavior of a starving lion, and he is said to "prowl" while seeking a victim to "devour" or "swallow up" (καταπίνω; see 1 Cor 15:54).[73] Peter's formidable description combats one of two interpretive errors that should be avoided—either imbuing Satan with greater power than he possesses or, conversely, ignoring his power and influence altogether.[74]

Peter, therefore, portrays Satan as the "adversary" to remind his readers of the cosmic battle in which they are engaged. Calvin observes: "He calls him the *adversary* of the godly, that they might know that they worship God and profess faith in Christ on this condition, that they are to have continual war with the devil, for he does not spare the members who fights with the head."[75] Like a ravenous lion, Satan is ferocious and dangerous—yet he categorically pales in comparison to the true Lion who will return in glory (Rev 5:5).[76] In response to the believer's recognition of Satan and his destructive appetite, the apostle gives two succinct commands: "be sober-minded" (νήψατε; see 1:13, 4:7; cf. 1 Thess 5:6, 8; 2 Tim 4:5) and "be watchful" (γρηγορήσατε; see Matt 24:42–43; 25:13; Mark 13:34–35, 37; Luke 12:37; 1 Thess 5:6; Rev 3:23; 16:15).[77] The admonition to "be sober-minded" occurs in both 1 Peter 1:13 and 4:7, giving the entire letter

---

72 Mounce, *Living Hope*, 88.
73 BDAG, s.v. "καταπίνω"; Mounce, *Living Hope*, 88.
74 Daniel M. Doriani, *1 Peter*, REC (Phillipsburg, NJ: P&R, 2014), 231.
75 Calvin, *Commentaries on the Catholic Epistles*, 150. Emphasis in original.
76 Doriani, *1 Peter*, 231n3.
77 Both forms are aorist active imperatives. See Thomas R. Schreiner, *1, 2 Peter, Jude*, NAC 37 (Nashville: Broadman & Holman, 2003), 241.

an eschatological sense and bringing particular attention to the larger "last days" setting within which Satan's assaults occur.[78]

Peter's second admonition is to "resist [Satan], standing firm in your faith." Though "resist" is the only verb present in the text, the passage likely indicates that believers are both to "resist" and "stand firm" in the manner of their resistance.[79] Similar to Paul's admonition to the Ephesians (Eph 6:10–12), the connotation appears to be that this command implies both individual and corporate effort by believers—every believer is admonished to stand, even while the church as a whole is called to stand together.[80] Satan's desire is to "devour," while Peter considers persecution against the church to be a constant threat "throughout the world" (3:9). The recipients of Peter's letter likely faced persecution from both family and state due to their newfound loyalty, and thus Satan is pictured as a lion who longs to "gulp" down his prey.[81] Satan attempts to intimidate believers through his fearful growl, showing his serpentine deception in his desire to cause believers to sin—yet ultimately, Satan's desire is to bring destruction to those who do not guard against his schemes.[82] Peter's conclusion reflects the content of the victory that Christ has won over Satan in service to God: "To him be the dominion forever and ever." (5:11). Though Satan continues his assaults against believers, Christ alone holds the final authority in *this age* and *the age to come*.

2 Corinthians 2:11

> SO THAT WE WOULD NOT BE OUTWITTED BY SATAN; FOR
> WE ARE NOT IGNORANT OF HIS DESIGNS. (2 COR 2:11)

Satan's attacks and schemes continue after his exorcism, but believers should not be unaware of his schemes. Paul makes this contention clear when writing to the Corinthian church, specifically in the context of a passage describing the emergence of conflict within the church and the resultant need

---

78 1 Peter 1:13 and 4:17 thus form an eschatologically oriented inclusio; see Schreiner, *1, 2 Peter, Jude*, 241; Mounce, *Living Hope*, 88.
79 Schreiner, *1, 2 Peter, Jude*, 242–43.
80 Doriani, *1 Peter*, 232.
81 Doriani, *1 Peter*, 227–28, 231; Mounce, *Living Hope*, 88.
82 Schreiner here warns against the danger of apostasy, while Doriani observes that Satan works through temptation, physical persecution, and obfuscation of the truth. See Schreiner, *1, 2 Peter, Jude*, 242; Doriani, *1 Peter*, 231.

for forgiveness and restitution. In this context of a call for forgiveness and reconciliation, Paul warns the Corinthians of the "designs" of their enemy, Satan—a theme the apostle revisits later in this letter (2 Cor 11:14; 12:7). Paul specifically admonishes the Corinthian believers to forgive one another in order that they might not be "outwitted" (πλεονεκτέω; i.e., "gained advantage" over) by Satan. Placing this warning against satanic assault in the larger context of this passage, Satan's "design" seems to be preventing restoration and impeding repentance in the Corinthian church, thus bringing about division from within.[83] Garland correctly observes that "Satan's goal is always to foil God's work of reconciliation," and this observation seems to be in keeping with the warning Paul gives in this passage.[84] While Satan can no longer deceive the nations with impunity, satanic attacks are still perceptible within the body of Christ when reconciliation is denied.

The satanic attack against the Corinthians is described as "designs" (νοήματα), conveying the sense of "schemes" or "plots" (see 2 Cor 3:14; 4:4; 10:5).[85] In this instance, Satan's scheme against the Corinthians is to twist a good and godly reaction (repentance) into a divisive and destructive evil (excessive grief).[86] Calvin provides insight into this passage: "For there was a twofold danger, that beset them from the stratagems of Satan—in the event of their being excessively harsh and rigorous, or, on the other hand, in case of dissension arising among them."[87] The Corinthians were therefore encouraged to beware of Satan's νοήματα, because they are not unaware of his divisive schemes. Believers do well to recognize Satan's schemes while simultaneously observing the comfort that Paul provides to the Thessalonians: "But the Lord is faithful. He will establish you and guard you against the evil one" (2 Thess 3:3).

---

83 Sam Storms, *Biblical Studies: Meditations on 2 Corinthians* (Edmond, OK: Sam Storms, 2016), 2 Cor 2:11; Garland, *2 Corinthians*, 131.

84 Use of the term "foil" ought not to be misconstrued as connoting the prevention of God's will and decree, which is a theological impossibility. See Garland, *2 Corinthians*, 131.

85 BDAG, s.v. "νοήματα." The former term is similar to μεθοδείαι (cf. Eph 6:11). Harris, "2 Corinthians,", 453–54.

86 Harris, "2 Corinthians," 454.

87 Calvin, *Commentaries on the Epistles of Paul to the Corinthians*, 2:152–53.

Satan's Cosmic War

Scripture depicts the current overlap of *this age* and *the age to come* as a time of cosmic spiritual warfare, one in which satanic persecution continues against believers. The descriptions of the battle and its participants vary based on the passage under examination, while the primary features remain: Christ has conquered, Satan has been defeated, Satan and his forces continue to make war on the elect, yet the elect will emerge victorious through persecution as Christ crushes Satan and consummates his victory. With this eschatological backdrop in mind, Revelation contains several depictions of this final battle, specifically concerning the interadventual state of satanic attack against believers.

Revelation 1:9

> I, JOHN, YOUR BROTHER AND PARTNER IN THE TRIBULATION AND THE KINGDOM AND THE PATIENT ENDURANCE THAT ARE IN JESUS. (REV 1:9)

In the opening chapter of Revelation, John introduces himself to "Christ's servants" (δούλοις; 1:1) and to the seven Christian churches in Asia (1:4) by describing himself as their "brother" and "partner" (1:9). John's partnership with them is in three related capacities, in areas that are introduced using a single definite article (τῇ): he is their "partner" in the tribulation (θλίψει) and the kingdom (καὶ βασιλείᾳ) and the patient endurance (καὶ ὑπομονῇ) in Jesus.[88] John's Christological focus is evident: Christ is the focal point, sustainer, and victorious conqueror upon whom the believers are to set their focus amid their suffering. John describes himself as a "fellow-partaker" (συγκοινωνός) with other Christians in this suffering—indicating that they share active participation in it, even while their suffering is sure to produce victory.[89] From the outset of Revelation, the interrelated concepts of trial, endurance, and kingdom triumph seem inseparably linked. Christians will experience kingdom triumph through the experience of suffering and tribulation in this age.[90]

Tribulation is eschatologically significant since it indicates the inbreaking advent of the kingdom amid this evil world (see John 16:33; Acts

---

88 Beale with Campbell, *Revelation*, 45.
89 BDAG, s.v. "συγκοινωνός"; Beale with Campbell, *Revelation*, 45.
90 So also Morris, *Revelation*, 56; Beale with Campbell, *Revelation*, 45.

14:22).⁹¹ Tribulation (θλῖψις; 1:9) is a defining characteristic of this age, and John considers it to be the anticipated experience of the believer in the overlap of the ages (Rev 1:9; 2:9–10; 2:22; 7:14; cf. Matt 24:9, 21, 29).⁹² John's depiction of the Christian's suffering reflects the Christological path of victory in this age. As Phillips notes, "John mentions the suffering of believers first because tribulation marks the path that leads us to the kingdom, just as for Jesus the cross preceded the crown."⁹³

The "kingdom" that follows the tribulation is the fulfillment of Christ ruling in this age: Christ is the "ruler (ἄρχων) of kings on earth" who has made believers "a kingdom (βασιλεία) and priests to his God and Father" (Rev 1:5–6).⁹⁴ Though the narrative backdrop is one of tribulation, John encourages his readers with the hope that as Christ's kingdom advances in this age, believers may partake in his victory over the false ἄρχων who has been exorcised from this world (John 12:31). John thus connects the interrelated concepts of "tribulation" and "kingdom" together since tribulation is the indicative sign of kingdom advance in this world. Believers experience kingdom advance, and kingdom advance is evidenced in the trials and tribulations that inevitably accompany it (see John 15:18–20; 16:33; Acts 14:22; 2 Cor 4:8–10; 6:4–10; Rev 3:21). John, therefore, encourages believers to stand with him in this age in "patient endurance" (ὑπομονῇ), bearing witness to the kingdom through their endurance in tribulation. Believers are to remember that while the temporal kingdoms of this age bring persecution, the eternal kingdom has come in the work of Christ, an eschatological development that calls for endurance on the part of the believer (see Rev 2:2–3; 2:19; 3:10; 14:12).⁹⁵ Phillips posits: "If tribulation is our road and the kingdom our destination, then patient endurance is our mode of travel, our manner of living."⁹⁶ Believers endure in this age by facing trials with boldness (2:9–11, 13; 3:8; 12:11) and by combatting the sins that manifest in their lives (chs. 2–3).⁹⁷

---

91   Ladd, *Commentary on the Revelation of John*, 29–30.
92   The tribulation closest to Christ's second coming will "merely intensify the tribulation that is always the Christians' lot." Richard D. Phillips, *Revelation*, REC (Phillipsburg, NJ: P&R, 2017), 59; see also Fee, *Revelation*, 13.
93   Phillips, *Revelation*, 59.
94   Phillips, 58.
95   Fee, *Revelation*, 13–14.
96   Phillips, *Revelation*, 60.
97   Beale with Campbell, *Revelation*, 46.

Revelation 12:17

> THEN THE DRAGON BECAME FURIOUS WITH THE WOMAN AND WENT
> OFF TO MAKE WAR ON THE REST OF HER OFFSPRING, ON THOSE
> WHO KEEP THE COMMANDMENTS OF GOD AND HOLD TO
> THE TESTIMONY OF JESUS. (REV 12:17)

Using apocalyptic language rich with imagery, the closing passage in Revelation 12 describes a "dragon" (representing Satan) engaging in "furious" warfare against the God-fearing offspring of the woman. The plot of the dragon has been described previously in menacing detail (12:3): his plot to devour the child of the woman has failed (12:4–6), and he has been defeated and cast down from heaven (12:9) with the declaration of Christ's kingdom (βασιλεία) and authority (ἐξουσία) in this age (12:10). The dragon is revealed to have been defeated and is restrained from accusing the believers (12:11–12), though John makes clear that this does not indicate a cessation of his activity: "But woe to you, O earth and sea, for the devil has come down to you in great wrath, because he knows that his time is short!" (12:12b). Satan is filled with fury in his exorcised state, and he, therefore, lashes out in vicious persecution against "those who keep the commandments of God and hold to the testimony of Jesus" (12:17). The church in this age and the individual believers who constitute it experience persecution not because the dragon has conquered—but precisely because of his defeat.[98] His attacks are furious yet temporary.

The dragon's rage against the woman's offspring draws on an eschatological theme that began in the Garden—as the serpent wars against the offspring (σπέρματος; Gen 3:15 LXX) of the first woman, so the dragon wars with fury against the offspring (σπέρματος; Rev 12:17) of the woman who follows Christ in *this age*. The dragon's persecution of the woman's offspring is a continuing prophetic fulfillment of the *protoevangelium* (Gen 3:15), as well as an escalation of the serpent's war in light of the defeat to which he has been subjected.[99] The dragon's rage is fueled by his recognition of his fallen and defeated state (see Rev 12:13), and he thus launches

---

[98] Beale notes the interpretive challenge between "the woman" and "her offspring"—he is probably correct to surmise that the "woman" is a heavenly depiction of the church, while her "offspring" speaks to the experience of individual believers. See Beale with Campbell, 262–63; also Phillips, *Revelation*, 359–60.

[99] Morris, *Revelation*, 160; Beale with Campbell, *Revelation*, 265. Beale especially notes the continuity of "deception" as a satanic theme in both Gen 3 and Rev 12.

a fierce and desperate assault that is directed against those who obey God's commands and cling to the testimony of Christ (12:17).[100] Those who are thus described as "obeying" and "clinging" to Christ can be readily identified as the children of God.[101] The vision of the woman, her children, and the dragon give the sense that although the people of God are kept and preserved by the power of Christ, individual believers who are yet in this age are called to endure fierce satanic attacks and persecution.[102] Satan is defeated and cannot spiritually destroy those who follow Christ, yet his attacks and persecutions are intense.

Revelation 11:7

> AND WHEN THEY HAVE FINISHED THEIR TESTIMONY, THE BEAST THAT RISES FROM THE BOTTOMLESS PIT WILL MAKE WAR ON THEM AND CONQUER THEM AND KILL THEM. (REV 11:7)

The final passage under consideration that describes the cosmic war in this age between Satan and the children of God takes place in the eleventh chapter of Revelation. This passage provides the description of the "two witnesses" followed by the "seventh trumpet," while its content gives a rich reflection on the church's steadfast testimony amid satanic persecution in this age.[103] The chapter's conclusion depicts the triumph of Christ in this world (in the symbolic language that is common to Revelation), along with the vindication of the persecuted saints over against the judgment of the wicked.[104]

The first figure of note is that of the "the beast" who rises from the "pit" (ἄβυσσος) to make war upon the two witnesses of Christ. The imagery

---

100 Phillips, *Revelation*, 360. Note that some translations include "And he stood on the sand of the sea" in 12:18b (ESV), while others include this phrase in 13:1 (NASB, NIV, KJV*, NRSV), though the narrative context remains unchanged.
101 Fee, *Revelation*, 176–77.
102 Fee, 176–77; Beale with Campbell, *Revelation*, 263; Phillips, *Revelation*, 353.
103 Phillips states, "The vision provides one of the most potent descriptions of the mightiness of the church in its witness and the violence of the world's warfare against the gospel." Phillips, *Revelation*, 318.
104 Regarding methodology, this chapter continues Revelation's theme of communicating through symbols and presenting the narrative of the period between Christ's first and second comings in a visionary, non-sequential, parallel format. See Storms, *Kingdom Come*, 29, 34–35, 387–402; Beale with Campbell, *Revelation*, 421; Hendriksen, *More Than Conquerors*, 10–15.

of the beast from the pit employs the language of the terrifying "fourth beast" of Daniel 7 (θηρίον; Dan 7:7 LXX), likely reflecting the manner in which satanic attacks manifest through the machinations of evil worldly empires.[105] Both Paul (2 Thess 2:1–12) and John (1 John 2:18–27; 4:1–6) describe the mysterious way in which satanic designs manifest through the operative forces at work in this world, even while an observable satanic figure remains absent from view. In Revelation 11, there is an escalation of the satanic work that is present in this age, as the beast is described as emerging from the pit to engage in "war." This does not signify a previous absence of activity but rather clarifies the manner in which the satanic machinations of evil earthly kingdoms in this age reach a culminating point, pictured here as the point when the beast itself rises from the pit to make war on the saints (cf. Dan 7:1–8, 19–27; Rev 17:8; 20:7).[106] Just as the Danielic beast made war against the saints and prevailed over them (Dan 7:21), the Johannine beast in similar fashion will make war against the saints in an attempt to "conquer" and even "kill" them (Rev 11:7, 19–21). The forces of Satan will persecute the saints even to the point of seeming to crush them in this age, while a final escalation is highlighted by John's depiction of the beast emerging from the pit that holds him (11:7).[107] Satan is a defeated foe, but his persecutions and attacks are fierce, and there is a period of eschatological intensification.

Satan's war against the saints is only permitted once their testimony has "finished" (τελέσωσιν)—that is, once their testimony has been completed and has accomplished its eschatological goal.[108] The setting of the church's culminating witness indicates that the final things in history are in view:

---

105 So Phillips, *Revelation*, 323.
106 Beale notes, "The beast in Daniel 7 represents an evil king and kingdom which persecute the saints, and so likewise the persecuting activity in Rev. 11:7 begins to take place through antagonistic earthly authorities. The same series of events (the final onslaught of the beast followed by his own demise) is described in 17:8, where the beast comes out of the abyss only to go to his destruction, and again in 20:7." Beale with Campbell, *Revelation*, 227.
107 Beale with Campbell, 227; Fee, *Revelation*, 152; Phillips, *Revelation*, 323. Phillips observes, "John, however, uses the present tense to speak of the beast's rising: this is a menacing reality current to his readers and to Christians throughout the church age, though it seems that the beast will take a most potent form at the end of the age before Christ returns."
108 Morris, *Revelation*, 145.

final judgment, final victory, and Christ's return.[109] The two witnesses (cf. Luke 10:1; also John 8:17; Deut 19:15) are "killed" by the beast, while their "dead bodies" (τὸ πτῶμα; singular) are left to lie in the street.[110] The beast makes war on the saints for a divinely appointed time and even conquers them, though his ostensible victory only hastens his ultimate defeat (cf. Dan 7:21, 23, 25; Rev 20:7–10).[111] Satan's apparent victory is vicious and violent, yet it is inherently ironic—though the saints will be killed and appear defeated in the eyes of the world (cf. Rev 6:9–11; 11:7–10), their deaths only seal the final defeat of the world and the satanic forces that lie behind it (11:11–13).[112] As the beast is finally released from the pit, his persecutions and attacks against the church will appear victorious in his vicious assault (see Matt 24:37–44)—but Christ's return, the vindication of the saints, and the final judgment are soon to follow.[113]

John speaks in the language of earthly kingdoms and powers (Sodom, Babylon, Egypt, Jerusalem) in order to depict the earthly manifestation of satanic powers that stand in spiritual opposition to the things of Christ.[114] Satanic warfare against the saints of Christ is frequently made manifest through the machinations of the powers at work in this world, evident through the murderous decrees of Herod (Matt 2:16–18), through the opposition of a corrupt religious establishment (Matt 23 // Luke 11:37–54; Rev 2:9), and through the crushing tyranny of imperial Rome (Luke 23:2)—in all these manifestations, Satan arrays the powers of this world to make war on the saints in this age. Though these earthly empires satanically oppose Christ, it is through such opposition that kingdom advance is realized (see Matt 16:21, 24–26; 20:17–19; John 15:18–25; 16:1–4).[115]

---

109 Beale with Campbell, *Revelation*, 226. Christ's return in judgment ties together the various parallel sections in Revelation: cf. Rev 1:7; 6:12–17 and 7:9–17; 11:15,18; 14:14; 16:20; 19:11; and 20:11. See Hendriksen, *More Than Conquerors*, 22–25.
110 Morris, *Revelation: An Introduction and Commentary*, 146.
111 Beale with Campbell, *Revelation*, 227; Fee, *Revelation*, 151; Phillips, *Revelation*, 319–20.
112 Beale with Campbell, *Revelation*, 226.
113 Beale with Campbell, 227–28; Phillips, *Revelation*, 323–24.
114 Phillips, *Revelation*, 323–24.
115 Walter A. Elwell and Barry J. Beitzel, "Persecution," in *BEB*, 1646.

Satan's Future and Final Defeat

Having considered the ongoing influence and attacks of Satan following his exorcism, the New Testament also depicts the final defeat that awaits Satan at the conclusion of *this age* and the consummation of *the age to come*. The satanic defeat of Christ's first coming is an inaugurated reality, while the consummative conclusion is described as a future reality and hope for believers in this age.

Romans 16:20a

> THE GOD OF PEACE WILL SOON CRUSH
> SATAN UNDER YOUR FEET. (ROM 16:20)

In the final chapter of Romans, Paul assures the believers in Rome that God "will soon crush Satan" under their feet. Having previously warned the Romans about false teachers and divisive people in their midst (Rom 16:17–18), Paul progresses into a section of commendation, wherein he lauds his letter's recipients for their obedience of faith (16:19) and subsequently comforts them with a promise of Satan's impending demise (16:20). Paul frames the mention of Satan's ultimate demise in the context of a larger conflict between good and evil. He calls the Romans to "be wise as to what is good and innocent as to what is evil" (16:19b) and speaks of an impending conclusion to the conflict in a definitive crushing of Satan (16:20).[116]

Paul conveys that the crushing of Satan will happen "soon" (τάχος; cf. Luke 18:8; 1 Tim 3:14; Rev 1:1; 22:6). Paul envisages that in an impending eschatological event, Satan, and by extension, all those who follow him, will be crushed underfoot by the power of God.[117] The coming event that will "soon" take place is a triumphant, conclusive victory—Satan will be "crushed" (συντρίβω) underfoot. This promise of Satan's impending defeat provided comfort to both the Roman situation being addressed in the immediate context as well as the larger eschatological narrative of Scripture—Satan's defeat is imminent, and God's final victory is already

---

[116] John R. W. Stott, *Romans: God's Good News for the World*, BST (Downers Grove, IL: InterVarsity Press, 1995), 400.
[117] BDAG, s.v. "τάχος."; Everett F. Harrison and Donald A. Hagner, *Romans*, rev. ed., in *The Expositor's Bible Commentary*, eds. Tremper Longman III and David E. Garland (Grand Rapids: Zondervan, 2011), 233.

being accomplished.[118] False teachers, divisive voices, and Satan himself are all considered opponents of God's peace and are thereby subjected to the crushing judgment that is to come.[119]

Paul specifies that Satan will soon be crushed by God, though he will be crushed under the feet of those addressed in the letter ("under your feet"). Standing in spiritual opposition against "what is evil" (τὸ κακόν; 16:19) is the "God of peace" (ὁ θεὸς τῆς εἰρήνης; cf. 15:33; Phil 4:9; 1 Thess 5:23)—a phrase that is laden with eschatological import, as it seems to connect the rise of the serpent (Gen 3) to the impending destruction of the satanic adversary at hand.[120] The picture of the "God of peace" crushing Satan (cf. Ps 91:13) infers that satanic defeat is directly tied to Christological triumph. Paul is likely making another overt allusion to the *protoevangelium* of Gen 3:15, though there is also the implication that God will use humanity in the completion of their commission to be the agents of Satan's crushing—hence, he will be crushed "under *your* feet" (ὑπὸ τοὺς πόδας ὑμῶν; see Luke 10:18–20).[121] Believers are made a new creation in Christ (Rom 5:12–21; Gal 6:15) and their victory is assured. As Keener remarks: "Their victory is certain, even if not yet consummated."[122] The believers' role in Satan's defeat is the outworking of Christ's establishment of authority in this age and the subsequent commissioning of his disciples (see Matt 28:18–20). God will crush Satan through the "feet" of believers in the power of Christ.

Revelation 20:7–10

> AND THE DEVIL WHO HAD DECEIVED THEM WAS THROWN INTO THE LAKE OF FIRE AND SULFUR WHERE THE BEAST AND THE FALSE PROPHET WERE, AND THEY WILL BE TORMENTED DAY AND NIGHT FOREVER AND EVER. (REV 20:10)

The vision that John describes in Revelation 20:7–10 anticipates the global unleashing of satanic deception, the subsequent rebellion of the nations,

---

118 John Calvin, *Commentary on the Epistle of Paul the Apostle to the Romans*, ed. and trans. John Owen (Bellingham, WA: Logos Bible Software, 2010), 551; Mounce, *Romans*, 279–80.
119 Moo, *Epistle to the Romans*, 932–33.
120 Harrison and Hagner, *Romans*, 233.
121 See Stott, *Romans*, 401; Sam Storms, *Biblical Studies: Romans* (Edmond, OK: Sam Storms, 2016), Rom 16:19–20.
122 Craig Keener, *Romans*, NCC (Eugene, OR: Cascade, 2009), 190.

and the conclusive victory of Christ. This passage is a consummation passage that forms a climax to the New Testament narrative of satanic persecution against the church. Satan is released from previous restraint in his exorcised status, and he is divinely permitted to deceive the nations and to instigate full-scale eschatological rebellion against Christ (see Rev 11:7, 18; 14:14–18; 16:13–16; 19:17–21). The timing of his release is not precisely noted—John says it will occur "when" (ὅταν; "whenever") the "thousand years" is concluded.[123] Though the angel had previously confined Satan to the pit (20:1) as a result of the satanic exorcism realized in Christ's first coming, the figure who releases him from the abyss is not specified—nevertheless, it is clear that Satan is released. The proliferation of satanic deception that occurs following Satan's release makes it clear that the root of man's destructive sinfulness rests in the rebellious and darkened heart that characterizes the fallen state of all men (cf. Eph 2:1–3).[124] Satanic influence operates through deception that leads to rebellion and ruin—which becomes clear when Satan is finally released, and deception, rebellion, and destruction immediately follow.[125]

John describes Satan's "release" (λύω; cf. Rev 5:2; 9:14; 20:3) from the pit, a release he has previously described as something that "must" happen (v. 3).[126] Satan's power is great, but he is still a finite creature, as his release implicitly highlights. It is important to affirm that Satan does not somehow "escape"—rather, he is released by the God who is sovereign over the deception and warfare that are soon to follow. The release of Satan "to deceive the nations" (v. 8) further clarifies the emphatic purpose of his initial restraint. He was previously restrained "so that he might not deceive the nations any longer" (v. 3). The specific eschatological nature of Satan's restraint is clarified by the prompt response to his release—Satan emerges to "deceive the nations" (πλανάω) and to "gather them for battle" (v. 8). The period of restraint has ended, and the short time of his release has come, as evidenced by his immediate work of deceiving multitudes into

---

[123] Morris, *Revelation*, 227; BDAG, s.v. "ὅταν." The "thousand years" symbolically refers to the interadventual period between Christ's first and second comings.
[124] So Ladd, *Commentary on the Revelation of John*, 269. Phillips observes: "We see that the sinful tendencies of the human heart do not evolve upward over time. As soon as God lifts his restraint on Satan, 'the nations' are deceived once more." Phillips, *Revelation*, 589.
[125] Phillips, *Revelation*, 589.
[126] BDAG, s.v. "λύω"; Phillips, *Revelation*, 588.

rebellion against Christ—rebellion that will inevitably bring about their own destruction.[127]

The army that Satan deceives into making war against those who follow Christ is described as a considerably large multitude.[128] Satan will draw the nations from "the four corners of the earth, Gog and Magog, to gather them for battle; their number is like the sand of the sea" (v. 8). The depiction of the "four corners" depicts an area of global significance, indicating that the entirety of the known world is in view (Rev 7:1; Isa 11:12; cf. Ezek 37:9; Dan 7:2).[129] The nations (τὰ ἔθνη) are further identified as "Gog and Magog" (τὸν Γὼγ καὶ Μαγώγ), language that calls to mind the biblical nations that rebelled against God in times past. Just as the evil "great horde" of Ezekiel's prophecy rebelled against God and made war against his people (Ezek 38:2–7, 15, 22; 39:4), so the current reference to "Gog and Magog" is now greatly escalated. As opposed to individual nations, Gog and Magog are now used as shorthand for the totality of the gathered evil ("four corners") that is arrayed for battle against believers.[130] Their identity as "Gog" and "Magog" clarifies the nature of their intentions: they represent the peoples of this world who have been deceived, who have risen in opposition to God, and who have attempted to destroy God's people.[131]

The satanic army is gathered for "the battle" or "the war" (τὸν πόλεμον), the final great war that Satan will launch against those who follow Christ, which is called "Armageddon" (Ἁρμαγεδών) in an earlier passage (Rev 16:16; cf. 11:7; 16:14; 19:19; also 13:7).[132] Following the description of Satan's exorcism and restraint early in the chapter (20:1–3), John later describes the final conflict and consummative defeat of Satan and his forces. While there may be a degree of narrative anticipation for a fierce battle to occur, John's succinct description reveals that the battle is not a fight between equals. The great satanic army surrounds the saints and their city,

---

127 Phillips, *Revelation*, 588; Beale with Campbell, *Revelation*, 452.
128 While Revelation ch 16 focuses on the destruction of the sinful, and ch 19 depicts the beast's defeat, ch 20 especially focuses on the horde arrayed in this final battle that all three passages describe. See Phillips, *Revelation*, 205.
129 Beale with Campbell, *Revelation*, 452; Fee, *Revelation*, 285.
130 Fee, *Revelation*, 285; Ladd, *Commentary on the Revelation of John*, 269; Morris, *Revelation*, 227; Beale with Campbell, *Revelation*, 452–53.
131 The phrase τὰ ἔθνη refers to human people, not demonic spirits (cf. Rev 19:15).; See Beale with Campbell, *Revelation*, 453.
132 Beale with Campbell, *Revelation*, 452; Phillips, *Revelation*, 589.

but their defeat is both decisive and abrupt: "Fire came down from heaven and consumed them" (v. 9; cf. Ezek 38:22).[133] Following the army's defeat, "the devil who had deceived them" is thrown into the pit of fire, where he will remain in torment for all eternity. Satan's final deception has cosmic consequences, and it leads to his final defeat and eternal punishment.

1 Corinthians 15:24–27

> THE LAST ENEMY TO BE DESTROYED IS DEATH. (1 COR 15:26)

After the previous discussion of 1 Corinthians 15 in the context of satanic exorcism in this age, some closing observations on this passage are important with regard to how the New Testament describes the final defeat of Satan. There is a palpable eschatological tension in this passage—Christ has defeated sin and death both *now* and *not-yet*, resulting in an eschatological state that is inaugurated while not yet consummated. Paul directs his readers to the impending coming of "the end" [τὸ τέλος]—in this case, referring to the teleological or consummative conclusion of all things.[134]

Christ's victory is one that is inaugurated in his first coming, while the consummative end (τέλος) is realized in his second coming. Death (ὁ θάνατος) is defeated now in the atoning work of Christ (John 3:5; Rom 5:12–21; 8:37–39; 2 Cor 5:16–19; Eph 2:15–16), while the final τέλος comes through the conclusive, ultimate defeat of death—what Paul describes as the "last enemy" (ἔσχατος ἐχθρὸς). The inaugurated advent of the age to come entails Christ's defeat of all rulers, authorities, and powers (see Eph 1:21; 2:2; 6:12; Col 1:13, 16; 2:15)—the same spiritual entities whose exorcism from this world precedes the final defeat of Satan himself.[135] Similarly, the kingdom is present now through the work of Christ in this age (Matt 3:2; Matt 4:17 // Mark 1:15; Mark 9:1; Rev 11:1; cf. Dan 2:44; 7:14, 27), while the τέλος represents the time in which Christ will deliver the kingdom to the Father.

The current overlap of *this age* and *the age to come* is a time of spiritual warfare, yet it is also a time in which Christ victoriously treads every

---

133 Morris, *Revelation*, 228; Beale with Campbell, *Revelation*, 451; Fee, *Revelation*, 285.
134 This term refers to the final act in the cosmic drama. BDAG, s.v. "τέλος."
135 Verbrugge, "1 Corinthians," 397. See also Storms, *Kingdom Come*, 145ff; Mathison, *From Age to Age*, 549; Strachan, *Reenchanting Humanity*, 367ff.

enemy underfoot (1 Cor 15:25–27; cf. Ps 8:6; Gen 1:28; Heb 2:5–8).[136] Christ is victorious now, yet his final victory is realized when every enemy (1 Cor 15:25; cf. Ps 110:1) is destroyed in the final death of death itself (Rev 20:14).[137] John details the unfolding of this eschatological τέλος in the fact that both "death" (ὁ θάνατος) and "Hades" (ὁ ᾅδης) are consigned to the second death (Rev 20:14). The last enemy (ἔσχατος ἐχθρὸς; 1 Cor 15), death itself, is ultimately destroyed. Paul makes clear that the death of death is a result of Christ's comprehensive victory, as Christ subjects "all" (πᾶς) underfoot: "all" rule and authority and power (15:24), "all" enemies (15:25), and "all" things (five occurrences in 15:27–28).[138] Martin Luther observes:

> When the hour strikes, [Paul] wishes to say, in which we who are Christ's are to rise and follow him, then all is accomplished, and the end to which Scripture points is at hand. This earthly life with all its misery and misfortune will cease, the vile devil with his rule will come to an end, yes, also both the secular and the spiritual offices will terminate. In sum, all things on earth will come to an end, and that which we together with all saints have desired and waited for since the beginning of the world will be ushered in.[139]

The "end"—that is, the τέλος to which Christ's victory leads—entails the final defeat of Satan and death itself, as Christ reigns triumphantly over "all."

---

136 Verbrugge, "1 Corinthians," 397.
137 Sproul, *Reformation Study Bible: English Standard Version*, 2040.
138 Compare the use of "all things" (πάντα ὑπέταξας) in Ps 8:6 (8:7 LXX). See Verbrugge, "1 Corinthians," 398.
139 Martin Luther, Commentary on 1 Corinthians 15:20, *Luther's Works* 28:123-24, cited in Manetsch, George, and McNutt, *1 Corinthians*, 371.

Chapter 7

Conclusion

This study has examined the theological concept of satanic exorcism in this age as an inaugurated eschatological theme. Satanic exorcism describes a divinely instituted limitation of satanic power and authority through the work of Christ's first coming while still recognizing the persistence of satanic persecution and attack as *this age* is passing away and being replaced by *the age to come*. Satan is defeated *now*, even though his final defeat is *not-yet* realized. Satanic defeat may rightly be referred to as an exorcism because it shares striking similarities with demonic exorcisms, only writ large on a cosmic scale. Christ's public ministry was illustrated by demonic exorcisms as God's kingdom advanced in this world, while the culmination of Christ's first coming involved the cosmic exorcism of Satan himself. Satanic exorcism describes a spiritual reality between Christ's first and second comings—an eschatological state that has been inaugurated while not yet consummated. Scripture depicts this eschatological state as an overlapping of *this age* and *the age to come*, ushering in realities that are inaugurated in Christ's first coming that await the consummation of his return. Therefore, there are many tangible eschatological consequences to Satan's exorcism through Christ's first coming, even while his exorcism and restraint do not entail a complete cessation of all satanic activity.

This study's approach to examining satanic exorcism shares much in common with Graham Cole's method of scriptural grounding. Scriptural grounding is an approach that primarily stresses the analysis of biblical material, as opposed to relying on extra-canonical source material as the foundational source material for study.[1] The outworking of scriptural ground-

---

[1] Cole, *Against the Darkness*, 19–20. Cole also recognizes a reliance on Charles Scobie's work in this regard, see Cole, *Against the Darkness*, 19n14. On "scriptural grounding," see

ing is the construction of systematic-theological conclusions that flow from a foundation of exegetical theology. This study likewise shares the eschatological approach of Charles Scobie's work, particularly regarding his effective use of cross-canonical biblical eschatology.[2] Scobie develops the eschatological themes in Scripture from Genesis through Revelation, observing the unity of the biblical revelation through the lens of biblical eschatology. Particularly regarding the identity of Satan, Scobie correctly observes that a close reliance on biblical revelation is necessary in order to avoid undue theological speculation regarding this figure.[3] Satan is presented in Scripture as a defeated foe who warrants recognition and caution, even while every detail of his existence is not made abundantly clear.

Summary of Findings

This study traces satanic power and authority throughout the biblical canon, though the primary focus is given to the effects of satanic exorcism that exist between Christ's first and second comings—in the overlap of *this age* and *the age to come*. Chapter 1 began this discussion by examining the eschatological consequences of satanic exorcism, particularly as it manifests as an inaugurated defeat. There is an eschatological tension in Satan's defeat—he is a defeated foe who has been cast down from his previous place of power, and yet his attacks are still present, and his persecutions against believers are still felt. Satan is a murky figure in the biblical narrative, rarely presented as the focus of any given passage and with a paucity of details provided—which calls for a degree of exegetical caution. Though his complete background is unknown, Satan is clearly a created being whose power and authority have been curtailed by the work of Christ. Satan's defeat is inaugurated in Christ's first coming, his powers of deception are limited in this age, and his work is subject to the sovereignty of God. Martin Luther thus reportedly observed that Satan is ultimately "God's Devil."[4]

Chapter 2 examined the field of scholarship in the area of eschatology, with specific attention paid to the area of satanic defeat. Notable works include the eschatological approaches of G. K. Beale and Anthony

---

also Köstenberger and Patterson, *Invitation to Biblical Interpretation*, 576–77.
2   Scobie, *Ways of Our God*. The "narrative" eschatological approach of Mathison is also beneficial regarding methodology. See Mathison, *From Age to Age*.
3   Scobie, *Ways of Our God*, 243.
4   George, "Where Are the Nail Prints?," 253; cf. Lutzer and Sproul, *God's Devil*.

Hoekema, both of which effectively employ facets of satanic defeat in their conception of inaugurated eschatology. Geerhardus Vos is a foundational theologian in this regard, as he explicates and expounds on the nature of two-age eschatology as it occurs within the New Testament (particularly the Pauline writings). The work of William Cook and Charles Lawless concerning exorcisms and spiritual warfare is especially helpful, as their study provides a groundwork for examining demonic exorcisms in the New Testament. Though several scholars address the concept of satanic defeat, few expound on the effects of satanic defeat within the New Testament. There are even fewer studies that note the theological and exegetical links between satanic defeat and exorcism in the New Testament, leaving significant room to explore the concept of satanic defeat as a cosmic spiritual exorcism in this age. A theology of New Testament satanic exorcism reveals a robustly Christological eschatology—believers experience victory through suffering, conquering Satan by the word of their testimony (Rev 12:11; 1 John 5:4).

Chapter 3 discussed the theme of satanic exorcism as it occurred in Christ's first coming. Satan emerges at various times in Scripture prior to Christ's first coming, primarily operating in the spiritual realm and appearing to exercise a pronounced degree of power and authority. Satan also appears to stand ready to levy accusations against God's people, accusations that are intended to bring about humanity's judgment or destruction (Gen 3; Job 1–2; Zech 3). With the advent of Christ's first coming, the advance of God's kingdom is paralleled by exorcisms of demons—a form of precursory victories over the forces of darkness that culminate in Satan's eventual cosmic exorcism. Christ achieved victory and conquest over Satan and expelled him from his previous place of power and influence.

Following the work of Cook and Lawless, four major Gospel exorcisms were examined in this study: the Capernaum Synagogue (Mark 1:21–28 // Luke 4:31–37), the Gadarene/Gerasene demoniac (Matt 8:28–34 // Mark 5:1–20 // Luke 8:26–39), the Syrophoenician woman's daughter (Matt 15:21–28 // Mark 7:24–30), and the demonized boy (Matt 17:14–20 // Mark 9:14–29 // Luke 9:37–43). These major demonic exorcisms show five common elements present in demonic exorcisms, which also inform our understanding of satanic exorcism. First, the kingdom of God advances forcefully in this world, coming directly into conflict with the forces of evil. Second, demonic entities exercise a high degree of influence and power, while immediately recognizing and submitting to Christ's superior authority. Third, evil forces often work in conjunction with one another and exhibit certain territorial tendencies regarding the victimized. Fourth, there is a visceral and violent reaction to expulsion of the demonic/satanic from its host. Fifth and finally, the evil forces at work in this world submit to the authority of Christ and those who are sent in his authority. The demonic exorcisms in the Gospels prepare the way for the satanic exorcism that is to follow, evidenced by the eschatological references to the strong man (Matt 12:22–30 // Mark 3:22–27 // Luke 11:14–23), the ruler (John 12:31), and Satan falling (Luke 10:18–19). Satan's defeat in the work of Christ's first coming is described using the language of demonic exorcism, and his binding and expulsion bear evidence of the spiritual effects of his exorcism. As in demonic exorcism, there is a change in authority in satanic exorcism, and the evil spirit is removed from its previous place of influence. Exorcisms, both demonic and satanic, bear witness to eschatological control in this world being wrested from satanic control through the work of Christ.

Chapter 4 discusses the eschatological liberation that Christ's victorious and conquering work brought to those in bondage to sin and death in this world, in the context of the overlap of the ages. The current eschatological state of believers occurs in a time between the ages—that is, during the continuing overlap of *this age* and the inaugurated inbreaking of *the age to come*. Christ's first coming accomplished an eschatological reversal—rebuking Satan's attempt to grant him authority (Luke 4:6) while instead proclaiming his true possession of all authority (Matt 28:18), and subsequently issuing his disciples his authority over the forces of Satan (Luke 10:19). Satan previously exercised a degree of authority in *this age*, though a defining characteristic of the inaugurated *age to come* is Christ's reclamation of all authority in this world. Satanic forces have previously exercised authoritative influence in the realm of *this age*, while Christ's introduction of the new-creational reign of *the age to come* has brought inaugurated liberation with anticipation of the consummative second coming. Christ's victory has now brought believers deliverance from this age (Gal 1:3b–4), establishing Christological authority over the evil rulers and powers in this world (Col 2:15; Eph 1:20–23; 3:10; 6:11–12), including Satan, the ruler of the forces of evil (Heb 2:14; 1 John 3:8; 2 Cor 4:4).

Chapter 5 examines the spiritual implications of the curtailment of satanic power and authority through the work of Christ's first coming. Satanic exorcism does not imply that Satan is physically or spatially restrained, but rather that his exorcism has cast him from his previous place of power and influence and correspondingly limited the power and authority that he once exercised. Satan successfully accused believers before the very throne of God prior to Christ's first coming (Job 1; Zech 3), though his ability to indict those who are in Christ has been curtailed due to Christ's atoning work (Rom 8:33, 38; cf. Rev 12:7–12). Satan cannot successfully accuse believers before God—Christ's work has liberated believers and removed Satan's ability to accuse them (Rom 8:1). Because his authority has been powerfully reclaimed by the work of Christ, Satan no longer holds sway over the nations and thus cannot prevent the spread of the gospel message (Matt 28:18–20; Luke 10:1–20). Satan is also restrained from deceiving the nations into prematurely revolting against Christ and his followers until the appointed time of his final release and ultimate defeat (2 Thess 2; Rev 20:7–10). Opposition to the church continues in this age, but the final eschatological rebellion is held at bay. The New Testament thereby proclaims that Satan no longer possesses authority over death, he cannot prevent the gospel message from reaching the nations, and he cannot deceive the nations into premature eschatological rebellion.

Chapter 6 concludes this study by observing the ongoing reality of satanic assault that persists in this age. Believers are called to pray for the Father's protection from "the evil one" (Matt 6:13), recognizing Satan's desire to remain active in this world and to pursue his destructive purposes (see Matt 12:43–45 // Luke 11:24–26). Satan's influence in this world is ongoing, and believers are called to be on guard and ready for the persistent satanic attacks that characterize this age. Believers are made aware of Satan's designs and are therefore called to be prepared and guarded against his evil attacks. Satan continues to work through his children, through the mechanisms of lies, deception of the world, and false teaching that is brought in against the church. Satan is in the final stages of a cosmic spiritual war against Christ and his children, even while Satan's final defeat is assured. When this eschatological narrative concludes, the ancient serpent will finally be crushed underfoot, thrown into the lake of fire, and destroyed for all time (Rom 16:20; Rev 20:7–10; 1 Cor 15:24–27). Therefore, the call of believers in this age is to be ready for satanic attack and to persevere amid persecution. The perseverance and faith of believers serve as an eschatological witness, as John observed: "For everyone who has been born of God overcomes the world. And this is the victory that has overcome the world—our faith" (1 John 5:4).

Satan is a created spiritual being and a defeated sinister foe. The first coming of Christ has conquered him, and he is now described as cast out (John 12:31; 14:30; 16:11; Luke 10:18), defeated (Col 2:15; Heb 2:14; Eph 1:20–23, 3:10), and restrained (Matt 12:22–32; Gal 1:4; 2 Thess 2:1–12). Satan's exorcism has also produced tangible and substantial effects in this world—he is unable to accuse the elect successfully (Rev 12:7–12; Rom 8:33, cf. Rom 8:38–39), unable to prevent the spread of the gospel (Luke 10:1–20; Matt 28:18–20 // Mark 16:14–18* // Luke 24:44–49 // John 20:19–23), and unable to deceive the nations into premature apocalyptic rebellion (Rev 20:1–3).

Contribution to the Field

This study contributes to the field of eschatology by incorporating the theological construct of satanic exorcism within the field of two-age eschatology. Satanic exorcism is a key facet in eschatology, and the concept of satanic exorcism involves a cross-canonical[5] eschatological approach—observing satanic activity prior to, during, and following the first coming of Christ. Christ has defeated Satan, and this study has sought to uncover the theological dynamic of that satanic exorcism. Eschatology is the movement toward a final goal and an eternal new order,[6] and the exorcism of Satan in Christ's atoning work is a key facet of the eschatological storyline. Satanic exorcism is therefore, primarily, a New Testament concept, involving the time between Christ's first and second comings—a midpoint defeat in the eschatological narrative of spiritual warfare.

The period in which satanic defeat occurs is one of inauguration—a time in which the things of the age to come have commenced but are not yet consummated. This interadvental period is depicted in Scripture as an overlap of the ages, the time in which *this age* is passing away while *the age to come* has already dawned. Within this overlapping of the ages, Scripture

---

5 Such an approach may be termed "whole-Bible" eschatology. See Dumbrell, *Search for Order*, 9, 11.
6 Vos, *Pauline Eschatology*, 1; Hoekema, *Bible and the Future*, 6.

depicts Satan as a defeated foe, and Christ's victory is accomplished even while its blessings and benefits are not yet fully realized. There is a strain within the pages of the New Testament that depicts this ongoing tension—the things of the end have begun, yet there is an "end" or *telos* that is yet to come.

The eschatological concept of satanic exorcism also shows a depth of continuity in the work of Christ in the Gospels, connecting the preliminary demonic exorcisms with the cosmic satanic exorcism that would occur through the victorious conclusion of Christ's first coming. Demonic exorcisms denote an expanding presence of God's kingdom in this world, while the satanic exorcism that follows exemplifies the triumphant conclusion of Christ's work against the forces of darkness in this age. Satan's exorcism involves a transferal of power—the power that Satan exorcised prior to Christ's first coming has been curtailed, his power has been restrained, and he has been eschatologically cast down in the atoning work of Christ. As a result of this transferal of power and authority, Christ then commissioned his followers to go into the world in his authority with the commission of the gospel.

Finally, the category of satanic exorcism clarifies the nature of satanic deception, specifically regarding the future and final lifting of satanic restraint, which leads to cosmic deception and destruction. Satan is currently restrained in the interadventual period from deceiving the nations, concomitant with the kingdom promises regarding the work of the church. Satan's final release from his restraint leads to immediate deception, rebellion, and the final eschatological destruction of both Satan and all the nations who follow him.

Appendix 1

Lexical Parallels

archōn

John 12:31; 14:30; 16:11	"Now is the judgment of this world; now will the ruler of this world [*ho archōn tou kosmou*] be cast out."
	"I will no longer talk much with you, for the ruler of this world [*ho tou kosmou archōn*] is coming. He has no claim on me"
	"because the ruler of this world [*ho archōn tou kosmou toutou*] is judged."
Col 2:15	He disarmed the rulers [*tas archas*] and authorities [*tas exousias*] and put them to open shame
Eph 6:11–12	Put on the whole armor of God, that you may be able to stand against the schemes of the devil. For we do not wrestle against flesh and blood, but against the rulers [*tas archas*], against the authorities [*tas exousias*], against the cosmic powers over this present darkness, against the spiritual forces of evil in the heavenly places.
Rev 1:5	Jesus Christ the faithful witness, the firstborn of the dead, and the ruler of kings on earth [*ho archōn tōn basileōn tēs gēs*].

ballō

John 12:31	Now is the judgment of this world; now will the ruler of this world be cast out [*ekblēthēsetai exō* / lemma *ekballō*].

Rev 20:2–3	And he seized the dragon, that ancient serpent, who is the devil and Satan, and bound him for a thousand years, and threw [*ebalen* / lemma *ballō*] him into the pit, and shut it and sealed it over him, so that he might not deceive the nations any longer, until the thousand years were ended.
Rev 20:10	and the devil who had deceived them was thrown [*eblēthē* / lemma *ballō*] into the lake of fire and sulfur where the beast and the false prophet were

deō

Matt 12:29 [Mark 3:27; Luke 11:22]	Or how can someone enter a strong man's house and plunder his goods, unless he first binds [*dēsē* / lemma *deō*] the strong man? Then indeed he may plunder his house.
Rev 20:2	And he seized the dragon, that ancient serpent, who is the devil and Satan, and bound [*edēsen* / lemma *deō*] him for a thousand years

Appendix 2
Satanic Passages Analysis

The Old Testament

Gen 3:1	Now the serpent [*nāḥāš*] was more crafty than any other beast of the field that the Lord God had made.	Deception
Isa 14:12*	How you are fallen from heaven, O Day Star [*hêlēl*], son of Dawn!	Pride
Isa 27:1*	In that day the Lord with his hard and great and strong sword will punish Leviathan the fleeing serpent, Leviathan the twisting serpent [*nāḥāš*], and he will slay the dragon that is in the sea.	[Oppression]
1 Chr 21:1*	Then Satan [*sātān*] stood against Israel and incited David to number Israel.	Inciting
Job 1:6ff	Now there was a day when the sons of God [*benê hā elōhîm*] came to present themselves before the Lord, and Satan [*sātān*] also came among them.	Accusation, inflicting suffering
Job 2:1ff	Again there was a day when the sons of God [*benê hā elōhîm*] came to present themselves before the Lord, and Satan [*sātān*] also came among them to present himself before the Lord.	Accusation, physical torment
Ezek 28:14*	You were an anointed guardian cherub. I placed you; you were on the holy mountain of God;	Pride and violence

| Zech 3:1–2a | Then he showed me Joshua the high priest standing before the angel of the Lord, and Satan [*sātān*] standing at his right hand to accuse him. And the Lord said to Satan, "The Lord rebuke you, O Satan [*sātān*]! | Accusation |

* Disputed passages

The Gospels

Matt 4:1	Then Jesus was led up by the Spirit into the wilderness to be tempted by the devil [*diabolou*]	Temptation
Matt 4:5	Then the devil [*diabolos*] took him to the holy city and set him on the pinnacle of the temple	Temptation
Matt 4:8	Again, the devil [*diabolos*] took him to a very high mountain and showed him all the kingdoms of the world and their glory.	Temptation
Matt 12:29 [Mark 3:27; Luke 11:22]	"Or how can someone enter a strong man's house and plunder his goods, unless he first binds the strong man? Then indeed he may plunder his house."	Control / dominion
Matt 13:39	and the enemy who sowed them is the devil [*diabolos*]. The harvest is the end of the age, and the reapers are angels.	Sowing of 'tares'
Mark 1:13	And he was in the wilderness forty days, being tempted by Satan [*tou Satana*]. And he was with the wild animals, and the angels were ministering to him.	Temptation

Luke 4:2–5	forty days, being tempted by the devil [*diabolou*]. And he ate nothing during those days. And when they were ended, he was hungry. ³ The devil said to him, "If you are the Son of God, command this stone to become bread." And Jesus answered him, "It is written, 'Man shall not live by bread alone.'" And the devil took him up and showed him all the kingdoms of the world in a moment of time,	Temptation
Luke 8:12	then the devil [*ho diabolos*] comes and takes away the word from their hearts, so that they may not believe and be saved.	Taking away the word
Luke 10:18	And he said to them, "I saw Satan [*ton Satanan*] fall like lightning from heaven."	Fell from heaven
Luke 13:16	"And ought not this woman, a daughter of Abraham whom Satan [*ho Satanas*] bound for eighteen years, be loosed from this bond on the Sabbath day?"	Binding [a woman]
Luke 22:3	Then Satan [*Satanas*] entered into Judas called Iscariot, who was of the number of the twelve.	Possession [Judas]
Luke 22:31	"Simon, Simon, behold, Satan [*ho Satanas*] demanded to have you [pl.], that he might sift you like wheat"	Destruction
John 8:44	You are of your father the devil [*tou diabolou*], and your will is to do your father's desires. He was a murderer from the beginning, and does not stand in the truth, because there is no truth in him. When he lies, he speaks out of his own character, for he is a liar and the father of lies.	Murderer, Father of lies
John 10:10a	The thief comes only to steal and kill and destroy.	Steal, kill, destroy

John 12:31	"Now is the judgment of this world; now will the ruler [*ho archōn*] of this world be cast out."	Is cast out
John 13:2	During supper, when the devil [*tou diabolou*] had already put it into the heart of Judas Iscariot, Simon's son, to betray him	Instigation to betrayal
John 13:27	Then after he had taken the morsel, Satan [*ho Satanas*] entered into him.	Possession [Judas]
John 14:30	"I will no longer talk much with you, for the ruler [*ho archōn*] of this world is coming. He has no claim on me"	Rules this world
John 16:11	"because the ruler [*ho archōn*] of this world is judged"	Is judged

The Already—Defeated

2 Cor 2:11	"so that we would not be outwitted by Satan [*tou Satana*]; for we are not ignorant of his designs."	his plots are known
Eph 4:27	give no opportunity to the devil [*tō diabolō*]	Give no opportunity
Eph 6:11–12,16	[11] Put on the whole armor of God, that you may be able to stand against the schemes of the devil [*tou diabolou*]. [12] For we do not wrestle against flesh and blood, but against the rulers [*tas archas*], against the authorities [*tas exousias*], against the cosmic powers over this present darkness, against the spiritual forces of evil in the heavenly places. [...] [16] In all circumstances take up the shield of faith, with which you can extinguish all the flaming darts of the evil one;	Christians can stand against schemes of devil and demonic forces
2 Thess 3:3	But the Lord is faithful. He will establish you and guard you against the evil one [*tou ponērou*].	God guards us against the evil one

Heb 2:14	Since therefore the children share in flesh and blood, he himself likewise partook of the same things, that through death he might destroy the one who has the power of death, that is, the devil [*ton diabolon*]	Christ destroyed Satan through cross
Jas 4:7	Resist the devil [*tō diabolō*], and he will flee from you.	Resist Satan
1 John 2:13–14	I am writing to you, young men, because you have overcome the evil one. [x2]	Christians have overcome evil one
1 John 3:8	Whoever makes a practice of sinning is of the devil [*tou diabolou*], for the devil [*ho diabolos*] has been sinning from the beginning. The reason the Son of God appeared was to destroy the works of the devil [*tou diabolou*].	Christ destroyed works of Satan
1 John 4:4b	for he who is in you is greater than he who is in the world.	Christ greater than Satan
Rev 20:2–3a	And he seized the dragon, that ancient serpent [*ophis*], who is the devil [*Diabolos*] and Satan [*ho Satanas*], and bound him for a thousand years, and threw him into the pit, and shut it and sealed it over him, so that he might not deceive the nations any longer, until the thousand years were ended.	Satan is bound and unable to deceive

The Already—Not-yet

Acts 5:3	"Ananias, why has Satan [*ho Satanas*] filled your heart to lie to the Holy Spirit and to keep back for yourself part of the proceeds of the land?"	Fills heart to lie
Acts 10:38	He went about doing good and healing all who were oppressed by the devil [*tou diabolou*], for God was with him.	Oppresses

Acts 26:18	to open their eyes, so that they may turn from darkness to light and from the power of Satan [*tou Satana*] to God	Has power over darkness
1 Cor 5:5	you are to deliver this man to Satan [*tō Satana*] for the destruction of the flesh, so that his spirit may be saved in the day of the Lord.	Destroys flesh
1 Cor 7:5	but then come together again, so that Satan [*ho Satanas*] may not tempt you because of your lack of self-control.	Tempts
2 Cor 4:4	In their case the god of this world [*ho theos tou aiōnos toutou*] has blinded the minds of the unbelievers, to keep them from seeing the light of the gospel of the glory of Christ, who is the image of God.	Blinds eyes of unbelievers
2 Cor 11:3	as the serpent [*ophis*] deceived Eve by his cunning, your thoughts will be led astray from a sincere and pure devotion to Christ	Deceives [Eve]
2 Cor 11:14	Satan [*ho Satanas*] disguises himself as an angel [*angelon*] of light	Disguises as angel of light
2 Cor 12:7	a thorn was given me in the flesh, a messenger [*angelos*] of Satan [*Satana*] to harass me, to keep me from becoming conceited.	Harasses
Eph 2:2	the prince [*archonta*] of the power [*exousias*] of the air, the spirit that is now at work in the sons of disobedience	Works in sons of disobedience
1 Thess 2:18	but Satan [*ho Satanas*] hindered us.	Hinders
2 Thess 2:9–10a	The coming of the lawless one is by the activity of Satan [*tou Satana*] with all power and false signs and wonders, [10] and with all wicked deception [*apatē*]	Has power in false signs, wonders, and deception

1 Thess 3:5	for fear that somehow the tempter had tempted you and our labor would be in vain	Tempts
1 Tim 1:20b	whom I have handed over to Satan [*tō Satana*] that they may learn not to blaspheme	---
1 Tim 3:6–7	he may become puffed up with conceit and fall into the condemnation of the devil [*tou diabolou*] […] fall into disgrace, into a snare of the devil [*tou diabolou*]	Condemns and snares
1 Tim 5:15	For some have already strayed after Satan [*tou Satana*].	---
2 Tim 2:26	and they may come to their senses and escape from the snare of the devil [*tou diabolou*], after being captured by him to do his will.	Snares and captures
1 Pet 5:8	Be sober-minded; be watchful. Your adversary the devil [*diabolos*] prowls around like a roaring lion, seeking someone to devour.	Prowls and devours
1 John 5:18b–19	but he who was born of God protects him, and the evil one does not touch him. We know that we are from God, and the whole world lies in the power of the evil one.	Has power over world
Jude 9	the archangel Michael, contending with the devil [*tō diabolō*], was disputing about the body of Moses	Contends with angels
Rev 2:9b–10a	"those who say that they are Jews and are not, but are a synagogue of Satan [*tou Satana*]. Do not fear what you are about to suffer. Behold, the devil [*ho diabolos*] is about to throw some of you into prison, that you may be tested, and for ten days you will have tribulation."	Persecutes
Rev 2:13	"I know where you dwell, where Satan's [*tou Satana*] throne is."	---
Rev 3:9	"the synagogue of Satan [*tou Satana*] who say that they are Jews and are not, but lie"	---

Rev 12:13–14,17	And when the dragon saw that he had been thrown down to the earth, he pursued the woman who had given birth to the male child. But the woman was given the two wings of the great eagle so that she might fly from the serpent [*tou opheōs*] into the wilderness, to the place where she is to be nourished for a time, and times, and half a time. […] Then the dragon became furious with the woman and went off to make war on the rest of her offspring, on those who keep the commandments of God and hold to the testimony of Jesus.	Makes war against children of God

The Not–Yet

Rom 16:20	The God of peace will soon crush Satan [*ton Satanan*] under your feet.	Will be crushed
1 Cor 15:25–26	For he must reign until he has put all his enemies under his feet. The last enemy to be destroyed is death.	Death will be destroyed
Rev 20:7–8	And when the thousand years are ended, Satan [*ho Satanas*] will be released from his prison and will come out to deceive the nations that are at the four corners of the earth, Gog and Magog, to gather them for battle	Will be released, deceived, then destroyed

Bibliography

Akin, Daniel L. *1, 2, 3 John*. NAC 38. Nashville: Broadman & Holman, 2001.

Alexander, T. Desmond. *From Eden to the New Jerusalem: An Introduction to Biblical Theology*. Grand Rapids: Kregel, 2013.

———. *The City of God and the Goal of Creation*. Wheaton, IL: Crossway, 2018.

Arnold, Clinton E. *Ephesians*. ZECNT. Grand Rapids: Zondervan, 2011.

Augustine of Hippo. *Sermons on Selected Lessons of the New Testament*, Vol. 2. Library of Fathers of the Holy Catholic Church. Oxford: Parker, 1845.

Aulén, Gustaf, and A. G. Herbert. Christus Victor*: An historical Study of the Three Main Types of the Idea of Atonement*. London: SPCK, 1931. Repr., Eugene, OR: Wipf & Stock, 2003.

Aune, David. *Revelation 6–16*. WBC 52B. Grand Rapids: Zondervan, 2014.

Awwad, Johnny. "Satan in Biblical Imagination." *TR* 26.2 (2005): 111–26.

Baldwin, Joyce G. *Haggai, Zechariah, Malachi: An Introduction & Commentary*. TOTC 24. Downers Grove, IL: Inter-Varsity Press, 1972.

Barry, John D, David Bomar, Derek R. Brown, Rachel Klippenstein, Douglas Magnum, Elliot Ritzema, Carrie Wolcott, Lazarus Wentz, and Wendy Widder. *The Lexham Bible Dictionary*. Logos Research Edition.Bellingham, WA: Logos, 2016.

Bauer, Walter, Frederick William Danker, William F. Arndt, and F. Wilbur Gingrich, eds. *A Greek-English Lexicon of the New Testament and Other Early Christian Literature*, 3rd ed. Chicago: University of Chicago Press, 2000.

Bavinck, Herman. *Reformed Dogmatics, Volume 2: God and Creation*. Edited by John Bolt. Translated by John Vriend. Grand Rapids: Baker Academic, 2004.

Beale, G. K. *The Book of Revelation: A Commentary on the Greek Text*. NIGTC. Grand Rapids: Eerdmans, 1999.

———. "Eden, the Temple, and the Church's Mission in the New Creation." *JETS* 48.1 (2005): 5–31.

———. "The Millennium in Revelation 20:1-10: An Amillennial Perspective." *CTR* 11.1 (2013): 29–62.

———. *A New Testament Biblical Theology: The Unfolding of the Old Testament in the New*. Grand Rapids: Baker Academic, 2011.

———. *Redemptive Reversals and the Ironic Overturning of Human Wisdom*S-SBT. Wheaton, IL: Crossway, 2019.

———. "A Surrejoinder to Peter Enns." *Themelios* 32.3 (2007): 14–25.

———. *The Temple and the Church's Mission: A Biblical Theology of the Dwelling Place of God*. NSBT 17. Downers Grove, IL: InterVarsity Press, 2004.

Beale, G. K., and Benjamin L. Gladd. *The Story Retold: A Biblical-Theological Introduction to the New Testament*. Downers Grove, IL: InterVarsity Press, 2020.

Beale, G. K., and Mitchell Kim. *God Dwells among Us: Expanding Eden to the Ends of the Earth*. Downers Grove, IL: InterVarsity Press, 2014.

Beale, G. K., with David H. Campbell. *Revelation: A Shorter Commentary*. Grand Rapids: Eerdmans, 2015.

Beilby, James K., and Paul R. Eddy, eds. *The Nature of the Atonement: Four Views*. Downers Grove, IL: InterVarsity Press, 2006.

Bethancourt, Phillip Ross. "Christ the Warrior King: A Biblical, historical, and Theological Analysis of the Divine Warrior Theme in Christology." PhD diss., The Southern Baptist Theological Seminary, 2011.

Bird, Michael F. *Colossians and Philemon*. NCC. Eugene, OR: Cascade, 2009.

Bird, Michael, and Scott Harrower. *Trinity Without Hierarchy: Reclaiming Nicene Orthodoxy in Evangelical Theology*. Grand Rapids: Kregel, 2019.

Block, Daniel I. *The Book of Ezekiel: Chapters 25–48*. NICOT. Grand Rapids: Eerdmans, 1998.

Blomberg, Craig L. "Eschatology and the Church: Some New Testament Perspectives." *Themelios* 23.3 (1998): 3–26.

Blomberg, Craig L. *Matthew: An Exegetical and Theological Exposition of Holy Scripture.* NAC 22. Nashville: Broadman & Holman, 1992.

Bock, Darrell L. *Luke 1:1–9:50.* BECNT. Grand Rapids: Baker Books, 1994.

Bonhoeffer, Dietrich. *Creation and Fall; Temptation: Two Biblical Studies.* London: SCM, 1959.

Borchert, Gerald L. *John 1–11.* NAC 25A. Nashville: Broadman & Holman, 1996.

———. *John 12–21.* NAC 25B. Nashville: Broadman & Holman, 2002.

Boyd, Gregory A. *The Crucifixion of the Warrior God: Volumes 1 & 2.* Combined ed. Minneapolis: Fortress, 2017.

———. *God at War: The Bible & Spiritual Conflict.* Downers Grove, IL: InterVarsity Press, 1997.

———. *God of the Possible: A Biblical Introduction to the Open View of God.* Grand Rapids: Baker Books, 2000.

———. *Satan and the Problem of Evil: Constructing a Trinitarian Warfare Theodicy.* Downers Grove, IL: InterVarsity Press, 2001.

Brannan, Rick. *The Lexham Analytical Lexicon to the Greek New Testament.* Bellingham, WA: Logos Bible Software, 2011.

Brown, Colin, ed. *The New International Dictionary of New Testament Theology.* Vol. 3. Grand Rapids: Zondervan, 1975.

Brown, Derek R. "The Devil in the Details: A Survey of Research on Satan in Biblical Studies." CBR 9.2 (2011): 200–227.

Brown, Raymond E. *The Gospel According to John I–XII.* AB 29. New York: Doubleday, 1966.

Bruce, F. F. *The Epistles to the Colossians, to Philemon, and to the Ephesians.* NICNT. Grand Rapids: Eerdmans, 1984.

———. *The Gospel of John: Introduction, Exposition, and Notes.* Grand Rapids: Eerdmans, 1994.

Burge, Gary M. "Gospel of John." Pages 37–164 in *The Bible Knowledge Background Commentary*, eds. Craig A. Evans and Craig A. Bubeck. 1st ed., vol. 3. Colorado Springs: Cook, 2005.

Cairns, Alan. *Dictionary of Theological Terms.* Greenville: Ambassador Emerald International, 2002.

Caldwell, William. "The Doctrine of Satan: I. In the Old Testament." *Biblical World* 41.1 (1913): 29–33.

———. "The Doctrine of Satan: III. In the New Testament." *Biblical World* 41.3 (1913): 167–72.

Calvin, John. *Commentaries on the Catholic Epistles*. Edited and translated by John Owen. Bellingham, WA: Logos Bible Software, 2010.

———. *Commentaries on the Epistles of Paul the Apostle to the Philippians, Colossians, and Thessalonians*. Edited and translated by John Pringle. Bellingham, WA: Logos Bible Software, 2010.

———. *Commentaries on the Epistles of Paul to the Corinthians*. Vol. 2. Edited and translated by John Pringle. Bellingham, WA: Logos Bible Software, 2010.

———. *Commentaries on the Epistles of Paul to the Galatians and Ephesians*. Edited and translated by William Pringle. Bellingham: Logos Bible Software, 2010.

———. *Commentaries on the Twelve Minor Prophets*. Edited and translated by John Owen. Bellingham, WA: Logos Bible Software, 2010.

———. *Commentary on the Epistle of Paul the Apostle to the Romans*. Edited and translated by John Owen. Bellingham, WA: Logos Bible Software, 2010.

———. *Commentary on the First Book of Moses Called Genesis*. Vol. 1. Edited and translated by John King. Bellingham, WA: Logos Bible Software, 2010.———. *Commentary on the Gospel according to John*. Vol. 1. Edited and translated by William Pringle. Bellingham, WA: Logos Bible Software, 2015.Canoy, Robert W. "Time and Space, Satan (Devil, Ancient Serpent, Deceiver, and Accuser), and Michael in Revelation." *RevExp* 114.2 (2017): 254–65.

Carman, Jon. "The Falling Star and the Rising Son: Luke 10:17-24 and Second Temple 'Satan' Traditions." *Stone-Campbell Journal* 17.2 (2014): 221–31.

Carpenter, Eugene E., and Philip W. Comfort. *Holman Treasury of Key Bible Words: 200 Greek and 200 Hebrew Words Defined and Explained*. Nashville: Broadman & Holman Publishers, 2000.

Carson, D. A. *The Gospel according to John*. PNTC. Leicester: Apollos; Grand Rapids: Eerdmans, 1991.

———. "Matthew." 1st ed. Pages 3–600 in *EBC* 8. Edited by Frank E. Gabelein. Grand Rapids: Zondervan, 1984.

———. *When Jesus Confronts the World: An Exposition of Matthew 8–10*. Grand Rapids: Baker Books, 1987.

Case-Winters, Anna. "The End?: Christian Eschatology and the End of the World." *Int* 70.1 (2016): 61–74.

Chamblin, J. Knox. *Matthew: A Mentor Commentary*. 2 vols. Fearn, Scotland: Mentor, 2010.

Chapell, Bryan. *Ephesians*. REC. Phillipsburg, NJ: P&R Publishing, 2009.

Childs, Brevard S. *Biblical Theology of the Old and New Testaments: Theological Reflection on the Christian Bible*. Minneapolis: Fortress, 1993.

———. *Isaiah: A Commentary*. OTL. Louisville: Westminster John Knox, 2001.

Cole, Graham A. *Against the Darkness: The Doctrine of Angels, Satan, and Demons*, Foundations of Evangelical Theology Series. Wheaton, IL: Crossway, 2019.

Collins, C. John. *Did Adam and Eve Really Exist?: Who They Were and Why You Should Care*. Wheaton, IL: Crossway, 2011.

———. "The Place of the 'Fall' in the Overall Vision of the Hebrew Bible." *TJ* 40.2 (2019): 165–84.

Cook, William F., and Charles E. Lawless. *Spiritual Warfare in the Storyline of Scripture: A Biblical, Theological, and Practical Approach*. Nashville: Broadman & Holman, 2019.

Cooper, Lamar E. *Ezekiel*. NAC 17. Nashville: Broadman & Holman, 1994.

Copeland, Edwin Luther. "Great Commission and Missions." *SwJT* 9.2 (1967): 79–89.

Cotterell, Peter, and Max Turner. *Linguistics and Biblical Interpretation*. Downers Grove, IL: InterVarsity Press, 1989.

Cross, F. L., and E. A. Livingstone, eds. *The Oxford Dictionary of the Christian Church*. 3rd rev. ed. Oxford; New York: Oxford University Press, 2005.

Dahms, J. V. "Lead Us Not into Temptation." *JETS* 17 (1974).

Dempster, Stephen G. *Dominion and Dynasty: A Theology of the Hebrew Bible*. NSBT. Leicester, England; Downers Grove, IL: InterVarsity Press, 2003.

Doriani, Daniel M. *1 Peter*. REC. Phillipsburg, NJ: P&R Publishing, 2014.

———. *Matthew*. 2 vols. REC. Phillipsburg, NJ: P&R Publishing, 2008.

Dumbrell, William J. *The Search for Order: Biblical Eschatology in Focus.* Eugene, OR: Wipf & Stock, 2001.

Elwell, Walter A., and Barry J. Beitzel. *Baker Encyclopedia of the Bible.* Grand Rapids: Baker Books, 1988.

Erickson, Millard J. *Christian Theology.* 3rd ed. Grand Rapids: Baker Academic, 2013.

Evans, Craig A. "Inaugurating the Kingdom of God and Defeating the Kingdom of Satan." *BBR* 15.1 (2005): 49–75.

Evans, Craig A., ed. *The Bible Knowledge Background Commentary: Matthew–Luke.* Colorado Springs: Cook, 2003.

Evans, Craig A., ed. *The Bible Knowledge Background Commentary: Acts–Philemon.* Colorado Springs: Cook, 2004.

Evans, Craig A., and Stanley E. Porter Jr, eds. *Dictionary of New Testament Background: A Compendium of Contemporary Biblical Scholarship.* 1st ed. Downers Grove, IL: InterVarsity Press, 2000.

Farmer, Craig S., , ed. *John 1–12*.RCS 4. Downers Grove. IL: InterVarsity Press, 2014.

Farrar, Thomas J., and Guy Williams. "Diabolical Data: A Critical Inventory of New Testament Satanology." *JSNT* 39.1 (2016): 40–71.

———. "Talk of the Devil: Unpacking the Language of New Testament Satanology." *JSNT* 39.1 (2016): 72–96.

Fee, Gordon D. *Revelation.* NCC. Eugene, OR: Cascade, 2011.

———. *The First and Second Letters to the Thessalonians.* NICNT. Grand Rapids: Eerdmans, 2009.

Ferguson, Eamonn M. "The Devil in the Details: Satan in the Passion Narratives." *Logia* 28.1 (2019): 19–24.

Findlay, George G. "The Epistle to the Ephesians," in *The Expositor's Bible: Ephesians to Revelation*, ed. R. Robertson Nicoll. Hartford: Scranton, 1903.

Fitzmyer, Joseph A. *Romans: A New Translation with Introduction and Commentary.* AB 33. New Haven: Yale University Press, 2008.

Forbes, Chris. "Paul's Principalities and Powers: Demythologizing Apocalyptic?" *JSNT* 23.82 (2001): 61–88.

Fowl, Stephen E. *Ephesians: A Commentary*. NTL. Louisville: Westminster John Knox, 2012.

Frame, John M. *The Doctrine of God*. Phillipsburg, NJ: P&R Publishing, 2002.

France, R. T. *The Gospel of Mark: A Commentary on the Greek Text*. NIGTC. Grand Rapids: Eerdmans, 2002.

Fung, Ronald Y. K. *The Epistle to the Galatians*. NICNT. Grand Rapids: Eerdmans, 1988.

Garland, David E. *2 Corinthians*. NAC 29. Nashville: Broadman & Holman, 1999.

———. *Mark*. NIVAC. Grand Rapids: Zondervan, 1996.

Garrett, Susan R. "Christ and the Present Evil Age." *Int* 57.4 (2003): 370–83.

Gathercole, Simon J. "Different Chronological Views on Lk 10: Jesus' Eschatological Vision of the Fall of Satan: Luke 10,18 Reconsidered." ZNW 94 (2003): 143–63.

George Eldon Ladd. *A Commentary on the Revelation of John*. Grand Rapids: Eerdmans, 1972.

George, Timothy. *Galatians*. NAC 30. Nashville: Broadman & Holman, 1994.

———. "Where Are the Nail Prints? The Devil and Dr. Luther." *JETS* 61.2 (2018): 245–57.

Gershenson, Daniel E. "The Name Satan." ZAW 114.3 (2002): 443–45.

Gibson, John M. "The Gospel of St. Matthew." Pages 693–810 in *The Expositor's Bible* 4. Hartford: Scranton, 1903.

Goldingay, John. *Isaiah. Understanding the Bible Commentary*. Grand Rapids: Baker Books, 2012.

Graybill, Gregory B. *Philippians, Colossians*. RCS 11. Downers Grove, IL: InterVarsity Press, 2013.

Green, Joel B. *The Gospel of Luke*. NICNT. Grand Rapids: Eerdmans, 1997.

Green, Joel B., Scot McKnight, and I. Howard Marshall, eds. *Dictionary of Jesus and the Gospels*. Downers Grove, IL: InterVarsity Press, 1992.

Grudem, Wayne A. *Systematic Theology: An Introduction to Biblical Doctrine*. Leicester: Inter-Varsity Press; Grand Rapids: Zondervan, 1994.

Gurtner, Daniel M. "Ephesians." Pages 543–68 in *The Bible Knowledge Background Commentary: Acts–Philemon*, eds. Craig A. Evans and Craig A. Bubeck (Colorado Springs: Cook, 2004).

Hamilton, Victor P. *The Book of Genesis: Chapters 1–17*. NICOT. Grand Rapids: Eerdmans, 1990.

Harper, Brad. "Christus Victor, Postmodernism, and the Shaping of Atonement Theology." *Cultural Encounters* 2.1 (2005): 37–51.

Harris, Gregory H. "Does God Deceive?: The 'Deluding Influence' of Second Thessalonians 2:11." *TMSJ* 16.1 (2005): 73–93.

Harris, Gregory H. "Satan's Work as a Deceiver." *BibSac* 156.622 (1999): 190–202.

Harrison, Everett F., and Donald A. Hagner. "Romans." Rev. ed. Pages 19–273 in *Expositor's Bible Commentary* 11. Edited by Tremper Longman III and David E. Garland. Grand Rapids: Zondervan, 2011.

Hartley, John E. *The Book of Job*. NICOT. Grand Rapids: Eerdmans, 1988.

Heiser, Michael S. *Supernatural: What the Bible Teaches about the Unseen World and Why It Matters*. Bellingham, WA: Lexham, 2015.

———. *The Unseen Realm: Recovering the Supernatural Worldview of the Bible*. Bellingham, WA: Lexham, 2019.

Hendriksen, William. *John: New Testament Commentary*. Grand Rapids: Baker Books, 2002.

———. *Luke: New Testament Commentary*. Grand Rapids: Baker Books, 1978.

———. *Mark: New Testament Commentary*. Grand Rapids: Baker Books, 1975.

———. *More Than Conquerors: An Interpretation of the Book of Revelation*, 75th anniv. ed. Grand Rapids: Baker Books, 2015.

Hertig, Paul. "The Great Commission Revisited: The Role of God's Reign in Disciple Making." *Missiology* 29.3 (2001): 343–53.

Hiers, Richard H. "Satan, Demons, and the Kingdom of God." *SJT* 27.1 (1974): 35–47.

Augustine. *City of God*. Translated by Henry Bettenson. New York: Penguin Books, 2004.

Hodge, Charles. *Commentary on the Epistle to the Ephesians*. Grand Rapids: Eerdmans, 1994.

Hoekema, Anthony A. *Created in God's Image*. Grand Rapids: Eerdmans, 1994.

———. *The Bible and the Future*. Grand Rapids: Eerdmans, 2000.

Höhne, David A. *The Last Things. Contours of Christian Theology*. Downers Grove, IL: InterVarsity Press, 2019.

Horton, Michael. "Eschatology After Nietzsche: Apollonian, Dionysian or Pauline?" *IJST* 2.1 (2000): 29.

———. *The Christian Faith: A Systematic Theology for Pilgrims on the Way*. Grand Rapids: Zondervan, 2011.

Orr, James, John L. Nuelsen, Edgar Y. Mullins, and Morris O. Evans, eds. *The International Standard Bible Encyclopedia*. Chicago: Howard-Severance Company, 1915.

Johnson, Keith E. "Trinitarian Agency and the Eternal Subordination of the Son: An Augustinian Perspective." *Themelios* 36.1 (2011): 7–25.

Johnson, Luke T. *Hebrews: A Commentary*. NTL. Louisville: Westminster John Knox, 2012.

———. "Powers & Principalities: The Devil Is No Joke." *Commonweal* 138.17 (2011): 14–18.

Kaiser Jr., Walter C. "The Promise Doctrine and Jesus." *TJ* 4 (1975): 58–66.

Kanagaraj, Jey J. *John*. NCC. Eugene, OR: Cascade, 2013.

Keener, Craig. *Romans*. NCC. Eugene, OR: Cascade, 2009.

Kees, Jason P. "At the End of All Things: Identifying the Ideal-Reader of the Revelation." PhD diss., Midwestern Baptist Theological Seminary, 2018.

Keil, Carl Friedrich, and Franz Delitzsch. *Commentary on the Old Testament, Vol. 9: Ezekiel, Daniel*. Peabody, MA: Hendrickson, 1996.

———. *Commentary on the Old Testament, Vol. 10: Minor Prophets*. Peabody, MA: Hendrickson, 1996.

Kidner, Derek. *Genesis: An Introduction & Commentary*. TOTC 1. Downers Grove, IL: Inter-Varsity Press, 1967.

Kimble, Jeremy M., and Ched Spellman. *Invitation to Biblical Theology: Exploring the Shape, Storyline, and Themes of Scripture*. Invitation to Theological Studies. Grand Rapids: Kregel, 2020.

Kittel, Gerhard, and Gerhard Friedrich. *Theological Dictionary of the New Testament*. Translated by Geoffrey W. Bromiley. Vol. 1. Grand Rapids: Eerdmans, 1985.

Köstenberger, Andreas J., Alexander Stewart, and Apollo Makara. *Jesus and the Future: Understanding What He Taught about the End Times*. Bellingham, WA: Lexham, 2018.

Köstenberger, Andreas J., and Richard Duane Patterson. *Invitation to Biblical Interpretation: Exploring the Hermeneutical Triad of History, Literature, and Theology*. Grand Rapids: Kregel, 2011.

Köstenberger, Andreas J., and Scott R. Swain. *Father, Son and Spirit: The Trinity and John's Gospel*. NSBT. Downers Grove, IL: InterVarsity Press, 2008.

Kreitzer, Beth, Timothy George, Scott M. Manetsch, and David W. McNutt, eds. *Luke*. RCS 3. Downers Grove, IL: InterVarsity Press, 2015.

Krentz, Edgar. "'Make Disciples': Matthew on Evangelism." *CurTM* 33.1 (2006): 23–41.

Ladd, George Eldon. *A Theology of the New Testament*. Rev. ed. Grand Rapids: Eerdmans, 1993.

———. *The Gospel of the Kingdom: Scriptural Studies in the Kingdom of God*. Grand Rapids: Eerdmans, 2011.

———. *The Presence of the Future: The Eschatology of Biblical Realism*. Grand Rapids: Eerdmans, 1974.

Ladd, George Eldon, Anthony A. Hoekema, Herman A. Lloyt, and Loraine Boettner. *The Meaning of the Millennium: Four Views*. Edited by Robert G. Clouse. Downers Grove, IL: InterVarsity Press, 1977.

Letham, Robert. *Systematic Theology*. Wheaton, IL: Crossway, 2019.

———. *The Holy Trinity: In Scripture, History, Theology, and Worship*. Phillipsburg, NJ: P&R Publishing, 2004.

The Lexham Analytical Lexicon of the Septuagint. Bellingham, WA: Lexham Press, 2012.

Liefield, Walter L. "Luke." 1st ed. Pages 797–1059 in *Expositor's Bible Commentary* Vol. 8. Edited by Frank E. Gaebelein. Grand Rapids: Zondervan, 1984.

Löfstedt, Torsten. "Satan's Fall and the Mission of the Seventy-Two." *Svensk exegetisk årsbok* 76 (2011): 95–114.

Longman, Tremper, and Daniel G. Reid. *God Is a Warrior*. Studies in Old Testament Biblical Theology. Grand Rapids: Zondervan, 1995.

Luther, Martin. *Luther's Works*. Edited by Jaroslav Pelikan. Vol. 1. St. Louis: Concordia, 1958.

Lutzer, Erwin W., and R. C. Sproul. *God's Devil: The Incredible Story of How Satan's Rebellion Serves God's Purposes*. Chicago: Moody, 2015.

Luz, Ulrich. *Matthew 1–7*. Edited by Helmut Koester. Rev. ed. Hermeneia.his. Minneapolis: Fortress, 2007.

Magnum, Douglas, Derek R. Brown, Rachel Klippenstein, and Rebekah Hurst, eds. *Lexham Theological Wordbook*. Lexham Bible Reference Series. Bellingham, WA: Lexham, 2014.

Manetsch, Scott M., Timothy George, and David W. McNutt, eds. *1 Corinthians*. RCS 9A.. Downers Grove, IL: InterVarsity Press, 2017.

Mangum, Douglas, Miles Custis, and Wendy Widder. *Genesis 1–11*. Lexham Research Commentaries. Bellingham, WA: Lexham, 2012.

Marshall, I. Howard. *The Epistles of John*. NICNT. Grand Rapids: Eerdmans, 1978.

Martin, Michael D. *1, 2 Thessalonians*. NAC 33. Nashville: Broadman & Holman, 1995.

Martin, Ralph P. *2 Corinthians*. WBC 40. Waco, TX: Word, 1986.

Mathews, Kenneth. *Genesis 1–11:26*, NAC 1A. Nashville: Broadman & Holman, 1996.

Mathison, Keith A. *From Age to Age*. P&R Publishing, 2014.

Melick, Richard R. *Philippians, Colossians, Philemon*. NAC 32. Nashville: Broadman & Holman, 1991.

Michaels, J. Ramsey. *The Gospel of John*. NICNT. Grand Rapids: Eerdmans, 2010.

Miller, Stephen. *Daniel*. NAC 18. Nashville: Broadman & Holman, 1994.

Milne, Bruce. *The Message of John*. BST. Downers Grove, IL: InterVarsity Press, 1993.

Moltmann, Jürgen. "The End as Beginning." *Word and World* 22.3 (2002): 221–27.

Moo, Douglas J. *The Epistle to the Romans*. NICNT. Grand Rapids: Eerdmans, 1996.

Morris, Leon. *Revelation: An Introduction and Commentary*. TNTC 20. Downers Grove, IL: InterVarsity Press, 1987.

———. *The Gospel According to Matthew*. PNTC. Grand Rapids: Eerdmans, 1992.

Motyer, J. Alec. *Isaiah: An Introduction and Commentary*. TOTC 20. Downers Grove, IL: InterVarsity Press, 1999.

Mounce, Robert H. *A Living Hope: A Commentary on 1 and 2 Peter*. Eugene, OR: Wipf & Stock, 2005.

———. *Romans*. NAC 27. Nashville: Broadman & Holman Publishers, 1995.

———. *The Book of Revelation*. Rev. ed. NICNT. Grand Rapids: Eerdmans, 1997.

Myers, Allen C., ed. *The Eerdmans Bible Dictionary*. Grand Rapids: Eerdmans, 1987.

O'Brien, Peter T. "Great Commission of Matthew 28:18-20: A Missionary Mandate or Not?" *RTR* 35.3 (1976): 66–78.

———. *The Letter to the Ephesians*. PNTC. Grand Rapids: Eerdmans, 1999.

O'Donnell, Douglas Sean. *1–3 John*. REC. Phillipsburg, NJ: P&R Publishing, 2015.

Pagels, Elaine H. "The Social history of Satan, the 'Intimate Enemy': A Preliminary Sketch." *HTR* 84.2 (1991): 105–28.

Paul, Barnett. *The Second Epistle to the Corinthians*. NICNT. Grand Rapids: Eerdmans, 1997.

Phillips, Richard D. *John*. REC. Phillipsburg, NJ: P&R Publishing, 2014.

———. *Revelation*. REC. Phillipsburg, NJ: P&R Publishing, 2017.

Pink, Arthur W. *Exposition of the Gospel of John*. Grand Rapids: Zondervan, 1982.

Poobalan, Ivor. "Who Is the 'God of This Age' in 2 Corinthians 4:4?" *JAET* 24.1 (2020): 41–56.

Poythress, Vern S. "Currents within Amillennialism." *Presb* 26.1 (2000): 21–25.

———. "Genre and Hermeneutics in Rev 20:1–6." *JETS* 36.1 (1993): 41–54.

Pugh, Benjamin. "'Kicking the Daylights out of the Devil': The Victory Motif in Some Recent Atonement Theology." *EuroJTh* 23.1 (2014): 32–42.

Recker, Robert R. "Satan: In Power or Dethroned?" *CTJ* 6.2 (1971): 133–55.

Richardson, Alan, and John Bowden, eds. *The Westminster Dictionary of Christian Theology*. Philadelphia: Westminster, 1983.

Ridderbos, Herman N. *The Coming of the Kingdom*. Edited by Raymond O. Zorn. Translated by H. de Jongste. Phillipsburg, NJ: P&R Publishing, 1962.

———. *The Gospel according to John: A Theological Commentary*. Translated by John Vriend. Grand Rapids: Eerdmans, 1997.

Riddlebarger, Kim. *A Case for Amillennialism: Understanding the End Times*, Exp. ed. Grand Rapids: Baker Books, 2013.

———. *The Man of Sin: Uncovering the Truth About the Antichrist*. Grand Rapids: Baker Books, 2006.

Romanowsky, John W. "'When the Son of Man Is Lifted up': The Redemptive Power of the Crucifixion in the Gospel of John." *Hor* 32.1 (2005): 100–116.

Schreiner, Patrick. *The Body of Jesus: A Spatial Analysis of the Kingdom in Matthew*. LNTS 555. New York: T&T Clark, 2016.

———. *The Kingdom of God & the Glory of the Cross*. SSBT. Wheaton, IL: Crossway, 2018.

Schreiner, Thomas R. *1, 2 Peter, Jude*. NAC 37. Nashville: Broadman & Holman, 2003.

———. *New Testament Theology: Magnifying God in Christ*. Grand Rapids: Baker Academic, 2008.

———. *Romans*. BECNT. Grand Rapids: Baker Books, 1998.

Scobie, Charles H. H. *The Ways of Our God: An Approach to Biblical Theology*. Grand Rapids: Eerdmans, 2003.

Segal, Alan F. "Ruler of This World: Attitudes about Mediator Figures and the Importance of Sociology for Self-Definition." In *Jewish and Christian Self-Definition, Vol. 2: Aspects of Judaism in the Greco-Roman Period*, ed. E. P. Sanders with A. I. Baumgarten and Alan Mendelson (Philadelphia: Fortress, 1981), 245–68.

Shepherd, Thomas J. *The Westminster Bible Dictionary*. Philadelphia: Presbyterian Board of Publication, 1880.

Smith, Gary V. *Isaiah 1–39*. NAC 14. Nashville: Broadman & Holman, 2007.

Smith, Robert H. "Eschatology of Acts and Contemporary Exegesis." *CTM* 29.9 (1958): 641–63.

Smith, William, and Henry Wace, eds. *A Dictionary of Christian Biography, Literature, Sects and Doctrines*. London: Murray, 1977.

Souter, Alexander. *A Pocket Lexicon to the Greek New Testament*. Oxford: Clarendon, 1917.

Spicq, C. *Theological Lexicon of the New Testament*. Translated and edited by J. D. Ernest. 3 vols. Peabody, MA: Hendrickson, 1994.

Sproul, R. C. *A Walk with God: An Exposition of Luke*. Fearn, Scotland: Christian Focus, 1999.

———. *John*. St. Andrew's Expositional Commentary. Lake Mary, FL: Reformation Trust, 2009.

———. *The Purpose of God: Ephesians*. Fearn, Scotland: Christian Focus, 1994.

———, ed. *The Reformation Study Bible: English Standard Version*, 2015 Edition. Orlando: Reformation Trust, 2015.

Stein, Robert H. *Luke*. NAC 24. Nashville: Broadman & Holman Publishers, 1992.

Stokes, Ryan E. "Satan, Yhwh's Executioner." *JBL* 133.2 (2014): 251–70.

Stokes, Ryan E. "The Devil Made David Do It ... or 'Did' He? The Nature, Identity, and Literary Origins of the 'Satan' in 1 Chronicles 21:1." *JBL* 128.1 (2009): 91–106.

Stokes, Ryan E., and John J. Collins. *The Satan: How God's Executioner Became the Enemy*. Grand Rapids: Eerdmans, 2019.

Storms, Sam. *Biblical Studies: Colossians*. Edmond, OK: Sam Storms, 2016.

———. *Biblical Studies: Ephesians*. Edmond, OK: Sam Storms, 2016.

———. *Biblical Studies: First John*. Edmond, OK: Sam Storms, 2016.

———. *Biblical Studies: Meditations on 2 Corinthians*. Edmond, OK: Sam Storms, 2016.

———. *Biblical Studies: Romans*. Edmond, OK: Sam Storms, 2016.

———. *Biblical Studies: The Sermon on the Mount*. Edmond, OK: Sam Storms, 2016.

———. *Kingdom Come: The Amillennial Alternative*. Fearn, Scotland: Mentor, 2013.

Story, J. Lyle. "Jesus' 'Enemy' in the Gospels." *American Theological Inquiry* 6.1 (2013): 43–63.

Stott, John R. W. *Romans: God's Good News for the World*. BST. Downers Grove, IL: InterVarsity Press, 1995.

———. *The Cross of Christ*. Downers Grove, IL: InterVarsity Press, 2006.

———. *The Epistles of John*. TNTC 19. Grand Rapids: Eerdmans, 1964.

Strachan, Owen. *Reenchanting Humanity: A Theology of Mankind*. Fearn, Scotland: Mentor, 2019.

Swanson, James. *Dictionary of Biblical Languages with Semantic Domains: Greek (New Testament)*. Oak Harbor, WA: Logos Research Systems, 1997.

Tan, Kim H. *Mark*. NCC. Eugene, OR: Cascade, 2015.

Tasker, R. V. G. *The Gospel according to St. John*. TNTC 4. Downers Grove, IL: Inter-Varsity Press, 1960.

———. *The Second Epistle of Paul to the Corinthians*. TNTC 8. Downers Grove, IL: Inter-Varsity Press, 1974.

Taylor, John B. *Ezekiel: An Introduction & Commentary*. TOTC 22. Downers Grove, IL: Inter-Varsity Press, 1969.

Thielman, Frank. *Theology of the New Testament: A Canonical and Synthetic Approach*. Grand Rapids: Zondervan, 2005.

Thomas, Robert L. "The Great Commission: What to Teach." *TMSJ* 21.1 (2010): 5–20.

Thompson, J.A. *1, 2 Chronicles*. NAC 9. Nashville: Broadman & Holman, 1994.

Til, Cornelius Van. *Introduction to Systematic Theology: Prolegomena and the Doctrines of Revelation, Scripture, and God*. Edited by William Edgar. 2nd ed. Phillipsburg, NJ: P&R Publishing, 2007.

Toorn, Karel van der, Bob Becking, and Pieter W. van der Horst, eds. *Dictionary of Deities and Demons in the Bible*. 2nd ed. Grand Rapids: Eerdmans, 1999.

Twelftree, Graham H. *Jesus the Exorcist: A Contribution to the Study of the Historical Jesus*. Eugene, OR: Wipf & Stock, 2011.

———. *Jesus the Miracle Worker: A Historical and Theological Study*. Downers Grove, IL: InterVarsity Press, 1999.

———. "Paul's Experience of the Miraculous." *EvQ* 87.3 (2015): 195–206.

———. "The Miracles of Jesus: Marginal or Mainstream?" *JSHJ* 1.1 (2003): 104.

Unger, Merrill F. *Biblical Demonology: A Study of Spiritual Forces at Work Today*. Grand Rapids: Kregel, 2012.

Vanhoozer, Kevin J., Daniel Treier, and N. T. Wright, eds. *Theological Interpretation of the New Testament: A Book-by-Book Survey*. Grand Rapids: Baker Academic, 2008.

Venema, Cornelis P. *The Promise of the Future*. Carlisle, PA: Banner of Truth, 2000.

Verbrugge, Verlyn D. "1 Corinthians." Rev. ed. Pages 239–414 in *Expositor's Bible Commentary* 11. Edited by Tremper Longman and David E. Garland. Rev. ed. Grand Rapids: Zondervan, 2011.

Vlach, Michael J. "The Trinity and Eschatology." *TMSJ* 24 (2013): 199–215.

Vos, Geerhardus. *Biblical Theology: Old and New Testaments*. Grand Rapids: Eerdmans, 1988.

———. *The Pauline Eschatology*. Phillipsburg, NJ: P&R Publishing, 1995.

Wagner, C. Peter. *Confronting the Powers: How the New Testament Church Experienced the Power of Strategic-Level Spiritual Warfare*. Prayer Warrior Series. Ventura, CA: Regal, 1996.

———. *Territorial Spirits: Practical Strategies for How To Crush the Enemy through Spiritual Warfare*. Shippensburg, PA: Destiny Image, 2012.

Walvoord, John F. "Is Satan Bound?" *BibSac* 100.400 (1943): 497–512.

Ware, Bruce A. *Father, Son, and Holy Spirit: Relationships, Roles, and Relevance*. Wheaton, IL: Crossway, 2005.

Wessel, Walter W. "Mark." Pages 601–796 in *Expositor's Bible Commentary* 8. Edited by Frank E. Gabelein. Grand Rapids: Zondervan, 1984.

White, Benjamin L. "The Eschatological Conversion of 'all the Nations' in Matthew 28.19–20: (Mis)Reading Matthew through Paul." *JSNT* 36.4 (2014): 353–82.

White, R. Fowler. "Agony, Irony, and Victory in Inaugurated Eschatology: Reflections on the Current Amillennial-Postmillennial Debate." *WTJ* 62.2 (2000): 161–76.

Witherington III, Ben. *Grace in Galatia: A Commentary on St. Paul's Letter to the Galatians*. Grand Rapids: Eerdmans, 1998.

———. *The Letters to Philemon, the Colossians, and the Ephesians: A Socio-Rhetorical Commentary on the Captivity Epistles*. Grand Rapids: Eerdmans, 2007.

Wright, David F., Sinclair B. Ferguson, and J. I. Packer, eds. *New Dictionary of Theology*. Downers Grove, IL: InterVarsity Press, 1988.

Wright, N. T. *Colossians and Philemon*. TNTC 12. Downers Grove, IL: InterVarsity Press, 2008.

———. *The New Testament and the People of God*. 1st North Amer. ed. Minneapolis: Fortress, 1992.

Zeller, Paul, ed. *Calwer Biblical Lexicon: Biblisches Handwörterbuch* Illustriert. Stuttgart: Verlag der Vereinsbuchhandlung, 1912.

Ziegler, Philip Gordon. "'Bound Over to Satan's Tyranny': Sin and Satan in Contemporary Reformed Hamartiology." *ThTo* 75.1 (2018): 89–100.

On Campus & Distance Options Available

GRACE BIBLE THEOLOGICAL SEMINARY

Interested in becoming a student or supporting our ministry?
Please visit gbtseminary.org

www.ingramcontent.com/pod-product-compliance
Lightning Source LLC
Chambersburg PA
CBHW021853230426
43671CB00006B/374